WOMEN IN TRADE UNIONS
Organizing the unorganized

WOMEN IN TRADE UNIONS

Organizing the unorganized

Edited by
Margaret Hosmer Martens
and Swasti Mitter

International Labour Office Geneva

First published 1994

Martens, M.H.; Mitter, S.
Women in trade unions: Organizing the unorganized
Geneva, International Labour Office, 1994
/Woman worker/, /Trade union/, /Trade unionization/, /Nonunionized worker/, /Developed country/, /Developing country/. 14.04.2
ISBN 92-2-108759-X

ILO Cataloguing in Publication Data

ILO publications can be obtained through major booksellers or ILO local offices in many countries, or direct from ILO Publications, International Labour Office, CH-1211 Geneva 22, Switzerland. A catalogue or list of new publications will be sent free of charge from the above address.

Printed in Switzerland HEL

Preface

This volume is a product of the ILO's Interdepartmental Project on Equality for Women in Employment.

In order to facilitate analysis of attempts made at the national level to organize women workers in the unorganized sectors, and in particular the informal and rural sectors, the ILO commissioned a series of case studies. To the extent possible, these studies were compiled by the trade unionists directly concerned; in some instances they were prepared by those who have been working closely with the unions. The case studies thus provide a down-to-earth description but not necessarily a vigorous theoretical analysis.

Following an introductory chapter, the volume is divided into five parts on organizing female domestic workers (including migrants), homeworkers, rural women workers, the self-employed and informal sector women and women in export processing zones. Whereas more than half of the studies are from developing countries in Africa, Asia, Latin America and the Caribbean, four are from industrialized countries: Australia, Canada, Italy and the Netherlands.

Although there are common threads running through the studies, each case is unique and it might therefore be impossible to use any of them as a "model" to follow in organizing women workers. However, several themes emerge which not only affect women in the informal or rural sectors, but women in society as a whole. These are lessons for all those working with women, be it for development assistance in the Third World or organizing women workers in both industrialized and developing countries. Therefore, to better learn from these experiences, wherever possible, two or more instances of organizing within a given sector are provided. This is true of the part on homeworkers, which offers a comparison of organizing homeworkers in Australia, Canada and the Netherlands; the rural sector, with three examples of organizing rural women workers in Africa, Asia, and Latin America; two cases of organizing market women in Côte d'Ivoire and Burkina Faso; and three studies on organizing domestic workers in Brazil, Mexico and Namibia.

The need for a basis for comparison was evident in the report on organizing women in Mauritius export processing zones (EPZs). As this case was clearly not representative of situations in other countries, a brief comparison with organizing in other EPZs was added.

These case studies make it clear that organizing is a continuous process. In fact, it might have been more appropriate to call this report "Steps to organizing the unorganized" because there is far more involved here than giving a woman worker her union card. As organizers have found in Mauritius, it is the commitment to the potential and ideal of trade unionism rather than simply agreeing to become a member which is at stake.

This volume was coordinated and edited by Margaret Hosmer Martens and Swasti Mitter as part of a work item on "Participation of women in trade unions", under the responsibility of Elizabeth Goodson, within the ILO's Interdepartmental Project on Equality for Women in Employment under implementation in the 1992-93 biennium. The project was to promote, in a multidisciplinary way, the examination of some critical issues regarding gender equality in the employment field aimed at providing a solid basis for realistic plans and actions to improve the situation.

Eugenia Date-Bah,
Manager,
Interdepartmental Project on Equality for Women in Employment,
International Labour Office

Contents

Abbreviations used in the text

ACO	Catholic Workers' Action (Brazil)
ACTU	Australian Council of Trade Unions
ADWU	Asian Domestic Workers' Union (Hong Kong)
ANG	Austrian Agricultural, Food Processing and Catering Union
CASED	Collective for Solidarity Action with Domestic Workers (Mexico)
CATDA	Salaried Workers' Support Centre (Mexico)
CATU	Clothing and Allied Trades Union of Australia
CEBEMO	Relief organization in the Netherlands
CENAP	North-East Centre for Peoples' Animation (Brazil)
CGIL	Italian General Federation of Labour
CGT	Workers' General Confederation (Brazil)
CIDA	Canadian International Development Agency
CIDHAL	Communication, International and Human Development, Latin America
CIPAF	Research Centre for Female Action (Dominican Republic)
CISL	Italian Confederation of Workers' Unions
CUT	Workers' Central Union (Brazil)
DANIDA	Danish International Development Agency
DEW	Distant Early Warning
DIGNITÉ	Confederation of Free Trade Unions of Côte d'Ivoire
DIP	Demonstrative Intervention Project
EC	European Community
EPZ	Export processing zone
FAO	Food and Agriculture Organization of the United Nations
FENAZUCAR	Union representing sugar workers in the Dominican Republic
FESACI	Federation of Independent Trade Unions of Côte d'Ivoire
FILCAMS	Italian Federation of Commerce, Tourism and Service Workers
FILTEA	Italian textile and garment union affiliated to the CGIL
FNV	Netherlands Trade Union Confederation
GAPWUZ	General Agricultural and Plantation Workers' Union of Zimbabwe
CGEC	Greater Colombo Economic Commission
GROOTS	Grassroot Organization Operating in Sisterhood
HSC	Home Work Support Centre, the Netherlands
ICFTU	International Confederation of Free Trade Unions
IFPAAW	International Federation of Plantation, Agricultural and Allied Workers
ILGWU	International Ladies' Garment Workers' Union
INSD	National Institute for Statistics and Population (Burkino Faso)
Intercede	International Coalition to End Domestics' Exploitation
IRENE	International Restructuring Education Network Europe
ITGLWF	International Textile, Garment and Leather Workers' Federation

IUF	International Union of Food and Allied Workers' Association
JIT	Just in time
JOC	Young Catholic Workers (Mexico)
KIPZ	Katunayake Investment Promotion Zone (Sri Lanka)
KPAWU	Kenya Plantation and Agricultural Workers' Union
LIFE	Filipino Migrant Women in Domestic Work in Italy
MDR	Metropolitan District of Recife, Brazil
MLC	Mauritius Labour Congress
MT&GWU	Mauritius Textile and Garment Workers' Union
NDAWU	Namibia Domestic and Allied Workers' Union
NGG	Union of Food Processing and Catering Workers (Germany)
NGO	Non-governmental organization
NUDE	National Union of Domestic Employees (Trinidad and Tobago)
NUNW	National Union of Namibian Workers
NUPAW	National Union of Plantation and Allied Workers (Uganda)
OATUU	Organization of African Trade Union Unity
OECD	Organization for Economic Cooperation and Development
ONPE	National Office for the Promotion of Employment (Burkino Faso)
ONSL	National Organization of Free Trade Unions (Burkino Faso)
ORIT	Regional Inter-American Organization of Workers
OXFAM	Oxford Committee for Famine Relief (United Kingdom)
PSAC	Public Service Alliance of Canada
RWO	Rural workers' organization
SASK	Trade Union Solidarity of Finland
SEWA	Self-Employed Women's Association (India)
SOGEMAB	Commercial Bureau of the Burkina Market Management
SOS CORPO	Women's association in Recife, Brazil
SPMFZU	San Pedro De Macoris Free Zone Trade Union (Dominican Republic)
SUITRACAP	Single Independent Union of Workers in Private Homes (Mexico)
SYNAFSI	National Union of Informal Sector Women (Côte d'Ivoire)
TUCP	Trade Union Congress of the Philippines
UGTCI	General Union of Workers of Côte d'Ivoire
UIL	Italian Labour Union
UNICEF	United Nations Children's Fund
UNIFEM	United Nations Development Fund for Women
UNFPA	United Nations Fund for Population Activities
WID	Women in development
WWF	Working Women's Forum (India)
YCW	Young Catholic Workers (Recife)
ZACA	Ouagadougou Commercial Zone Organization Commission
ZCTU	Zimbabwe Congress of Trade Unions

Part I

Introduction

1

A comparative survey

*Swasti Mitter**

Why women?

It is difficult not to be aware of the dimensions of gender in evaluating strategies for organizing workers in the unorganized sector. In the poorer parts of the world, women generally find jobs not in organized workplaces but in small factories, sweatshops or home-based units – the types of establishment that are generally exempt or hidden from a country's employment and labour legislation. Alternatively, women in search of a livelihood become self-employed, selling petty commodities such as fruit, vegetables, *bidis* (cigars), or even their own bodies as domestic workers or as prostitutes. In plantation and agricultural work too, women receive the most vulnerable forms of employment; their dual role as wage earner and homemaker leaves them with little energy to engage in bargaining for better conditions through workers' organizations. For trade unions, it proves difficult to organize such women for collective action, as they are generally to be found in scattered workplaces and undertake numerous varieties of trade for survival. Men also are often compelled to find a livelihood in the less protected or unprotected trades and occupations, especially in the developing world. None the less, it is the male members that form the majority of the small and elite group of workers in the factories and offices of the organized sector.

In contrast, women are as numerous as men in the unorganized sector, in the poorer as well as in the richer parts of the world.[1] Legislation that grants generous benefits specific to women, such as maternity leave, child-care facilities or exemption from night work, make it more expensive to hire women in the formal sector, especially when such benefits are financed mainly by the employer.[2] Even in the richer parts of the world, there has been an understandable and persistent trend towards preferring men to women in permanent core jobs of the formal sector; women generally find employment in peripheral jobs of the larger units as temporary, contract or part-

* Professor Swasti Mitter holds a Chair at the Centre for Business Research at the University of Brighton, United Kingdom. She is also a Professorial Research Fellow at the United Nations University Institute for New Technology, Maastricht, the Netherlands.

[1] For a quantitative estimate, see Swasti Mitter: *On organizing workers in the informal sector*, Report prepared for the International Confederation of Free Trade Unions (ICFTU), Brussels, 1989; for an analysis, see idem: "On organizing workers in the informal sector: A global overview", in Sheila Rowbotham and Swasti Mitter (eds.): *Dignity and daily bread: Alternative forms of economic organization in the Third World and the First* (London, Routledge, 1994).

[2] Rohini Hensman: *Trade unions and the gender division of labour: A case study in India* (Brighton, Institute of Development Studies, Sussex, 1988).

time workers. Such workers, with their insecure employment contracts, are often described as flexible workers; they have rarely been targets of mobilizing strategies on the part of the unions. The culture and procedures of the trade union movement, a champion mainly of workers of the organized sector, have understandably, over time, assumed a male bias. In Chapter 3 of this volume, "Unions and domestic workers in Mexico City", Ruth Joffre Lazarini and Olivia Martínez significantly remind us that when women form the major membership of a union, it is described as a *sindicato femenil* or women's union; there is no comparable term such as *sindicato masculino*, even when all or most members are men. In Mexico, as elsewhere, "it was simply taken for granted that a trade union was by definition a male affair. The participation of women was exceptional, so that when membership was mainly female, [unions] made a point of the fact."

The activities of traditional trade unions elude not just the small-scale or scattered units of production. In common with the flexible workers of the informal sector, the workers of some new forms of corporate organization are also beyond the reach of conventional strategies of mainstream trade unions. Export processing zones (EPZs) are examples of such new enterprises where workers, although full-time employees of large-scale multinational companies, remain largely non-unionized because of the geographical isolation of such zones and host countries' special concessions to foreign investors. In the 1970s and 1980s, the growth and spread of EPZs gave rise to a new type of working class, who were initially unaccustomed to workplace militancy and negotiating skills.[3] The majority of them were women.

Innovative management practices in the last two decades have resulted in further informalization or casualization of employment through the decentralization of work. The Japanese "just-in-time" (JIT) method had become a norm to emulate, both in the developed countries and in the industrializing parts of the developing world. In order to achieve quick responses to uncertain markets, reliance on a network of subcontractors was viewed as a sound business proposition; in this way, large companies could ensure the supply of goods and raw materials just in time and avoid holding unnecessary stocks of materials or final products. The resultant rise in the number of satellite companies and factories has meant an expansion of the small-scale sector in most countries of the Organisation for Economic Co-operation and Development (OECD).

Italy's spectacular success in rejuvenating the economy on the strength of its industrial districts containing groups of small businesses has become a focus of discussion by management and theoreticians of the labour movements alike. The industrial districts of Emilia Romagna, Tuscany or Piedmont have thrived on the entre-

[3] For a study of the evolving struggles of women workers for the right to organize, see Women Working Worldwide: *Common interests: Woman organising in global electronics* (London, 1991), available from Box 92, 190 Upper Street, London N1, United Kingdom. See also Kumudhini Rosa: "Strategies of organisation and resistance: Women workers in Sri Lankan Free Trade Zones", in *Capital and Class* (London), No. 45, Autumn 1991, pp. 27-34; Hema Goonatilake and Savitri Goonesekere: "Industrialism and women workers in Sri Lanka: Working conditions inside and outside the investment promotion zones", in Noeleen Heyzer (ed.): *Daughters in industry: Work, skills and consciousness of women workers in Asia* (Kuala Lumpur, Asia and Pacific Development Centre, 1988); and J. Lochead: *Retrenchment in a Malaysian free trade zone. The history of a struggle of women workers* (Malaysia, University of Malaysia, Project KANITA, May 1986).

preneurial energy of small-scale entreprises, supplying a variety of goods to large retailers. The range of goods covers traditional items such as clothing and textiles to high-technology products such as electronic components of cars. The Italian way of networking among large and small companies has become known as the model of flexible specialization.[4]

The expansion of the small-scale sector benefits women in terms of quality of jobs; in Italy, as elsewhere, women have become the major recipients of the jobs in this sector.[5] Yet the owners or the managers are almost always men, as highlighted by Vicky Franzinetti in Chapter 16. The culture of new artisanal units, where employers and employees are both from the same community, makes conventional union strategies ineffective in meeting the workplace needs of women workers. Redress against sexual harassment, for example, becomes a more delicate and problematic issue in the context of a family firm.

Jane Tate, in Chapters 6 to 8 on organizing homeworkers in Australia, Canada and the Netherlands, also indicates that the decentralization of work has led to an increase in clandestine forms of employment, particularly among immigrant women in the developed world. A lack of relevant skills and language qualifications, and uncertainty over their residence status as wives of migrant workers, often compel migrant women to accept employment that is invisible to officials.

The rise of undeclared manufacturing home work, which is widespread among immigrant women, has been well documented in such countries.[6] The spread of such work has substantially weakened the membership and strength of traditional industrial unions. Living on the fringe of the formal economy, immigrant women perceive trade unions as irrelevant to improving the quality of their working and living conditions.[7]

Common elements of the unorganized sector

Unorganized labour is not only found in the poorer parts of the world. Nor is it linked with labour-intensive technologies, commonly associated with the so-called "informal sector". The growth of unorganized labour arises from the casualization of employment contracts; such casualization often takes place in response to a technical advance. Computer technology, for example, facilitates the decentralization of manufacturing work through miniaturization and modularization of products. Telecommu-

[4] F. Pyke et al.: *Industrial districts and inter-firm cooperation in Italy* (Geneva, International Institute for Labour Studies, 1992).

[5] Raffaele Gaeta et al.: "Pronta moda: the new business venture for women in Italy", in Swasti Mitter (ed.): *Computer-aided manufacturing and women's employment* (London, Berlin, New York, Springer-Verlag, 1992), pp. 103-116.

[6] Roeland Van Geuns: "An aspect of informalisation of women's work in a high-tech age: Turkish sweatshops in the Netherlands", ibid., pp. 125-137; Swasti Mitter: *Common fate, common bond: Women in the global economy* (London, Pluto Press, 1986), Ch. 3.

[7] For the challenges and prospects of organizing immigrant homeworkers, see *Proceedings of conference on homeworking*, sponsored by the International Ladies Garment Workers' Union and Public Service Alliance of Canada, Regis College, Toronto, November 1992.

nications technology makes it cost-effective to locate information-intensive service jobs to teleports in other countries or to the homes of teleworkers.[8]

What then are the common elements of the so-called "informal" jobs that include different levels of technology and a plethora of trades, skills and professions? These are the jobs that are not covered by the collective bargaining procedures of enterprise-based, industrial or professional unions. One can safely say that there is always a trend towards feminization when employment contracts and conditions in an occupation become flexible, and hence unbargainable in nature. Women, historically, have been given a marginal role in the trade union movement; hence, employers feel lesser threats of militancy from women than from men against insecure and unjust employment contracts. Being generally excluded from secure and bargainable jobs in the formal sector, women are willing to accept employment that offers them a livelihood, however insecure. In some cases, self-employment, home-based work, part-time employment or employment in family businesses allow women to have some flexibility in working hours that helps them to combine their conflicting duties as homemakers and workers. Women's demand for such work increases as recession, structural adjustment and technological change reduce the availability of jobs in the organized sector – especially in the poorer parts of the world.

In some parts of Latin America, and in most of Africa, it is the unorganized sector that acts as a shock absorber against the economic crises facing the developing world. The result, however, has been a marked decline in trade union membership and a rise in unregistered workers' organizations. Such developments do not bode well either for the trade union movement or for the women and men as workers.

Why trade unionism?

The major advantage of a trade union is that it is a legally registered organization; its members are entitled to certain rights and protections offered by the State to working members of the population. At the international level, additional rights are provided for in the various conventions on freedom of association and collective bargaining, the application of which is subject to scrutiny by the ILO supervisory bodies.[9]

There are numerous informal and unregistered workers' organizations in the developing world. Some of them describe themselves as unions. In his famous book, *The other path*, Hernando de Soto documents a number of such unregistered unions

[8] Swasti Mitter and Ruth Pearson: *Global information processing: The emergence of software services and data entry jobs in selected developing countries* (Geneva, ILO, Working paper SAP 4.14/WP.51 (rev.1), 1992), Part 2; Ursula Huws: *The new homeworkers: New technology and the changing location of white collar workers* (London, Low Pay Unit, 1984).

[9] See ILO: *Freedom of association and collective bargaining*, General Survey by the Committee of Experts on the Application of Conventions and Recommendations, Report III, Part 4B, International Labour Conference, 69th Session, 1983; and idem: *Freedom of association*, Digest of decisions and principles of the Freedom of Association Committee of the Governing Body of the ILO (Geneva, 3rd ed., 1985).

in Peru, such as the Union of Small Traders and Street Vendors.[10] These organizations, without a legal status, are often less than effective in giving workers an identity and collective power in improving their living and working conditions. The informality of unregistered associations also makes it difficult for the members to seek redress when the leaders manipulate their power to the detriment of the workers' welfare.

The absence of a legal status poses difficulties in strengthening institutions that aim to assist workers. Unregistered informal groups, for example, cannot acquire capital assets. The bank accounts of such groups have to be opened in the name of a particular member. This places an extra burden of responsibility on the individual; it also opens up ways of private control and private gain. The lack of legal identity of a workers' organization also limits its access to many government schemes. In India, for example, numerous anti-poverty schemes launched by the Government cannot be used by self-employed women unless the funds can be channelled through registered self-employed workers' organizations.[11]

International donors also tend to give financial support mostly to legally registered workers' associations or unions. As the case studies here illustrate, such funding is extremely important in the earlier stages of mobilizing women workers in the informal sector.

The lack of interest in unionism among women workers does not result from any inherent characteristic of women as such. The culture of mainstream trade unions, for historical reasons, does not sufficiently address the needs of working women. The issues of child care, sexual harassment, lack of access to capital, and social subordination of women are rarely central to the concerns of traditional unions; women, as a result, remain either unorganized or mobilize themselves in informal, unregistered associations that are free of daunting bureaucratic procedures.

Linking with cooperative structures

The expansion of unionism among casualized women workers thus requires innovative strategies on the part of the trade unions, as well as among women activists in trade unions. The case studies included in this volume highlight some possibilities and lessons for future actions in this direction. Different degrees of success in mobilizing women in legally registered unions depend on experimentation with methods of recruitment and with the institutional structures of unions. It is difficult, for example, to disseminate knowledge about unions around the workplace when the production is transferred to geographically scattered subcontracting units. Indeed, the strategies geared to the employees of large factories often prove irrelevant in organizing poor self-employed, home-based or domestic workers. Group activities planned around leisure, education, training and income-generating projects thus become the forum for raising workers' consciousness regarding collective actions. In making their image woman-friendly, unions consistently extend their area of actions beyond simple

[10] Hernando de Soto: *The other path* (London, I. B. Tauris, 1989), p. 81.

[11] Mitter: *On organizing workers in the informal sector*, op.cit., p. 34.

wage bargaining. As several case studies here illustrate, only a promise of an overall economic and social empowerment can make union activities attractive to poor casualized women workers.

In experimenting with institutional structures, the linking of cooperative economic activities with trade unionism has proved an effective means of mobilizing women, especially around income-generating projects for the poor self-employed. The big advantage of being a member of a trade union-cum-cooperative organization is that a casualized worker begins to perceive herself gradually as a proper "worker" entitled to rights similar to those that the State offers to the workers of the organized sector. Promises of viable and sustainable employment opportunities also capture the imagination of casualized and self-employed workers.

The women's union, the *Syndicat national des femmes du secteur informel* (SYNAFSI), affiliated to DIGNITE, one of the two national trade union confederations in Côte d'Ivoire, extends its scope by forming sellers' and buyers' cooperatives for the empowerment of market stall holders and petty vendors. Limited access to credit and finance is a constraint that poor women face in achieving a dignified livelihood. A novel system of group borrowing, initiated successfully by the Working Women's Forum (WWF) in India, and described in the case study by Claire L. Bangasser (Chapter 13), thus points to yet another way of establishing the unions' relevance among poor self-employed women.

For the majority of trade unions in poorer parts of the world, it is not always easy to undertake the responsibilities that the income-generating and financial activities of the cooperative movement entail. Their resources are extremely limited; extending trade union activities in this situation mainly involves widening the sphere of union concern to hurdles that women predominantly face in casualized jobs.

Women's unions or women in unions?

One way of achieving that goal is to form unions exclusively for women; this approach, however, could be diversionary and is unproductive in trades where a substantial proportion of the workers are men. The case studies of rural workers' organizations in Asia (Chapter 10), and in Central America and the Dominican Republic (Chapter 11), demonstrate the role that well-structured educational programmes could play in giving confidence and expertise to women, enabling them to demand and receive strategic positions in the bureaucratic hierarchy of unions. Training and development programmes, as the case studies illustrate, are immensely valuable in promoting leadership abilities among women trade unionists – a condition for changing the image of unions from being essentially male organizations.

In some situations, where women have been socially conditioned to be non-assertive, it is necessary, however, to initiate women in unionism in an all-female environment. In that sense, the Working Women's Forum in Madras or the Self-Employed Women's Association in Ahmedabad, both in India, have been notable successes in innovative unionism.

In societies where women have enjoyed relatively greater social freedom, women's unions have proved effective in lobbying women's causes and issues with the mainstream trade unions. In this volume, the Italian case of Sindacato Donna, the women's union in Biella in Piedmont, illustrates such an endeavour. The union has 2,000 members; one-third of them do not belong to industrial unions. The rest have double membership of the Sindacato Donna and of an industrial union. The role of the Sindacato Donna in Biella has been to act as a watchdog for ensuring equality of opportunity at work and for initiating women-specific demands in the collective bargaining of the industrial unions. Similarly, Jane Tate's case studies on organizing homeworkers in Australia, Canada and the Netherlands (Chapters 6-8) clarify the role of the Women's Union in the Netherlands, one of the 19 unions affiliated to the FNV, the Dutch trade union confederation. The Women's Union of the Netherlands is not an industrial union but a general organization for all women, whether in paid employment or not. Women workers can be members of the Women's Union, and at the same time members of an industrial union. The Union does not have negotiating rights and does not engage in collective bargaining for its membership. It campaigns, primarily, for women's interests within the FNV and with the Women's Committee of the FNV. It specifically devotes its action towards giving visibility to the challenge of mobilizing workers who are generally left out by mainstream trade unions, such as homeworkers, housewives and domestic workers.

For women active in the trade union movement, the fear of separatism poses a serious challenge; shifting the male bias in the existing union structure demands of them careful consideration and strategic plans. The documented case studies in this book, particularly those that deal with rural workers' organizations, highlight such innovative strategies undertaken by women in the trade union movement. They also show the role educational and training programmes – often funded by international agencies such as the ILO and the International Federation of Plantation, Agricultural and Allied Workers (IFPAAW) – have played in imparting skills that women need, in order to promote women's causes without weakening the trade union movement.

Organizing domestic workers: The role of women's movements

The nature of casualization is not the same among all casualized groups of workers, nor is it uniform among similar groups in different countries. It is important therefore to be aware of the prospects and problems of transferring the knowledge and experience of mobilization in different localities, times or political structures.

The domestic workers, although wage employees, are difficult to organize, as the nature of their employment prevents them from coming in contact with their fellow workers. In spite of this, in Namibia, with its history of anti-colonial rule, it has been relatively easy to organize domestic workers in trade unions. The national centre, the predecessor of the National Union of Namibian Workers, was mobilizing such workers even before independence and at a time when trade unionism was illegal. Since 1990, as a legal institution, the Namibian Domestic Workers' Union has recruited 4,000 members out of an estimated number of 12,000 such workers; 70 per cent of its members are women. The workers are proud of their vocation and of having an identity as workers. The anti-colonial struggle has given these women, the majority of whom are over 40 years of age, confidence to work with men on an equal footing even in unions. The major bottleneck that the union faces is in obtaining funds, as the members are extremely poor. Grants from international donors, such as Oxfam in the United Kingdom or the Trade Union Solidarity Fund of Finland, play strategic roles – especially in exploring alternative employment opportunities through cooperatives. The help of the Namibia Broadcasting Corporation in informing workers of the existence of the union has been highly effective and offers an example of the successful use of the media in spreading the union message among scattered workers.

The experience of Recife in Brazil is different. The study by Marie Anderfuhren on the Union of Women Domestic Employees (UWDE) (Chapter 2) shows that in a more advanced economy, women domestic workers are generally young and view their economic position without pride. They hope that this type of employment will be a temporary phase in their lives, which will last only until they get married or find another job. Mobilization, therefore, entails giving the young workers an esteem for their employment and occupation. It is important in this context to assess the roles of the Catholic youth workers and charismatic leaders, such as Lenira Carvalho, in extending the message of collective action among domestic workers. The UWDE was formed in 1989 and has a membership of 2,000; it has seen a marked rise in membership since then, and through its struggle and persistence has managed to obtain rights on a par with those of formal sector workers, so long as its members can show a record of service. These rights include the right to organize, maternity leave, minimum wages, a pension and a period of notice for job termination.

It is not easy to implement the rights of domestic workers even when they are legally granted. However, the counselling services and the legal advice that the UWDE offers in the field make the union attractive to its members. The vocation-specific training courses are launched and used by the union as vehicles for generating self-esteem among chambermaids, cooks or crèche attendants.

The case of the UWDE, Brazil, illustrates in this volume the strategic challenges that women in trade unions face in organizing workers. The UWDE is affiliated to the Workers' Central Union (CUT), one of the four trade union confederations; none the less, the UWDE finds some difficulty in collaborating with CUT. The rigid hierarchy and inflexible meeting hours make it impossible for domestic workers to take part in it. The education and training materials are exclusively geared to the needs of educated male workers and hence fail to make sense to illiterate or uneducated domestic workers. In contrast, the feminist movement SOS CORPO – even with its middle-class bias – has proved to be an important ally of the UWDE. Women in the UWDE, in solidarity with the women's movement, highlight the importance of issues such as abortion, sexual harassment or domestic violence in determining women's position in the world of paid work. The dilemma is that in dealing with SOS CORPO, women workers find they are collaborating with middle-class women who themselves are employers of domestic servants.

The experience of the ATABAL Collective in Mexico City, as documented in Chapter 3 of this volume, is an example of a rewarding alliance of a feminist movement with the mobilizing activities of poor domestic workers. ATABAL is an organization of professional women with a feminist political purpose, namely to fight for the social recognition of the value of domestic service and the social and political

Corrigendum

Women in trade unions

Hosmer Martens and Mitter, ISBN 92-2-108759-X

Cover photographs: Top left, bottom left and bottom right - Sharmini Boyle, Sri Lanka; top right - ILO Photo Library (J. Maillard); middle right - ILO Photo Library (P. Sutcliffe).

rights of domestic workers. The work of promotion, support and training, given by these middle-class women, has given rise to the Group of Domestic Service Workers "La Esperanza" (meaning "hope"). The educational programme of "La Esperanza" is oriented towards giving domestic servants a collective awareness of the need for organization to defend their interests.

Mobilizing the self-employed

Traditional shop-floor recruitment practices are equally irrelevant for mobilizing self-employed poor women, whose collective actions for economic and social empowerment are not likely to be directed towards an identifiable employer. Trade unionism becomes worthwhile only if it allows them to address the problems that place them in vulnerable economic and social positions. The example of the Working Women's Forum (WWF) in India in this respect deserves close attention. With 80,000 members on its roll, it has proved immensely successful; central to its success has been the cooperative banking system, which offers an innovative way of freeing women from the exploitation of traditional money lenders and from their marginalization by the mainstream banks. The "sustainability" of unionism, as stressed by Claire L. Bangasser in Chapter 13, lies in developing the leadership qualities of the members themselves. The traditional union bureaucratic procedure is thus replaced by members' participatory action. To offer its members the necessary business and leadership skills, the WWF launches training courses specifically geared to "make them realize their state of powerlessness and the power of their empowerment". The Forum, in promoting this consciousness, takes a broader view of unionism that includes a wide variety of actions, ranging from giving street vendors and the self-employed information about legal rights or sources of credit, to campaigning for better civic amenities, free contraceptives and immunization for their young children. By giving support to inter-caste weddings and by organizing non-violent demonstrations against the dowry system, the union helps the members to challenge discriminatory practices that keep women in an inferior social status. The holistic approach of the WWF is geared towards improving the overall quality of working and living conditions. The leadership training, the core of WWF's strategies for mobilizing, prepares women for a harmonious life. As one member states: "The training [for assertiveness] does not teach you to disrespect people, but to fight injustice."

Women's newly acquired boldness and economic power are often conducive to improving relationships with their husbands, who also struggle against poverty and degradation. In the words of a Forum leader, "money and a good husband are very necessary for a woman".

The WWF, along with the Self-Employed Women's Association (SEWA) of India, has been studied as a successful example of women organizing in the informal sector.[12] In order to evaluate its replicability, however, one needs to look carefully at the role of the leaders, who generally belong to the middle class and have a deep

[12] Kalima Rose: *Where women are leaders: The SEWA movement in India* (New Delhi, Sage Publications, 1992).

understanding of the country's political power structure. Not every country in the developing world has such a tradition of middle-class female political activists committed to casualized and self-employed workers.

The case concerning the Cissin-Natenga Women's Association and the organization of women traders in the market of Ouagadougou in Burkina Faso (Chapter 14) offers models of organizing women in a society that strictly follows traditional social norms. Women join unions mainly because they offer a chance of economic empowerment.

The case study of SYNAFSI (National Union of Women in the Informal Sector) – the union of casualized and self-employed women workers in Côte d'Ivoire – also shows in Chapter 15 that women readily become members of unions when the membership leads to profitable and sustainable participation in cooperative business activities. The training programmes of SYNAFSI do not highlight shop-floor bargaining procedures; instead they promote expertise in household management and family budgeting, basic administrative procedures and business skills.

The case of rural and plantation workers

Income-generating projects are not so relevant when mobilizing workers of certain trades or occupations. The rural workers in Asia, Central America and the Dominican Republic, for example, are familiar with the activities and potential benefits of trade unionism. The passive role of women in the relevant organizations arises not because of women's unfamiliarity with unionism as such, but because of the marginalization of women's voices and needs in the trade union structure. As Maritza González recounts in her case study of workers' education for women in RWOs in Central America and the Dominican Republic (Chapter 11), women's roles are limited in the RWOs because existing cultural patterns deny women a voice in decision-making bodies of the relevant unions and because trade union education and training programmes are usually drawn up without taking into account women's domestic responsibilities, such as child care, education, household tasks and helping with farm labour.

The educational and training programmes in leadership and self-development launched by international agencies such as the ILO and the IFPAAW can make some progress in this direction by giving women confidence and zeal in taking a more active part in trade unions. The most important aspect of the programmes has been the training of people who can act as catalysers by inspiring other women in collective action. The case study of workers' education for women members of RWOs in Asia (Chapter 10) shows what a well-structured programme, as launched in India, the Philippines and Sri Lanka, can produce:

> A cadre of women who have been trained to fulfil an important role in training other women at grass-roots levels including an awareness of their rights as women and as members in their own organizations. The corps of women activists ... have received specialized training and have been brought to the decision-making levels of the unions.

A case of failure: The Mauritius export processing zone

An unorganized labour force can be found even in large factories, owned and run by national and multinational corporate organizations. The women workers of export processing zones (EPZs) are examples of such non-unionized workers; in some countries, as in Sri Lanka, trade unions are not encouraged to form branches within the zones.[13] In Malaysia, on the other hand, workers in the electronics industry are allowed to join only in-house unions.[14] But even in Mauritius, where workers of the zones enjoy freedom of association, trade unionism is remarkably low. Whereas the unionized workforce represents 27 per cent of total workers in Mauritius, in the zones it is less than 12 per cent.

The case study of the Mauritius EPZs highlights the factors that account for such a low level of unionization. Sixty-six per cent of workers in the zone are women, and they generally feel inertia about forming trade unions. In spite of being the major breadwinners in Mauritius, women remain responsible for household tasks and child care; understandably, they find little time and energy to take part in union activities:

> Workers in EPZs are required to work regularly beyond normal hours (45 hours a week plus ten hours compulsory overtime) possibly to rectify the labour shortage and meet delivery deadlines. ... EPZ women workers spend between ten and 12 hours daily away from home and by 6 a.m. they must be on their way to work. In the evening, after a hard day's work, they must again spend between one and two hours travelling home ...

The demanding work schedule and lack of time for union activities make it difficult to raise a collective consciousness among women workers through educational activities, such as were organized by the Mauritius Labour Congress in the past. In addition, veiled threats from male supervisors inhibit women who, in any case, perceive trade union activities as belonging to the men's world. The increasing use of new institutions, such as the internal works council, erodes the collective bargaining power and hence the economic leverage of the unions.

In this situation, unions need to broaden their scope of activities beyond wage bargaining and be "women-friendly", catering to needs and demands specific to women. The health hazards of long working hours, and issues of sexual harassment and of child care – the concerns that have helped mobilize women in the unorganized sector in other countries – are likely to alter the image of a trade union as a male institution. The union structure needs reassessment as well: in the Mauritius EPZ women are rarely office bearers and hence have practically no influence in the running of the unions. In the absence of a change in the image and direction of trade unions, it will be difficult not to agree with the pessimistic view of the Education Director of the Mauritius Labour Congress, the author of the case study on the Mauritius EPZ (Chapter 17), that it "... is impossible for the trade unions to organize the remaining 88 per cent of the unorganized labour force in the EPZ sector ... when 66 per cent of the EPZs consist of female workers".

[13] Goonatilake and Goonesekere, op.cit., and Rosa, op.cit.

[14] K. S. Jomo: *Growth and structural changes in the Malaysian economy* (London, Macmillan, 1990), pp. 119-120.

The developed world: Distant early warning

The need to change the image of trade unions is becoming apparent also in the developed world. The trend towards decentralization in the high-technology era is creating a feminized workforce whose workplace demands are different from those of traditional male workers in the organized sector. The structure of the existing trade unions, however, is still not geared to improving the quality of women's working lives. CGIL-FILTEA is the active union in the Biella region of Italy, and 85 per cent of its members are women. Yet, Vicky Franzinetti points out in her case study of textile and garment workers (Chapter 16), there is no woman official and no full-time worker to recruit union members and meet the needs of women in a thriving cottage industry sector.

A conscious or unconscious marginalization of women workers' interests in the mainstream unions leads to a changed structure of employment that affects men as well as women. The three chapters (6-8) by Jane Tate document the current restructuring in the developed world that has resulted in a dramatic growth in home-based production, especially in the textiles and clothing sector. Her description of the situation in Australia, Canada and the Netherlands shows that a sizeable proportion of manufacturing employment now takes place in the informal sector of the developed world. The major recipients of such jobs are women; often they are immigrant women. The spread of such jobs understandably places strains on the resources of trade unions, as they lose membership from the organized sector. In order to survive, some unions are adding explicitly to their agenda the interests of new groups of workers, who are disadvantaged by ethnicity and gender.

Significantly, such unions in developed countries are looking at community-based, holistic approaches to mobilization, as are generally followed in the developing world. Jane Tate, in her study on Canada, cites Alex Dagg, of the ILGWU, Canada, who emphasizes the need for a patient, long-term approach to organizing, with a focus on campaigns that may last for years. To do this, it is imperative that the union work within the community. Some of the most creative organizing is originating from grass-roots women's organizations rather than traditional trade unions.

The growth of home-based and other forms of non-bargainable jobs is spreading rapidly in banking, finance and other service occupations, partly because of the growth of decentralized forms of work and partly in response to computer technologies. Teleworking, for example, covering a wide range of skills and expertise, leads to vulnerable forms of employment similar to those found in manufacturing home work when there is no mechanism for collective action.

The experiences of casualization among women workers of the traditional sectors are now being monitored by networks such as Distant Early Warning (DEW), significantly by unions of professional workers even in the developed world.[15] It is thus an opportune moment to incorporate transnational experiences of mobilizing unorganized women workers into the educational materials of the ILO's Workers' Education Branch.

[15] For the response of Public Service Alliance of Canada to current flexibilization of service work, see Alex Dagg: *Organising homeworkers into unions*, paper presented at the Conference on Homeworking, Nov. 1992, Toronto (also published in *Yorkshire and Humberside Low Pay Unit Newsletter* (Batley, Yorkshire), No. 15, Feb. 1993.

Part II

Organizing women domestic workers

2

The Union of Women Domestic Employees, Recife, Brazil

*Marie Anderfuhren**

This chapter is based on research conducted in Recife, North-East Brazil, on the Union of Women Domestic Employees (UWDE) in the Metropolitan District of Recife (MDR). While the study's focus is on organizing domestic employees in Recife, it also gives background information on developments at the national level. In particular, we attempt to show the interrelationships of the union with the trade union movement as a whole, as well as with the women's movement in the region.

Employment in Brazil's North-East region

Previously an important region for agriculture, North-East Brazil is today one of the poorest in the country. The new industrial sector has been unable to absorb the workforce after massive urban migration. In 1980 it was estimated that 48.5 per cent of the active population between the ages of 15 and 59 worked in the formal sector and that the remainder earned a living in other ways. As noted by ETAPAS (1991, p. 21): "The history of the population of Recife is one of precarious employment, domestic service, itinerant traders, small retailers, fisherfolk, in a word all those who are forced to generate their own small incomes in order to survive ... ."

Domestic workers in Brazil

There are about 3 million domestic workers in Brazil out of a total female workforce estimated at 18 million in 1985. (Sindicato dos Empregados Domésticos na Area Metropolitana da Cidade de Recife (Recife, 1990)). In the State of São Paulo there are about 515,000 domestic workers, in Rio de Janeiro 400,000, and in the North-East 600,000. In Recife the UWDE claims around 100,000 for the MDR. More women are employed as domestic workers than in any other occupational category in the country. Between 1970 and 1980 their number grew rapidly but, as a proportion of overall female employment, domestic workers shrank from 26 per cent to 20 per cent. Many young people are employed as domestics. A study in Recife in 1991 (IPESPE, 1991) showed that this sector contained equal numbers of migrants and local people, whereas in the past the majority had always been migrants.

* Engaged in postgraduate research at the Institut universitaire d'études du développement, Geneva.

Domestic service offers an entry into the labour market, but it is hard to use as a stepping-stone to more prestigious occupations and the rate of unemployment is high.The 1991 study also revealed that very few domestic workers realized that a trade union even existed. Of the 300 persons interviewed, 87 per cent had not heard of it, while 4.3 per cent had heard of it but had no idea what it was or how it functioned. An estimated 10 per cent of workers are unionized in Brazil but only one out of these ten is considered active. Comparable figures among domestic workers in Recife are 1.2 per cent unionized and about 0.06 per cent active members.

Whatever the criteria used to define domestic service, by far the majority of employees are women. A study carried out in 1985 (Dabat and Oliveira, 1985) estimated that there were about 60,000 persons in domestic service in Recife, of whom only 2 per cent were men; this proportion was reflected in the union membership.[1]

The struggle to organize domestic workers in Brazil

In some of the larger cities in the early 1960s domestic workers, with the help of the Young Catholic Workers, began to meet and discuss their lives and working conditions. Eventually through these meetings they decided to form associations. The São Paulo association was officially registered in March 1962 and that of Rio de Janeiro in March 1963. During this period there were many workers' organizations struggling to improve working and living conditions.

In Recife the Young Catholic Workers movement (YCW) also began organizing domestic employees in 1960. The present UWDE President in the MDR, Lenira Carvalho, was involved in these beginnings, having joined the YCW in 1962. Upon learning that domestic workers were often ashamed of their jobs and did not like to speak up when with groups of other workers, the YCW formed a group specifically for them. This whole period was notable for the aid given by the Church, which collaborated a great deal with the working classes in their efforts to organize. On 1 May 1963 domestic workers in Recife marched in a parade as workers for the first time.

Unfortunately the military putsch of 1964 dealt a heavy blow to the movement just beginning to blossom. In Recife, all who collaborated with the domestic workers in this movement were arrested. It was impossible to offer any resistance. Ms. Carvalho preferred to work in districts where she was unknown, since people were afraid to be seen with anyone recognized as a figure in the popular movement. A Jesuit priest organized a group of workers which used to meet just after the Mass. Ms. Carvalho took part in these meetings, and to this day three women from the original group are still working in the UWDE.

Over the years from 1964 until 1985 the workers struggled to form associations. In Recife it took two years to form a legal association because they could not find 20 domestic workers who could show a signed record of service. The association was finally registered in 1970. From 1978 onwards there was a marked need for a coordinating body at the national level and it was eventually decided to rotate the

[1] Ed. note: It is interesting to note here and in the case of Mexico that, although 2 per cent of the members are men, the union is known as one for women domestic workers.

responsibility among organized cities. This body eventually became the National Council with one, and more recently, two representatives per State.

The Domestic Workers' National Congress in 1985 raised the question of changing groups and associations into trade unions. Until the new Constitution was adopted in 1988, however, this claim could not legally be put into effect. In those days freedom of association was not guaranteed. As a hangover from the labour law of the 1930s there could only be one trade union for each occupation in a given area, the geographical unit being the municipality. Today these vary between small, barely organized groups, registered associations which have no representative power before the law, and trade unions, which do possess such power. The reasons for the retention of these three levels are sometimes more financial than organizational. In Recife the UWDE has also retained its association status that enables it to receive money from international agencies which would not make such donations to a union. Everybody is well aware of the artificiality of this arrangement.

The return to democracy in Brazil was accompanied by enormous social effervescence throughout 1987 and 1988. The process was accomplished by a Constituent Assembly, among other institutions, which was responsible for preparing the new Constitution that was adopted in 1988. During this time domestic employees were very active in Brasilia, the capital, in their attempt to secure the same rights as other workers. They spent time in lobbying members of the Constituent Assembly. In Recife the preparation for this work was greatly facilitated by the increasingly close bonds between the union and the women's movement, as will be seen later.

This nation-wide effort served to make the National Council of Women Domestic Employees more aware of workers' movements outside the country and the necessity of forming linkages. In 1988 the Council sent four representatives to the First Latin American and Caribbean Domestic Workers' Conference, which was held in Bogotá.

The last National Congress, held in 1989, was notable for a plethora of resolutions and tasks to be undertaken. One of the principal subjects was the need for more political education. Other challenges which the 1989 National Congress decided to take up concerned the need:

— to found trade unions;
— to fight for regular working hours and a compensation fund;
— to outlaw the employment of persons under the age of 15;
— to establish a collective contract entailing specific rights and obligations.

In Recife, 1989 was the year when the UWDE finally became a trade union, which was essential in order to work with the Ministry of Labour (although it also retained its status as an association). The year 1991 was notable for the introduction of courses on trade union activities, run jointly by an organizer from the union and two representatives from SOS CORPO, a women's association in Recife. A very useful training manual resulted from the programme and there is now a project afoot to standardize training along the same lines elsewhere in the country. This was also the year of the study on the conditions of domestic workers (IPESPE, 1991), which has proved a very useful working document for the union.

In August 1992 the Recife union decided to affiliate with the Workers' Central Union (CUT),[2] the largest of the four trade union confederations in the country. Each region's domestic employees' union decides for itself whether and with which union to affiliate. Although the CUT is the most usual choice, some unions are affiliated to the Workers' General Confederation (CGT) or to Força Sindical, two somewhat smaller confederations.

Recognition of domestic workers' rights

In the struggle during the 1980s for human and workers' rights, the work done in the Constituent Assembly was of decisive importance. Since that time domestic workers have enjoyed most (but not all) of the rights accorded to other workers, including the right to form trade unions. More specifically, these rights are as follows:

— the right to organize;
— a minimum wage;
— a thirteenth month's wage;
— weekly time off with pay;
— annual holidays;
— maternity leave;
— notice of termination;
— a retirement pension.

The achievement of these rights represents a significant advance in the recognition of the value of domestic service and marks the beginning of an important change in attitude for domestic workers and in particularly with regard to exercizing their rights as workers, and specifically as domestic workers. It is a long, slow process, given that the occupation is held in very low esteem, even to the extent that these people do not want to be recognized as domestic workers. Wages are low.

From another perspective, however, one may also see the change as rapid and profound, inasmuch as the number of domestic workers who now come forward to claim one right or another, taking their case to court if necessary, has increased dramatically. Radio and television programmes discuss domestic service, bringing it before the eyes of the public, and the union's membership is growing day by day. As we shall see, all this does not happen without problems, but the movement seems to have got under way.

[2] Until the adoption of the new Constitution the legal status of the CUT was simply that of a non-profit organization. Only in 1988 did it officially become a union confederation, even though it had been acting in this capacity for some considerable time.

The Union of Women Domestic Employees

Structure

The Union of Women Domestic Employees (UWDE) of Recife has:

— an Executive Committee of 20 people elected for three years, which meets once a fortnight; and

— a Training Group consisting of three people who are also members of the Executive Committee, which meets once a week.

It participates in an advisory group consisting of representatives from six women's groups from the North-East which share their problems and seek joint solutions. It is advised by a women's organization SOS CORPO (see below).

Until the next National Congress (i.e. initially for a period of four years) the Recife UWDE is serving as the secretariat of the National Council of Women Domestic Employees, the coordinating body for all the relevant groups, associations and trade unions in the country. Three members of the UWDE Executive Committee respectively assume the responsibilities of President, Secretary and Treasurer of the Council, a burden for the union but an essential task. The National Council meets three times a year. The cost of these meetings represents a real drain on the very modest finances of the country's domestic service unions. The National Council benefits from the advice of a CUT adviser who offers his services free of charge.

Financing

Finance is a problem for the union at every level, given that the occupation of domestic service does not qualify for trade union taxation rates (calculated on the basis of one day's wages per member, 60 per cent of which goes to the union), nor for breakdown figures on individual pay-slips.

Fees or salaries are paid to the legal counsel, one person in the training group, one personal adviser, five part-time staff and the UWDE's secretary.

One of the characteristics of the occupation is the low level of remuneration. It is rare for membership dues to be paid regularly, and in any case they do not cover the cost of the union's activities. Its sources of income are broken down as follows:

— membership dues (2 per cent of wages);

— fees for advice and for calculation of entitlements in case of dismissal (2 per cent of last monthly wage);

— 3 per cent of the sum involved in case of a wage dispute settled in court (1 per cent payable by the employee and 2 per cent by the employer);

— receipts from bazaars, social events, etc.;

— loans from the Catholic diocese;

— individual donations;

— international donations (from CEBEMO, the Netherlands; OXFAM, United Kingdom; and the Global Fund, United States).

The UWDE also benefits from many free services such as advice from SOS CORPO, courses provided by the CENAP (North-East Centre for Popular Animation), secretarial courses, production of the bulletin, voluntary labour, and so on. Funds for travel expenses on the occasion of National Congress sessions are supplied by the Ford Foundation.

Funding problems are equally acute at national level in view of the fact that the tasks of coordination and organizing meetings are particularly onerous.

The UWDE receives no funds from the international trade union movement.

The international agencies are now insisting that the UWDE seek ways and means of financing itself, but there is no solution to this problem owing to the characteristics of the occupational group.

Membership

In the MDR the union has 1,200 members out of a potential estimated at around 100,000. This is only a small number, but it represents a twofold increase in six years. According to its President, the UWDE is now growing very fast. This is because any worker approaching the union for legal help almost automatically becomes a member. As mentioned above, the union dues are 2 per cent of wages, while fees for legal aid are also levied. These fees are unavoidable because of the costs entailed by legal aid, personal assistance and case-by-case information.

This type of recruitment naturally does not provide any assurance that the newly enrolled member will play an active part in the union's activities — far from it — nor indeed that she will pay her dues regularly. In any case, the low level of wages typical of this occupation make the regular payment of dues, however modest, unlikely by the membership as a whole. For example, of the 1,200 members, 500 are duly registered, and only 100 or so contribute regularly.

According to the union, one of its problems is the way it is viewed by domestic workers. A majority of them, even those who are members, consider it as just another kind of public service or a form of social assistance run by the State. It is true that the Brazilian trade union tradition, dating from the time of President Vargas, has encouraged an aid-oriented union culture. The employee comes to claim her rights, but sees no reason to take any part in activities. This is particularly the case among the young. Although there is no doubt that they are the most exploited group, young women are also the least represented among the membership. This is a serious problem, and the President has formed several theories regarding it:

— the young domestic employee dreams that she will soon change to a different kind of job and thus sees no point in fighting for an occupation from which she wants to escape;

— the burden of the struggle is so heavy that, in spite of her enormous potential, the young worker is too discouraged to get involved;

— the union has not yet found the right approach to young people; it needs to

convey a sense of mission so that it is not only social occasions which attract them;
— almost all workers perceive unions as aid centres external to their own lives, and not as places to make a contribution.

It is hoped that the nation-wide study on domestic employees' working conditions will produce a member profile which will help to increase their participation. Currently, the union in Recife has two types of activity which attract young people: certain types of vocational training and a theatre group (see below).

Another category of domestic employee that the union has not been able to contact is that of child workers. The union has no figures, but there are known to be large numbers of them. Entirely new methods will have to be devised in order to gain their confidence and attempt to work with them.

In addition to the very young, there is another class of domestic servant which the union has hardly succeeded in penetrating, the daily workers or "*diaristas*". These workers are considered to be self-employed and thus cannot make claims on the same basis as employees (currently only the worker makes social security payments). In Ms. Carvalho's opinion, however, if their numbers increase appreciably (as is currently the case), either they will need to form a trade union or else the UWDE should constitute a special section where it can organize and work with the daily workers to solve their particular problems.

Once a domestic employee becomes a union member she is bound in principle to pay her dues. She must also attend at least those meetings where important decisions are taken, such as the adoption of accounts or elections to the Executive Committee. For Executive Committee members the question of succession is a serious problem.

Union activities and services

Workers' education

Following the decision of the 1989 National Congress to recognize the need for political education, the UWDE of Recife formed an Education Group responsible for organizing courses for union members on trade union policies and on the nature of political institutions in general. For example, two sessions were held on debating entry into the Central Unica dos Trabalhadores (CUT).

The Education Group has meetings once a month and explores such subjects for training as:
— Does domestic service have any value?
— Why join a trade union?
— Why insist on defined working hours?
— What rights do we have?

Counselling for members and dispute resolution

Providing individuals with information is a union service which absorbs an enormous amount of time and energy. Six people shoulder this heavy burden, in addition to the lawyer who deals with disputes which go to court. One of the major problems for the union is that this service is also used by employers, who have no active organization of their own in Recife. Thus the union's energies are partly devoted to counselling and informing employers, since failure to do so would almost certainly make life worse for the employee. Several methods to put an end to this paradoxical situation have been envisaged, among them refusal to supply further information while advising employers to form their own association, or handling their requests once a week in a group session. In the end, however, urgent reality has always overcome good resolutions.

Vocational training

It is traditionally rare for a domestic servant in Recife to be responsible for more than one task in a household. Since its beginning as an association, the UWDE has offered vocational training to improve workers' skills so that they are qualified in all facets of domestic work (such as training a laundress to become a cook, which offers more prestige and money). The latest cooking course on learning how to prepare food for deep freezing, for example, has proved highly popular. One of the reasons for this success has been a desire to specialize in selling deep-frozen meals and thus to escape from domestic service. In the President's view, the UWDE alone cannot solve the problem of raising the vocational skills of such a large occupational category. The situation should improve as the State of Pernambuco has plans to set up a domestic training school in conjunction with a local NGO which has discussed the subject with the union. The UWDE is quite happy for this task to be handled by the State.

The view of the CUT, on the other hand, is that occupational training is *the* major challenge which the union should take up. Professionalism represents the way to lift domestic service out of the low esteem in which it is held and will, furthermore, endow the employee with more weight in negotiations. Since the employee has no access to any other source of training, the CUT believes that the union should assume the task.

Leisure activities

These activities are fundamental to the life of the union. It is important for domestic workers to be able to break out of their isolation, and they sometimes even have the courage to insist on the time off to which they are entitled. From time to time there are festivals with dancing. There is debate in the union over which types of leisure activity could be offered to attract young domestic workers. One important innovation is the union's theatre group. The group sometimes performs during Sunday night meetings to help illustrate particular themes and also puts on public performances and street entertainment.

Interregional activities

Approximately twice a year, the UWDE takes part in interregional activities with delegates from unions and associations from the States of Bahia and Paraíba. These meetings become more frequent when preparations are under way for the National Congress. The problem is that each meeting entails heavy transport costs and the working hours of domestic staff are not easily adaptable.

Other activities

Producing and distribution a bi-monthly bulletin is a new activity for the union. The union's Political Training Group is responsible for its contents. It is distributed at union headquarters, and also by a dozen persons in various districts of the city, thus giving rise to discussion among domestic workers.

Among the places where it is possible to reach a large number of women, both employers and employees, are crèches and schools. Provided those in charge allow it, the union uses such premises for the diffusion of information regarding the rights of domestic workers.

In the Recife municipality of Olinda the union has held many meetings in a college run by nuns. Courses are held on employees' rights and on the organization of workers in domestic service. This activity has had to be suspended for the time being for lack of members able to provide the instruction.

Building links

Relations with the national centre (CUT)

From the UWDE's perspective

Even when it was no more than an association, the UWDE of the MDR had links with the CUT; it had first approached the national centre when envisaging its own constitution. Union members took part in CUT congresses and were invited to join in its various activities. However, it was only in 1991, when the idea of affiliation was discussed during the union's workers' education seminars, that the idea of joining the confederation began to be seriously considered. The argument in favour of joining was the need for status within the trade union world. According to the UWDE, however, problems with regard to being taken seriously have begun to crop up already in the process of affiliation. The CUT does not seem particularly interested in having the union as a new affiliate. Contacts are kept to a minimum, and CUT representatives have failed to turn up at meetings expressly convened to discuss its role with the domestic employees. It seems to the union that this attitude arises from their occupation's lack of status, so that the union is not taken really seriously, regardless of its organizing power. Once affiliated, the union will need to be able to make its voice heard, no easy matter. This is already a source of worry, for various reasons:

— The CUT is structurally a highly complex confederation with an infinite number of currents of opinion. In order to get anything done, it is essential to grasp the content and aims of these internal disputes, but domestic workers have an extremely low standard of education and political sophistication. Most of them do not really understand what the CUT is. In these circumstances it will be difficult for the union to play its proper role.
— Other workers often hold domestic service in low esteem.
— In the labour movement in general, and the CUT is no exception, sexual discrimination is widespread. Women have difficulty in making their voices heard or in acceding to posts of responsibility. This being so, a small union with a 98 per cent female membership is certain to run into difficulties.
— The level of education among other unions, and notably among their representatives at CUT meetings, is often fairly high. In this context it will be a challenge for the women to make their voices heard, understand what is being said and feel accepted by the others.
— Domestic workers do not have regular hours of work. Although there is supposed to be time off on weekends, it is not always granted. This will complicate attendance at CUT meetings.

In spite of all these foreseeable problems, the UWDE considers it vital to enter more fully into the world of labour. In order to prepare for this change, it has decided to engage the services of a trade union adviser.

From the CUT's perspective

The CUT seems to take a less sombre view of its relations with the UWDE. In the eyes of the Secretary of the Pernambuco CUT Education Section, the entry of the UWDE into the confederation will help the trade union movement as a whole in resisting its own tendency towards corporatism, a tendency which has increased considerably in recent years. The UWDE has always been invited to all functions where formal affiliation to the confederation was not a strict condition of attendance. Two members of the union's advisory group are also members of trade unions affiliated to the CUT and make its policies known. The UWDE has good status and firm links with the other trade unions, and has never hesitated to invite them or ask for their help. It is in no way isolated either from the confederation or from society in general, where it makes its views known both in the press and in the audiovisual media. That said, it is true that in the trade union movement as a whole there do exist certain prejudices concerning domestic workers, who are held to be lacking in education.

This state of affairs has created a problem in so far as such prejudice is not acknowledged, much less explicitly discussed. In addition, there exists in practice a pecking order based on social standing. Mainly female unions do have more problems. There is also a kind of ranking depending on "economic weight", i.e. the size and social importance of a union and the occupation it represents. In this unofficial hierarchy the UWDE is severely handicapped by being a women's union in a sector whose economic value is not recognized.

A further problem which the union will have to face is that it is always represented by the same persons, who are ageing. Young people play practically no part at all in the external representation of the union. This problem has already been raised, but it is obviously crucial to the future of the UWDE.

From the CUT's point of view the affiliation of a trade union representing a very numerous occupation mainly composed of illiterate and semi-literate women with no social status, whose working hours do not correspond to those of other workers, represents a challenge. These characteristics have to be incorporated into the confederation's scheme of activities. For example, the kind of training called for is different from that designed for members with a higher level of education. The CUT has a certain tendency to give a rather uniform kind of instruction, but this case, like that of women rural workers, must be considered a special one, and the training adapted to it.

The confederation appears to be attempting to affiliate organizations which represent very underprivileged classes of the population. The affiliation of the UWDE is thus a genuine challenge and a new step forward.

Relations with the feminist movement

From the UWDE's perspective

The relationship between the feminist movement and the UWDE in Recife is one of a gradual evolution where suspicion gave way to participation and mutual enrichment.

There were numerous grounds for suspicion. In the first place, domestic workers come into regular contact with the "mistress of the household". As a result, the concept of group solidarity based on sex and women's oppression as a whole is an abstract idea[3] which is difficult to grasp, and a reality which at first sight appears contrary to the facts.

The first meetings of the two groups were highly inauspicious. The feminists espoused radical ideas which the trade unionists considered taboo. The union saw little reason to continue but the feminists persisted, inviting the union to all their meetings.

Since those beginnings SOS CORPO and the UWDE have developed a close

[3] Ed. note: Some migrant domestic workers complain that "all the talk about women's 'double day'" does not apply to women in Western countries because it is the migrant workers who assume the burden for them.

working relationship. SOS CORPO has helped the union in many ways and in turn the trade unionists have taught the feminists the importance of class struggle — how a person's sex is just one of many determining factors in a woman's outlook.

It was in particular the invaluable assistance of SOS CORPO during the work for the Constituent Assembly to revise the Constitution which turned out to be decisive in building an alliance between the two groups. The mobilizing capacity of the organized domestic workers was obvious to the feminist movement, which gave abundant help in training employees through courses and group seminars. SOS CORPO has helped the UWDE to set up its bookkeeping system; it is assisting in preparations for the next National Congress; it provides advice for the Education and Training Group and has been very involved in the preparation and evaluation of training methods for the union. A further aspect which has encouraged the UWDE to work more closely with the feminists is that they often invite the union to meetings where projects are conceived which can subsequently be worked out in collaboration. There is a will to cooperate.

Nowadays the union has become a full partner in the women's movement. The nation-wide study carried out on the working conditions of domestic employees (Conselho Nacional dos Trabalhadores Domésticos do Brasil, 1993), which will serve as the basis of discussion at the next National Congress, is the fruit of collaboration between the union at the national level and SOS CORPO. This collaboration, still at the local level for SOS CORPO, will strengthen the bonds between the feminists and domestic employees at the national level also.

The UWDE considers that the feminist movement will bring about changes in the way society views domestic service. Women will become increasingly aware of the low esteem in which the work which all of them do in the home is held and will fight to obtain recognition of its usefulness. In the union's opinion, any hope of improving the status accorded to domestic service lies in this direction.

From SOS CORPO's perspective

As far as SOS CORPO is concerned, its collaboration with the UDWE is excellent. In the "women's forum of Pernambuco"[4] the union regularly plays an active part, and also produces very good reports of its proceedings. In its manner of working, moreover, the UDWE echoes the concerns and methods which the feminist movement seeks to propagate and the contacts between the two organizations have enabled SOS CORPO to evolve its own methods of approaching working-class women.

Inasmuch as it seeks to preserve its independence vis-à-vis the groups with which it works, the union has rarely asked the SOS CORPO for money. All requests for advice and support are made with the intention of acting independently afterwards.

Nevertheless, the fact remains that in its dealings with SOS CORPO, as in-

[4] The "women's forum", founded in 1987 in the State of Pernambuco, serves as a platform for discussion and coordinated action by women at state level. It consists mainly of various women's organizations, as well as a few individuals.

deed with practically all the social movements with which the union collaborates, its members find themselves working with people who, in their private lives, employ domestic workers. They are constantly aware of this fact, which sometimes occasions crises, not in the collaboration as such but in the minds of the UDWE members concerned. There is a constant desire on the part of the women to come back to the question of class relations and their immediate relations with their employers. Working together in social movements more or less implies thinking along the same lines, whereas in other circumstances attitudes are opposed. There exists in the UDWE an ability and a strong will to differentiate between times and places where this question must be faced and those where the common cause takes priority. Nevertheless, remembering this distinction is a constant effort, which is not made any easier by the economic crisis. For example, the union is affiliated to the CUT, which, in view of the recession, has negotiated a drop in wages against an undertaking to preserve jobs. In practice this means that CUT members who employ domestic workers are either going to dismiss them, pay them less, or otherwise reduce their hours of work. The antagonism is real.

Relations with other movements

One of the difficulties in giving precise information on relations with other movements stems from the fact that they are often informal. Even though they may be perceived by the other movement, association or trade union as inter-institutional relations, this does not necessarily mean that they are so regarded by the UWDE.

As an example, one might mention the advice sometimes given by persons who are friends of the union and also active in the CUT or the ACO (Catholic Workers' Action), an NGO such as the Josué de Castro Centre, the Catholic CENAP, or again people working in one of the CUT schools. The informal, personal nature of such contacts is very strong. For the union, it signifies that it has succeeded in establishing an important support and exchange network.

This informal and personal character also applies to certain activities developed by one member or another of the union's Executive Committee. For example, in 1988-89 the President collaborated in a personal capacity in a study on the living space of domestic workers (Teles, 1988). Even though her participation in the study was the result of a personal decision, as a member of the union she was indispensable to the inquiry. It would be possible to mention numerous other examples.

Relations with the State

The successes of the domestic workers' movement in having its claims become law are remarkable and numerous. They bear witness to the changes that have taken place in the occupation, changes which they have helped to bring about. In particular, the claiming of rights by many domestic workers has only been possible because their associations (in the pre-union stage) fought for them during the work of the Constituent Assembly.

However, there is still much to be done, as was pointed out in the 1989 National Congress. Rights still remaining to be won are:

— fixed working hours; the draft legislation provides for 44 hours per week with extra payment for overtime;
— unemployment benefits;
— a written record of any employee-incurred expenses to be deducted from wages (not to exceed 5–7 per cent of wages);
— standards with regard to room and board in cases where the employee lodges at the workplace.

The most difficult of these will be fixed working hours, in that they imply some sort of mechanism for monitoring. The UWDE feels that very strong pressure will be needed if this provision is to have any hope of becoming law. The opposition will also be strong. The domestic workers' unions will have to formulate specific proposals if the law is to come into force, as well as suggestions for the settlement of subsequent litigation. So far they have not been successful.

Until the adoption of the new Constitution in 1988, Brazilian trade unions were subject to supervision by the Ministry of Labour. This was why the domestic employees' organizations not recognized as representing an occupation could not become trade unions. Since that time the Ministry no longer exercises such control and the contacts between it and the union are few.

Relations with employers

As already mentioned, the union's troubled relations with employers stem from the number of telephone calls and requests for information, and the fact that there is no employer's association able to bargain on a collective basis. The Recife Employers' Association performs absolutely no function as a spokesperson for employers of domestic workers vis-à-vis the UWDE.

An outstanding personality in the struggle of domestic workers: Lenira Carvalho

The current President of the UWDE of the MDR has been an outstanding personality in the struggle for the recognition and status of the occupation and for the acquisition of rights.

Born in 1932, she came to Recife and began work as a domestic servant at the age of 14, remaining with the same family for 16 years. In 1960 she joined the CYW which helped her to realize that as a woman and as a domestic employee she had value — a fundamental enlightenment for a woman working in an occupation which, up to then, had been accorded no value at all. Following two years as a CYW missionary, she returned to her former employment, and since that time has never ceased to play a part in the upward struggle of domestic workers. For a long time she worked as a daily helper, which enabled her to combine the duties of a militant with the need to earn her living. She is one of those exacting trade unionists who insist not only on the struggle to obtain rights, but also on the need to educate employees and make them aware of their innate value as women and as workers. The acquisition of self-confidence and a consciousness of the value of the domestic servant and the service she performs are constantly recurring themes in this kind of trade unionism.

Bibliography

Britto da Motta, A. 1989. *Emprego doméstico: revendo o novo* [Domestic service: Selling back the new], XII Annual Meeting of Assoçiação nacional posgraduação em scienzas sociais (AMPOCS), Caxambu, 23-27 October 1989, working group on women in the labour force.

———. 1985. *Emprego doméstico em Salvador* [Domestic service in El Salvador], Final research report, El Salvador, Federal University of Bahia.

Castro, M. G. 1989. "Empregadas domésticas a busca de uma identidade de classe" [Domestic workers in search of class identity], in *Cadernos do CEAB* (El Salvador), No. 123, Sep./Oct.

———. 1991. *A alguimia das categorias sociais-gênero, raça e geraçao-na produçao de sujeitos politicos: o caso de lideres do sindicato de trabalhadores domésticos em Salvador* [The alchemy of social/gender, race and generation in the production of political debate: The case of the leaders of the domestic workers' union in El Salvador], XV Meeting of AMPOCS, Caxambu, Minas Gerais, October 1991, working group on social and gender relations.

———; Chaney, E. M. (eds.). 1988. *Muchachas no more. Household workers in Latin Ameriça and the Caribbean* (Philadelphia, Temple University Press).

Conselho Nacional dos Trabalhadores Domésticos do Brasil. 1993. *Pesquisa: O novo perfil da trabalhadora doméstica brasileira* [Research: A new profile of the Brazilian female domestic worker], Final report (Recife).

Dabat, Chr.; Oliveira, G. 1985. *As mulheres nas organizações profissionais* [Women in professional organizations] (Recife, Associação dos sociologos de Pernambuco (ASPE), Centro de Estudo da Mulher (CEM)).

Entidade Assesoria Pesquisa Ação Social (ETAPAS). 1991. *Miseria urbana, uma radiografia da região metropolitana do Recife* [Urban misery, a portrait of the Metropolitan District of Recife] (Recife).

Instituto de pesquisas sociais, politicas e econômicas (IPESPE). 1991. *Realidade social da empregada doméstica apôs a nova constituiçao* [The social reality of domestic work following the new Constitution] (Recife).

OXFAM, SOS CORPO, MMTER SERTÃO CENTRAL-PE, MMTR BREJO-PB, CEAS. 1990. *Porque trabalhar com mulheres?* [Why work with women?] (Recife).

Sindicato dos Empregados Domésticos na Area Metropolitana da cidade de Recife. 1990. *Domésticas, uma categoria da classe trabalhadora: seus direitos, suas lutas, suas propostas* [Domestic workers, a category of the working class: Its rights, its struggles, its proposals], Programme for the promotion of women, CNDM/UNICEF meeting (Recife).

Sindicato dos Trabalhadores e Trabalhadoras domésticas do Recife. 1991. *Livros de formação sindical* [Union training volumes], Vols. 1 and 2 (Recife).

Teles, Leda (ed.). 1988. *Pesquisa: Dependência de empregada; o espaço da exclusão: estudo de caso no Recife* [Research; The maid's room, space or exclusion: A case study of Recife], Final report, preliminary draft, Centro Josué de Castro, presented at IAF (Recife).

3

Unions and domestic workers in Mexico City

Ruth Joffre Lazarini and Olivia Martínez *

Introduction

The Federal District of the city of Mexico is the major socio-economic and political centre of Mexico. About 50 per cent of the country's economic and social activity takes place in the capital. In 1980 the city had a population of 17 million, and by 1995 the figure is expected to be 30 million. This enormous growth and concentration of resources has also given rise to a great many problems, including excessive centralization, a shortage of housing and services, inadequate road networks and transport facilities, and appalling environmental pollution.

In spite of all this, Mexico City continues to be the place where many migrants hope to improve their standard of living and leave behind them the prevailing poverty of the barren parts of Mexico. For unmarried countrywomen, domestic service represents the only hope of employment and of working in the city. According to the 1990 census, 97 per cent of domestic servants are women.

The current economic crisis has increased the number of female wage earners not only from the country but also from working-class districts of the city. Women who were formerly housewives are forced to seek work to supplement a family budget for which their husbands' wages no longer suffice. With their lack of education and skills, it is very difficult for them to find a place in the labour market. Thus they remain condemned to underemployment as pedlars, beauty assistants or domestic servants.

Added to the lack of available jobs is the fact that the middle class cannot afford to employ domestic servants, or only at a very low wage. Thus a situation of greater supply and less demand is building up in the domestic-service sector. Now, more than ever before, domestic workers must be skilled, aware and united in order to stand up for their rights and to improve their living and working conditions.[1]

* ATABAL Collective.

[1] Colectivo ATABAL: *Proyecto General de Apoyo y Promoción a la organización de la Trabajadoras del Servicio Doméstico en la Cd. de México* (General Plan for Support and Promotion of the Organization of Domestic Service Workers) (Mexico City), 1992, 1993 and 1994.

General characteristics of the domestic service sector

Working conditions

— differing requirements with regard to working arrangements depending on the culture and customs of the employer family, imposition of alien manners and culture;
— in many cases bad treatment, having to put up with the employer's or the family's whims and ill-humour;
— discrimination against servants on account of their humble background and different culture;
— in many cases sexual abuse by the employer or his elder sons;
— servants are generally regarded with suspicion and are unjustifiably threatened with accusations of theft if they request what is due to them;
— little or no communication with employers;
— relations of servitude, inequality and inferiority with regard to employers;
— both working and living conditions are a cause of labour instability.

The social and political context

— Domestic servants are usually young women. In our experience most of them are single, some of them unmarried mothers, or separated from their husbands or abandoned. There are also some married women.
— All those who work as domestic servants do so for reasons of financial need; some in order to earn their living and not be a burden to their families, others to contribute to the family budget. When unemployment rises among male workers, the supply of candidates for domestic service increases accordingly. This accounts for the instability of part of the domestic-service sector.
— The great majority of servants are of peasant origin and have little education. Some studies state that 15 per cent are illiterate and that 42 per cent are "functionally illiterate" (i.e. did not finish their primary education), while only 31 per cent completed primary school. Few of them continue studying, and then only in order to escape from domestic service.
— In general, servants are not qualified to do any other work. They have learnt their domestic skills in the family circle since childhood, so that their standards of cooking and cleanliness are those of a peasant society characterized by a minimum of social amenities – crowded lodgings, lack of drinking-water and electric light, and so on. As a result, their work is completely underestimated and much criticized. Thus they undervalue their own work and have difficulty in obtaining social and legal recognition for it by means of organization and solidarity.
— Owing to the social origins of domestic servants, the sector suffers from grave

economic, social and political lacunae. While its members live and work in widely differing circumstances, they nevertheless share a general ignorance with regard to their occupational rights and obligations, and to the social structure of which they form part. They have little or no access to cultural, sporting or recreational activities.

— Members of the sector have no awareness of belonging to a specific labour group. It is difficult to keep up any kind of association or organization owing to the isolation in which they work and the daily proximity to their employers, a situation which prevents them from perceiving class differences analytically.

— Several years ago there existed only a few schools for domestic servants in Mexico City, together with some employment agencies. However, the work of these institutions was based on the ideological interests of the system. In other words, their goal was to raise the cultural level of the workers in order to adapt them to the environment in which they worked, rather than tackling subjects which might foster their self-esteem, the defence of their rights or a critical and independent state of mind.

Subjective factors hindering association and organization

— suspicion regarding invitations to meetings with strangers;

— fear of forming part of a group working towards organization, this word meaning little to most domestic servants, less even than "trade union", "political struggle" "strike", etc.;

— apathy before the prospect of having to act in order to initiate change or having to play an active part;

— lack of motivation owing to the absence of any precedent of struggle and organization in their place of origin;

— lack of the necessary self-discipline in order to study and go to all the bother of thinking, proposing and coming to decisions;

— diffidence with regard to others doing the same work (e.g. shyness or difference of age);

— a need to be protected and defended;

— job insecurity (difficulty in keeping contact).

All these items highlight both the scale of the sector's needs and the *enormous difficulty* of organizing action groups within it.[2]

Early history of organizing

Proposals to organize domestic servants into trade unions first began in various parts of the country in the 1920s. Twenty years later there were unions in at least

[2] ibid.

eight states or provinces of the country. Less than half of them were made up exclusively of domestic servants; the majority also included tortilla vendors and hotel and restaurant employees. Although some of these unions consisted entirely of women, most of those consisting solely of domestic servants contained both men and women, although the proportion of men was not very high – less than 15 per cent. By the 1940s at least four unions consisted only of women members.

Unions were formed both in major cities and in small towns. In urban centres such as Guadalajara and Mexico City they represented only a very small minority of domestic workers, perhaps 2-5 per cent. Domestic workers' trade unions were recognized as associations and, as such, came under the jurisdiction of the states where they were located. Some were affiliated to regional federations and national confederations.

In looking through the history of the movement the names of the unions raise a number of interesting questions. Although the term "servant" or "maid" might be widely used, it is noticeable that the unions all use terms such as "domestic" or "domestic worker". Perhaps this reflects the terminology of the Federal Labour Act, or it may represent an attempt to claim the status of workers and to reject the subordination implicit in the word "servant". Another noticeable point is that the names of some groups emphasize the fact that they are female, as in the case of the Female Union of Domestic Workers of the Port of Veracruz or the Red Female Union of Domestic Servants and Related Workers of Ahuey de Angostura. As far as we know, there has never been a single comparable case where an organization has stressed the maleness of its members. We do not find a Male Union of Petroleum Workers, but rather the Union of Petroleum Workers (although one might suppose that all the members were men). It was simply taken for granted that a trade union was by definition a male affair. The participation of women was exceptional, so that when the membership was mainly female, they made a point of the fact.

These attempts to form unions seem to have succeeded in overcoming some of the organizational obstacles typical of the sector. The mere fact of seeking and obtaining registration represents a step forward in the reclassification of domestic service as work.

Some of the difficulties of organizing women domestic workers in this early period are illustrated in the box opposite.

More recent organizing attempts

A second phase of organizing began towards the end of the 1940s with various attempts to promote and foster the organization of women in domestic service in some of the major cities of Mexico. This movement was advanced by various organizations. Some of them were Catholic; others stemmed from social assistance and NGOs.

Domestic servants of Cautla: A early attempt to organize

Towards the end of the 1920s an attempt was made to unionize the domestic servants of Cautla, together with boarding-house kitchen staff, cooks, washerwomen and chambermaids. A woman worker of that period describes her experiences:

I worked as a scullerymaid in a guest-house run by a Polish lady. I think we earned about $25 a month, one way and another, because it was a guest-house. They were very kind to me. Then I heard about the union, and all my companions said that everybody in service would join. However, my employers said: "If you join, you needn't come back here." And frankly, I didn't see any reason to join, because they were very good to us. My brothers were all against it, too. They said: "Don't join the union!" My employers gave me everything the union people were claiming, working hours and days off, time to eat our meals. I didn't understand why they wanted to form a union. They said we should work shorter hours.

The influence on the young woman of her family and her employer is evident in her remarks. She felt she owed something to her employers for giving her work and wanted to avoid sources of conflict with them and her relations. She therefore stopped seeing her friend who was organizing the union. This union did not last long and never succeeded in getting registered.

National Association of Domestic Workers

The Association was founded in the city of Mexico in 1948 with a registered membership of 100,000 women, 30,000 of whom were active members. In the words of its founder, its object was "to qualify the membership to render better service to society".

The Association continued functioning for its members more or less until 1983. Nowadays, in the words of a founder member, "it has turned into a business in the hands of the founder's children which does not concern itself with the interests of women workers at all". In 1956, a kind of hostel for the workers was set up. No fee was charged over and above the membership dues.[3] It was this association which proposed the feast of Santa Zita "the patron saint of servants", as a national holiday (27 April).

[3] Martha Patricia Vélez Tapia: "Las trabajadoras de casa particular... hacen historia" [Workers in private homes... make history], in *Correo del Sur* (Cuernavaca), 9 Aug. 1992.

Domestic Servants' Centre

The first meeting was convened with 15 domestic servants of the town of Cuernavaca de Morelos in 1977, and two years later the association (Hogar de Servidores Domésticos) was founded with 300 members. The purpose of this group was "to open a social centre" where the town's domestic workers could be offered the necessary minimum of services to solve pressing problems such as a place to go on days off, or during working hours; a crèche where they could leave small children; a working fund with the backing of the association, claiming just treatment, better wages and shorter working hours for members; and general training courses for the improvement of skills and working standards.

The main aim was to form a female domestic servants' trade union.[4] In 1987 a new working group changed the original name to that of Salaried Workers' Support Centre (CATDA). Currently, the Labour and Training Exchange continues its activities, lending the crèche premises to the domestic servants so that they can organize child-care services. The main objective is still to form a trade union, and to this end officials are being trained at a school of management. A constituent assembly of 26 women was set up, and in November 1991 it presented the Conciliation and Arbitration Board with a petition for registration of the Single Independent Union of Workers' in Private Homes (SUITRACAP). This petition was turned down by the Board on the grounds that the petitioners had not proved their claim to be workers, even though the petition was drawn up in accordance with the provisions of the Federal Labour Act. A new petition for registration is being prepared making use of every last legal resource in case it meets the same response in spite of the constitutional guarantee of civil rights.[5]

[4] Mary Goldsmith: "Experiencas de organización: Hogar de Servidores Domésticos A.C." [Experiences of organization: Domestic Servants' Centre], in *Revista Feminista*, Vol. IV, No. 16, Sep. 1980-Jan. 1981, pp. 44-46.

[5] Martha Patricia Vélez Tapia: "A propósito de celebraciones en CATDA ... (reflexiones sobre nuestras experiencias)" [Concerning celebrations in CATDA ... (thoughts about our experience)], in *Correo del Sur*, 6 Sep. 1992; "Inicia escuela de promotoras populares" [First School for grass-roots promoters], ibid.; CATDA, Carta circular a la Confederación Latinoamericana y del Caribe de Trabajadoras del Hogar [Newsletter to the Latin American and Caribbean Confederation of Domestic Workers], Oct. 1992.

Young Catholic Workers (JOC)

The Young Catholic Workers (JOC) promoted collaboration with domestic servants in Guadalajara around the mid-1970s and in Mexico City towards the end of 1979. Its general approach was to educate young workers to defend their rights. Its specific aim was to help domestic workers to realize that they were workers just as much as any others.

In the Federal District, six domestic workers were trained as organizers to attract others to the movement. Leaflets, periodicals and a pamphlet were published.[6]

Collective for Solidarity Action with Domestic Workers (CASED)

This feminist group was formed in 1979 and operated in Mexico City up to 1985. Its objective was to coordinate the organization of domestic servants and to create awareness in society of the problems faced by women working in private households. In practice it worked in two districts. The work consisted of:

— giving weekly advice to women domestic employees wishing to complete their primary or secondary studies in the adult education system;
— holding discussion groups with these workers concerning their work situation, their experience in other kinds of work, their relations with their employers, and so on;
— organizing activities such as walks, museum visits, etc.

One achievement was the organization of an employment exchange and a telephone support network among domestic workers in case of problems. Research on domestic service was carried out, various articles were published, an audiovisual cassette was made, and a song was composed.[7] The organization is no longer active.

Christian Union of Young Domestic Workers (Unión Juvenil de Empleadas de Hogar Cristiano)

This group was formed in 1986 with five members, one man and four women, in the Cañada district. Its aim was to foster friendships and confidence among domestic workers to keep them from feeling alone in the city and to promote awareness of the dignity, rights and obligations of workers. Retreats and Bible readings were organized where people could speak about their personal situations, their work, the community, and so on. The group was sponsored by the JOC[8] and

[6] Elena Urrutia: "Experiencias de organización", interview with Tesasa Valdivia, Director of the JOC, in *Revista Feminista*, op. cit., pp. 37-43.

[7] Mary Goldsmith: "Experiencias de organización: Una opción", ibid., pp. 46-48.

[8] Interview with members of the Unión Juvenil de Empleadas de Hogar Cristiano, Mar. 1987.

took part in workshops and meetings on the national level until it ceased functioning in 1988.

Organizing today

The ATABAL Collective

In 1986 two promoters of the Domestic Servants' Centre of Cuernavaca investigated which groups were working with the domestic-service sector in Mexico City. Until that time it had only been possible to make contact with the Christian Union of Young Domestic Workers and one ex-member of the former CASED. Through the contacts of these two groups a project was formed to hold a workshop on workers' rights which was attended by 20 participants. The group met to celebrate Domestic Service Day on 27 April 1987.

In April 1987 the ATABAL Collective for Support and Promotion of the Organization of Domestic Service Workers was formed in Mexico City by two activists and one of the founders of the Domestic Servants' Centre. It was registered as an association in September 1992. ATABAL worked in close collaboration with the Christian Union of Young Domestic Workers until the latter ceased functioning in 1988. The workers of this group then transferred to another one which was forming as a result of the workshops held by the ATABAL Collective, and which became known as the Group of Domestic Service Workers "La Esperanza" (meaning "hope") – see below.

The ATABAL Collective is an organization of professional women which serves women domestic workers. It has a feminist political purpose, namely to fight for the recognition of domestic service and, in particular, the social and political rights of women who work in it.

Difficult as it is to find answers to the complex problems of the sector, the ATABAL has drawn up some strategic guidelines. Its strategy is to put the real chances of organizing the sector through the ATABAL into perspective. The aim is to exert influence in order to create awareness of the mutual responsibilities of domestic servants, employers and society in general, so as to obtain emancipation of the workers in their capacity as women, enabling them to claim their rights as workers, and act as members of society. ATABAL believes that, with the help of proper training and on the basis of their own experience, it will be the domestic employees themselves who will work out strategies to amplify the protection and manage the organization of the sector, and who will adopt other forms of organization within the broad context of the movement.

General and strategic objectives

Both the general and the strategic objectives take account of various social agents with whom to share the enormous social problems represented by the undervaluation of household work and, as a consequence, of domestic service. These agents include: (a) female domestic servants; (b) domestic employers; employment agencies or other intermediaries; lawyers; legislators; government labour authorities; (c) NGO support centres; women's organizations; rural workers' organizations; trade unions; Christian organizations; political parties; (d) academics; researchers; students; national and private educational institutions; and (e) public opinion.

The goals which ATABAL has set itself in order to carry out its project are as follows:

The general goal: to fight for public recognition of the value of domestic service and, in particular, the social and political claims of the women who work in this sector.

The strategic goal: to incite domestic employees to organize in pursuit of their human and labour rights and the social recognition of their work; to campaign for the various sectors of society to recognize, on the basis of their day-to-day functions, the social, economic and political status of women domestic workers.

In order to achieve these goals, ATABAL has drawn up five lines of action, namely:

— the formation and strengthening of groups;
— popular education and training in organization;
— the promotion of organization;
— an awareness campaign regarding the problems of the sector;
— systematization of experience in general.

Of these, we consider the first three to be strategic and the latter two tactical.[9]

As mentioned above, the work of promotion and support that ATABAL has carried out over the last five years with groups that have come together for training has given rise to the domestic workers' group "La Esperanza".

ATABAL and "La Esperanza" are conceived as two separate entities acting as interdependent but autonomous and self-managing groups. Each has its own policies but is directly involved in and co-responsible for that of the other.

"La Esperanza"'s approach is to build up its capacity to promote the rights and defend the grievances of the domestic-service sector, whereas ATABAL sees itself as adviser in training and organization, and as a resource pool (whether human, financial or infrastructural, this last towards the consolidation of its own project) to help domestic workers achieve recognition of their status. ATABAL is to act on behalf of the domestic-service sector by assisting in its organization and promoting its recognition throughout society, while "La Esperanza" is to provide feedback and support to ATABAL's strategy.

[9] Colectivo ATABAL: *Proyecto General ...*, op.cit.

"La Esperanza"[10]

We are a group of women in domestic service in private households. We have been meeting since 1987 within the framework of the training workshops given by the ATABAL Collective in response to our concerns about organizing. These workshops have helped us to analyse our personal and collective situations as women and as workers in society. They dealt with workers' rights; the female identity; woman in society; human relations; methods of organization; and trade unions.

ATABAL helped us to stay together, to develop a sense of our identity as a group and to take part in our common goal, the formation of a trade union. However, as almost all of us are in live-in employment and can only get out for educational or planning purposes on Sundays, our lack of time has made it difficult to expand our group to achieve our goal.

To us, a trade union represents a form of struggle to obtain workers' rights which have hitherto been denied us, even though the Federal Labour Act has recognized just a few. So far, each of us has had to negotiate individually for observance of her own rights, when indeed (thanks to the workshops) we knew what they were, but from our point of view it would be better for all of us simply to have the same rights as other workers.

The general objectives of "La Esperanza" are as follows:

— to obtain *de jure* and *de facto* recognition, and our place in the community, as a labour and social sector providing society with an important service;

— to equip ourselves to carry out our work with professional skill by specializing in some branch of domestic service;

— to raise our level of education and thus be in a position to cope with change and the development of the country;

— to assume our place in the labour market with mutual solidarity to confront the hazards of unemployment and the vagaries of supply and demand more effectively;

— to make contact with more workers so as to join together and establish a trade union of domestic service employees.

In view of the long time it is taking to recruit more workers to our cause and to launch the union, we are trying to find ways to attract them to the group. We want to teach them about our basic rights and to create a collective awareness of the need to organize to defend our interests. After much thought we have decided to set up a meeting-place where we can discuss our real needs together, namely: better working conditions; training and education both to improve our work performance and to foster our progress both as women and workers; and the recognition of our cultural background and recreational needs.

With this in mind, we have developed a very ambitious project, to establish a training and overall development centre for domestic service employees. The centre

[10] This case study was written in the first person by the members of the group "La Esperanza".

will provide: an employment exchange; a training centre in technical skills and specialization in domestic service; an open school; and a cultural and recreation centre. It will be a place for women workers wanting to study and improve themselves as long as they continue working in the domestic-service sector. Together with ATABAL we have drawn up a working plan with the aim of extending these services to the entire conglomeration of Mexico City.[11]

At present there are 15 of us in "La Esperanza" who are committed to this project, and six are responsible for its coordination. Most of us are unmarried mothers. We see ourselves as promoters of the group and are in touch with about 70 women in the sector whom we bring together for social occasions and with whom we maintain contact regarding information and support in matters of education, publicity and organization.

We have six areas of work in connection with the project: (a) administration; (b) service to the public; (c) training in labour organization; (d) training in occupational skills; (e) entertainment and culture; and (f) internal group organization. Each of us looks after one of these tasks, making sure that the work goes ahead. This involves a lot of responsibility, but we try to involve newcomers in work assignments. We meet for four hours on the first and third Sundays of each month for training and organizational purposes.

We have also built up a small savings fund so as to afford support to our members in case of emergency. Three times a year we organize raffles in order to raise money for the organization's most basic needs. One part of our goal, the employment exchange, has already been achieved. The group which is going to study in the open school has already been formed, and we are in the process of forming a folk-dancing group to provide entertainment for social occasions. We organize social events at least three times a year.

In order to make contact with more domestic employees we hold publicity drives promoting the services we offer, distributing invitations to the events we are organizing and chatting with the girls when possible. As a rule we do this on Sundays in parks and other places frequented by our colleagues. We also take part in radio and television programmes and give press interviews where we make our problems known and explain what we are doing. In recent years some of us have joined in the Independent March on Labour Day, to show the flag for our sector.

In addition, we are promoting a project for the reform of Chapter XIII of the Federal Labour Act 1969 (concerning domestic service). In view of the fact that its provisions are in many cases very vague, domestic servants do not receive the same protection as other workers in Mexico.

Finally, in 1988 we formed a confederation with women's trade unions and associations in 11 other Latin American and Caribbean countries. Our aim is to achieve recognition by international trade union organizations and by our governments, in the hope that they will enact legislation recognizing us as workers. One of our undertakings to the confederation is to convene its Third Congress in Mexico in

[11] Grupo de Trabajadoras del Servicio Doméstico "La Esperanza": *Proyecto General, Centro de Capacitación y Desarrollo Integral para Trabajadoras del Servicio Doméstico en la Ciudad de México y Area Conurbada* [General Plan, Integrated Empowerment and Development Centre for Domestic Service Workers in the City of Mexico and Urban Conurbation] (Mexico City, Oct. 1992).

1994. As a result, we are working to build up as many members as possible so that they too can take part in the Congress.

We understand very clearly that if we and our allies do not struggle to get ahead, nobody is going to solve our problems for us. We also know that we must struggle in various ways and on many fronts. So far we have devoted our efforts to equipping ourselves and to developing our awareness of social and political reality, but now we need to undertake practical steps to organize. The formation of a trade union is one such step, but it is not everything. No one activity alone will solve our problems, and this is why we propose following up all of them.

In order to carry out our project properly we need financial resources which we do not possess, but we are seeking them in conjunction with the ATABAL Collective.

4

The Namibia Domestic and Allied Workers' Union

Magano Nagombe *

The socio-economic conditions of women domestic workers

The Namibia Domestic and Allied Workers' Union represents workers, for the most part women, who have recently emerged from a long independence struggle in which families were forced to separate, often for good. Independence was finally achieved in March 1990 after a long and drawn-out war. Women particularly suffered under apartheid laws which saw men leave the countryside for the urban areas in search of contract labour. They were left behind to scratch a living from the earth and wait for irregular and inadequate payments from the men to feed all those left behind.

Women in the cities were no better off, and usually the only employment available was as domestic workers for the White population with poor wages and unsatisfactory working conditions. Most noticeable was the utterly inferior education available to Blacks, which remains a handicap to them today in trying to enter the labour market. Also appalling was the striking difference in per capita gross domestic product, which ranged from US$5,035 for the mainly white modern sector to a mere US$21.5 for the traditional agricultural and informal sectors. Domestic workers are clearly at the very bottom of this range. Additionally, because of the long war for independence, many women are widows and single heads of families. It is these working women who are represented by the NDAWU.

The NDAWU represents domestic workers scattered throughout the country in individual homes, including gardeners and private messengers. Seventy per cent of the members are women and 30 per cent men. Most of the women are heads of families with four or five children; many lost their husbands during the struggle for independence. The Union's members average between 40 and 60 years of age. This comparatively older membership (in relation to other workers) is because this is the group which received the least education prior to independence. Their generation has little other choice of work.

The founding of the NDAWU

The national centre, the National Union of Namibian Workers (NUNW), had been concerned for some time about the plight of domestic workers in Namibia: the

* Official of the Namibia Domestic and Allied Workers' Union.

daily threat of dismissals, low salaries, long hours of work and slave-like working conditions. Under colonial labour law conditions were harsh. Domestic workers did not get paid leave, bonuses, pensions, or medical assistance. Salaries were much below those of the average worker.

In June 1987 an organizing committee met with a delegation of domestic workers and helped them to select a subcommittee in Windhoek. This subcommittee proceeded to organize domestic workers throughout the capital and in nine other urban areas outside the capital from 1987 until 1989.

As the country was still under colonial rule at that time and trade unions were forbidden, the subcommittee was eventually disbanded and some of its members arrested for trying to organize workers. Today, of that original subcommittee, only one woman remains active in the union. The national centre was forced to begin again to organize domestic workers and elected a new subcommittee of ten members for this task. Once the organizing had resumed and new members were joining, the NUNW provided basic courses on trade unionism to help the workers understand the role of trade unions.

In 1990 the NDAWU formally came into being at the first national congress of domestic workers on 21 April. The union adopted its constitution, structure, emblem and motto. The delegates elected members to the National Central Committee and the National Executive Committee. One hundred workers from throughout Namibia attended that first congress.

The NDAWU today

Today the union is formally affiliated to the NUNW and claims a membership of 4,000 out of an approximate 12,000 domestic workers throughout the country. Most of the membership comes from the larger centres of Windhoek, Swakopmund, Walvis Bay, Tsumeb and Keetmanshoop.

NDAWU has branch committees for the various regions as well as section committees. The branch committee meets once a month and the section committee twice a month. The union structure is similar to that of other unions. However, at the local level it has section stewards rather than shop stewards since, because of the nature of their jobs, most of the members work in individual homes. Owing to financial problems the union has only three full-time officials: the General Secretary, the National Chairperson, and the National Educator.

With women in the majority and in senior positions in the union, some of the male members were asked for their reaction to this arrangement. They replied that they felt confident in being represented by women because domestic workers in Namibia are very active and not at all shy about working with men.

When asked why they joined the union, members responded that they had never been considered as having "real" jobs like workers in the formal sector. They wanted to be treated with the same respect as any labourer and to have the same benefits.

There is no collective bargaining structure yet because the union is still young and at the time of writing the labour code was still in the preparatory stage. As a result, employers do not recognize the union and this makes it difficult to solve the workers' problems. Nevertheless, NDAWU does help its members through negotiating with their employers whenever possible. Union officials contact the employers by telephone and if they are unable to come to an agreement they ask to meet the employer in person. They have succeeded in resolving some of the cases, but where this is not possible they refer cases to the Ministry of Labour.

Organizing and workers' education

One of the union's first concerns was to increase membership and inform the workers of their rights. To help in this effort, the NDAWU arranged a radio interview with the Namibia Broadcasting Corporation to inform the listeners about the union. A union official spoke about how the union was founded, its aims and objectives, and how workers could apply for membership. The interview was a success because since then many domestic workers have applied for membership. The union relies heavily on individual workers' telling others about the benefits they derive from joining.

Education is one of the essential functions of the union. The NDAWU believes strongly in the importance of workers' education for its members to inform them of the basic tenets of trade unionism and to make them aware of the types of labour problem which arise. The NDAWU has organized study circles on Saturday afternoons to teach the rank-and-file members to understand what unions can do for their members. At present 80 per cent of the members are illiterate, and a literacy project is planned for the future. The members and staff are kept busy with various seminars, workshops and general meetings within headquarters and the regions.

Financing and income-generating activities

The biggest constraint for the union is its lack of financial resources. The members earn very little and it is hard for them to pay dues regularly; perhaps only 5 per cent manage to pay their dues in an average month. This is particularly difficult for them because many are single women with children. Dues are R1 per month, while the enrolment fee is R2.

Because of this lack of financing the union has had to turn to outside help. Trade Union Solidarity of Finland (SASK) has provided support to the NDAWU for its education project so that it may provide more basic trade union education to its members. OXFAM has provided assistance for a cooperative project. The members are learning about cooperatives so that they will be able to form their own cooperative in the future.

The union has been able to start a catering service as an income-generating activity. Catering is provided for various trade union activities such as national meetings of the unions and the federation. This project was started with the help of the Finnish Embassy. Three domestic workers who lost their jobs have been employed in the catering service.

The national centre recently organized a women's bureau. The bureau is quite active in dealing with women's issues and NDAWU works closely with them.

5

Migrant women as domestic workers

Margaret Hosmer Martens *

A traditional alternative for young women jobseekers

Just as young men have customarily been able to find work as day labourers, domestic work has historically been a means for rural women to find jobs in the city, usually when the hardships of rural life became too great or the city too alluring. In the latter half of this century women have migrated not just from the countryside to the city but from one country to another. For many this is the only way they can earn enough to support themselves and their families back home. However, this is not without a great deal of personal cost as the women are forced to work far from home, often under exceedingly difficult circumstances.

A significant number of migrant women are qualified for professional work in their own countries but end up as domestic workers after they emigrate. They take up the household jobs which are left unfilled by the citizens of the host country — jobs with low wages, little labour protection and little possibility for advancement. Many live and work illegally where there are large support networks of these women who congregate by nationality. As they rarely meet immigration requirements they enter as tourists and remain in the country clandestinely, living in groups in small apartments in immigrant areas of the cities. Some Filipino women living in European capitals complain that it is too dangerous to commute to work in the more affluent suburbs. They risk being stopped for an identification check when going any distance on public transport or walking in neighbourhoods where their "foreignness" stands out. Working clandestinely makes their bargaining position extremely weak.

The home country is anxious for the foreign exchange and wishes to relieve the pressure of large numbers of unemployed. During the Gulf War in 1991, several countries from Asia and the less affluent Arab States with large numbers of nationals working in the Middle East saw their economies reel from the blow. Not only did foreign exchange cease to flow, but they had to manage tens of thousands of their unemployed citizens who fled from the Gulf. Many of these were Asian women employed as domestic workers.

Migrant female domestic workers are reported to be exploited both in the sending and receiving countries. In quite a few countries, overseas migration has developed into a well-organized private business, particularly for female domestic workers. The majority of women go through private recruitment agencies to find

* Women in development specialist with extensive field experience.

work abroad and in many cases they are taken advantage of by unscrupulous agents who demand exorbitant fees. Although domestic work is poorly paid, economies in some Asian countries are so depressed that women can make up to four times what they could earn at home in more professional jobs. The attraction is obvious. However, they are often forced to live and work under impossible conditions. Some of the worst experiences for migrant female domestic workers are reported regularly in the Middle East,[1] where women have fled to their embassies for protection from their employers.

Findings of a survey on Filipino women in Italy

A recent ILO publication of a survey conducted by LIFE, a Filipino NGO in Italy, reported on the living and working conditions for 101 Filipino migrant women employed as domestic workers throughout Italy.[2] The report provides a close look at these women's lives as domestics working under better conditions than those found in most receiving countries. The immigration laws in Italy for non-EC workers and labourers have thus far been more lenient and protective than those in other EC countries where it is extremely difficult for non-citizens to obtain a work permit.[3] Migrants in possession of a residence permit (usually for two years) are free to work with the same protection as EC citizens, although the needs of the national economy must be taken into account and adequate financial resources and administrative support must be available to take care of their needs.

One of the findings of the study shows that Filipino migrant women in Italy are qualified to make a significant contribution to the workforce outside their usual roles as domestic workers (almost half the 101 women in the survey had college degrees). Only 2 per cent of the women lacked the necessary residence permit and as such were working illegally. Compared to the many clandestine workers in other countries in Europe and North America, the other 98 per cent have no fear of being stopped for identity checks. Yet most are still living and working in isolation far from their families. Their average age was 34 and only 36 out of 101 were married; 61 per cent of these had husbands living in the Philippines. The average period of time they had spent in Italy was four years. The 101 women had a total of 108 children, with an average age of 13, but only 9 per cent had their children with them in Italy. Thus, under relatively good working conditions, more than half of these young women had not married and the majority of those who had married lived far from their families while they worked for years to save enough money to send home.

Some of these migrant female domestic workers (not those employed in Italy) were interviewed in the Philippines after they had finally returned home. One

[1] See, for example, "Sri Lanka to Kuwait and back: The crisis of domestic workers", in *World of Work* (Geneva, ILO), Apr. 1993, pp. 8-9.

[2] Lega Italo-Filippina Filippini Emigrati Domesticas (LIFE): *Filipino migrant women in domestic work in Italy* (Geneva, ILO, WEP working paper, 1991).

[3] This was the case when research for the report was conducted in 1990. However, in April 1993 there were signs that it may be more expensive to employ domestic workers. A discussion is currently under way on whether or not to consider domestic workers as luxuries for tax purposes in Italy.

woman who had worked for three years in Saudi Arabia left her husband and three young children to work as a domestic abroad. Her eyes filled with tears when she recalled leaving her young daughter behind. But in spite of the pain of separation and hardships endured, she explained that there had been no alternative for the family. At the time, she had lost her assembly line job in a firm that made cigarettes and she knew that the family could not survive on her husband's meagre salary.[4] Through her work in Saudi Arabia they were able to save enough money to build a small house and buy some pigs to raise.

Obstacles to hiring migrant domestic workers

In some countries governments make it particularly difficult for migrant workers to find employment as domestics. Over 65,000 foreign domestic helpers in Singapore, including Filipinos, were expected to be adversely affected by an edict that imposed higher levies on employers hiring foreign maids, the Department of Labor and Employment of the Philippines reported.[5] The Singapore Ministry of Labor had announced that it intended to increase the levy from S$200 a month to S$300 effective 1 April 1992. According to the Philippines Labor Secretary, the immediate effect of the increase in the levy would be on the salaries of the domestic helpers. She said that it would dampen the possibility of any increase in wages among domestic helpers. The Labor Secretary added that the Singapore Labor Minister attributed the levy increase to a "surging demand" for domestic helpers, which grew by more than 20 per cent during the previous year, and that the move was aimed at easing the negative socio-economic effects of allowing the 200,000 Singaporean married women in the workforce to have free and unregulated access to foreign domestic helpers.

Moves to organize migrant domestic workers

In spite of the difficulties in organizing migrant domestic workers, a number of positive developments have occurred in various countries and areas.

In Hong Kong, migrant female domestic workers have made great strides in organizing themselves. The Asian Domestic Workers' Union (ADWU) in Hong Kong was formed at the end of 1988. Seven domestic workers succeeded in officially registering the union in May 1989 and today the organization has over 1,700 members. The members are women from Thailand (1,050), and the Philippines (600), with smaller numbers from India, Indonesia, Malaysia, Nepal, Pakistan and Sri Lanka.

A vital aspect of ADWU's work consists in assistance with grievance cases of which some 400 have been handled thus far with largely positive results. These have involved labour disputes (e.g. maltreatment and underpayment), police cases (e.g. physical and sexual assault, accusa-

[4] She had been the shop steward in her factory and, although she could not prove it, was sure that she had been let go for her union activities. Today her husband raises pigs and she works as a union organizer and is president of her union.

[5] From *Philippine Labor*, Vol. XVIII, No. 5, May 1992.

tions of theft), and immigration cases (illegal work, overstay, change of employment). The union also offers telephone counselling for domestic workers experiencing difficulties on the job — an important service as members work alone in individual households.[6]

The organization is run by members who devote their one free day a week to the union. In addition to help with grievance cases, they offer general assistance; but this is difficult when they have so little time free to commit to the union. Most of the work, including coordination and administrative work, is handled by the union's part-time organizer. The ADWU Executive Committee has 12 members who meet at least once a month.

The ADWU rents office space which members are free to use when they need a place to rest on their weekly day off. Members try to promote diverse Asian cultural traditions and understanding among Hong Kong's women domestic workers.

A much earlier case of migrant women organizing occurred in 1981 in Canada where women fought for and won the right to stay in the country. Previously they could only obtain temporary permits and were forced to leave the country after three years. Under pressure from Intercede (International Coalition to End Domestics' Exploitation), based in Toronto, the Canadian Government granted domestic workers the right to apply for "Landed Status" after two years' working in the country. Foreign domestic workers on temporary permits now have the same rights under labour laws as Canadian citizens. Intercede began in 1979 as a coalition of community groups for domestic workers' rights, soon to become a multiracial organization of domestic workers with community support.[7]

Another step towards migrant women organizing, although not necessarily domestic workers, was the holding of a conference on Philippine women in Europe entitled "Empowering Filipinas in Europe". The conference was held in Barcelona, Spain, in September 1992.

In Europe some of the unions affiliated to the International Union of Food and Allied Workers' Association (IUF) have domestic workers as members, such as the Austrian Agricultural, Food Processing and Catering Union (ANG), the German Union of Food Processing and Catering Workers (NGG) and the Italian Federation of Workers in Commerce, Tourism and Services/Italian General Confederation of Labour (FILCAMS/CGIL). These have all concluded collective agreements covering domestic workers. The FILCAMS/CGIL has published a sample domestic workers' contract, "Il contratto de lavoro domestico", in nine languages.

Recognition for migrant domestic workers

The many migrant women who work illegally as domestics live in constant fear of being discovered by the local authorities. Worst of all, they are at the mercy of their employers as they have absolutely no bargaining power over their working con-

[6] International Union of Food and Allied Workers' Association: *IUF News Bulletin* (Petit-Lancy, Switzerland), No. 1-2/1993.

[7] C. Mather: "Good enough to stay", in *International Labour Reports* (Geneva, ILO), Sep.-Oct. 1986, p. 17.

ditions. This is not to say that conditions for these women are inevitably bad, but what is inacceptable is that they have no ability to negotiate the circumstances of their own labour. A favourite topic of conversation among these women is how they hope to regularize their situation and arrange a work permit. This is sometimes possible if work is found with a diplomatic family, but it is exceedingly complicated and even then not always accomplished legally.

For those migrant women who are not working illegally as domestics, life is comparatively easier. However, the basic problem remains: whether as domestics they are recognized as workers and given the same protection as other workers receive. It is the job of domestic worker itself which is far too often unrecognized. The ILO standards apply equally to national and foreign workers alike and, therefore, this should also be the case for foreign domestic workers. The right to equal treatment as to wages, hours of work, social security coverage, days off, weekly rest, collective bargaining, and protection under law against abuses and maltreatment, should be in line with the general standards practised in each country for all other categories of workers. However, this is frequently just as much a problem for local citizens, as seen in the case of the National Union of Domestic Employees (NUDE) in Trinidad and Tobago, which was reported to be challenging the Government's determination of domestic workers as "non-workers". Currently they are denied any of the rights and privileges accorded to others under the country's Industrial Relations Act.

Conclusions to Part II

Margaret Hosmer Martens

The incentive to organize

Although domestic workers have long been considered difficult to organize because of the comparatively isolated nature of their work, we have seen here that, given the right conditions, they will come forward. Domestic workers will organize because, as in the case of Namibia, they are tired of not being considered as having "real" jobs like others in the formal sector.

There is a stigma associated with domestic work. Many, as in Brazil where a youth group was formed especially for domestic workers, are ashamed of their jobs and uncomfortable about socializing with other workers. Some young domestic workers go to great lengths to keep their friends, particularly boyfriends, from learning how they earn their living. Understandably many who are outraged by such a situation believe that the only acceptable alternative for domestic work would be the formation of cleaning cooperatives where workers would negotiate with employers as a group. Some insist that domestic work is dismissed as "real employment" because society considers women's work in their homes as little more than a natural extension of their lives. Thus, the fact that someone else might be paid to perform these tasks does not automatically imply that this is recognized as "real" work. The job's invisibility tends to remain intact as in the case in Trinidad, where the NUDE is fighting the Government's determination of them as "non-workers".

Regardless of what the future may offer, the problem now is that the casualized nature of the work puts domestic workers at an extreme disadvantage. Organizing is essential to obtain protection through legislation, to inform the public of their plight and to provide domestic workers with an understanding of their rights as workers and, most important, a sense of dignity in their occupation.

The support for organizing

In Namibia it was the NUNW that elected a subcommittee to organize domestic workers. Today, only three years after its formation, the NDAWU has succeeded in organizing one-third of the potential domestic worker population in the country.

Although in Brazil the movement was originally started through the assistance of church groups, it was especially the hard work and dedication of some of the members, such as Ms. Carvalho in Recife, which brought the union to life. Since its inception the UWDE has been helped by a variety of linkages with other groups including the trade union confederation, CUT, but it has had a particular boost from the women's movement through SOS CORPO. The account of the gradual development of the alliance between the UWDE and SOS CORPO, as well as the subtleties of class versus gender relationships, is very instructive.

The movement in Mexico has also been greatly influenced by the women's movement. The ATABAL Collective was begun by two women activists and the founder of a previous domestic workers' association. The ATABAL Collective and the domestic workers' organization, "La Esperanza", have an interesting working relationship, and this association bears watching to see how others might learn from its experience in the future.

Relations with the trade union movement

In Namibia there is an understandably close working relationship between the NDAWU and the confederation, NUNW. In Mexico the situation is more problematic. Essentially the unions thought that such workers were potentially too difficult to organize and that their lack of education could inhibit their full participation as members.

When these same potential drawbacks were suggested to the officials of CUT in Brazil, it was admitted that the UWDE would present a challenge to the confederation but they were ready to take it on. The issues raised with the CUT are important, and in some respects they are representative of any attempt to affiliate an organization in which the majority of members are women. In particular, as "women have difficulty in making their voices heard or in acceding to posts of responsibility" within the confederation, what will be the fate of a small union with mostly female membership? The extent to which the UWDE's affiliation with the CUT is successful will be significant.

Other issues for organizing domestic workers

One issue which came up often in the literature and in the Brazil and Mexico case studies is the role of the union and vocational training. What type of training can and should the union provide? Whereas most trade unions provide training for their members on their rights as members and workers, vocational training is often seen as a special service which attracts domestic workers to the union. Then the question arises: Should vocational training be provided which will improve their work in the domestic sector or which can be used as a means to leave the sector?

Another important issue for this sector seen particularly in Brazil is the age of the members themselves. The UWDE is very concerned that the young, who most need the union's protection, are not easily convinced of the need to become active members. The leadership has recognized social activities as an incentive. This is particularly important for domestic workers because of their isolation and lack of ease with other workers.

Other special services for domestic workers included employment exchanges, telephone support networks, a place to congregate on days off, sometimes a crèche, and both legal advice and general advice, the latter because as the women are so isolated, they need to feel supported.

The future

Although the chapter on Mexico shows the long history of domestic workers' organizations forming and then disappearing, Latin America has been making big strides in this sector. There are trade unions and associations for domestic workers in 12 Latin American and Caribbean countries, and in 1988 they joined together to form the Latin American and Caribbean Democratic Workers' Confederation which will hold its third congress in 1994.

Domestic workers' organizations and, to some extent, unions are to be found throughout the world but they suffer many handicaps. Money will always be a problem because their members are among the poorest paid in the world. A particular frustration of many domestic workers' unions, as seen for the UWDE in Brazil, is the lack of an organized employers' group although this has reportedly been achieved in areas of Germany.

Most important is the fight to win recognition of domestic work as "real work" with the same rights as any other occupation. To achieve this goal it is necessary to have the firm support of the entire trade union, as well as other groups such as those depicted in the case studies.

Part III

Organizing homeworkers in the informal sector

Introduction to Part III

Jane Tate *

One of the challenges of the trade unions in the 1980s and 1990s has been how to find ways of working in the expanding informal sector, a term which is used in this book to include home work. Home work, or outwork as it is often called, has always been a difficult issue for trade unions. Homeworkers are by definition scattered in their own homes and are difficult for unions to organize. Unions have generally been strongest where large numbers of workers are brought together in one workplace. The majority of homeworkers have always been women who make up a captive workforce, and are sometimes tied to the home by their family responsibilities. In some industries in the countries studied for these case studies, homeworkers have often been minority or migrant women who face a number of barriers in finding work outside the home. As a result, homeworkers have been seen as cheap labour, who undercut those working in organized workplaces.

Historical background

The traditional union response to the challenge of home work has been regulation. The campaigns against the "sweated trades" of the late nineteenth and early twentieth centuries came up with different forms of state intervention. In Australia and the United Kingdom, the answer to the problem of home work was seen to be regulation, through the use of minimum wage legislation and other laws allowing, for example, the inspection of workplaces for health reasons. The other form of regulation, which has been the official position of most trade unions in this century, has been for a total ban on home work, or a limited ban in certain trades. In some countries, for example the United States, the unions successfully fought for a ban to be imposed.

The call for a ban on home work was also repeated in the First Tripartite Technical Meeting for the Clothing Industry, held by the ILO in 1964, which stated that: "Industrial home work in the clothing industry should, as a matter of principle, ultimately be abolished, except as to certain individuals, for example physically handicapped persons — who cannot adapt themselves to factory work" (cited in Johnson and Johnson, 1982, p. 123). The same meeting further acknowledged that total abolition was not yet "practicable"and called for strict regulation in the meantime.

* Yorkshire and Humberside Low Pay Unit, Batley, United Kingdom. A founder member of the Yorkshire Homeworking Unit, she is the author of several publications on homeworking and is now involved in setting up a European Coordinating Group on Homeworking.

Underlying these calls for regulation of home work was the view that homeworkers, as well as other workers in the "sweated trades", were impossible to organize. Regulation was seen as an alternative to organization and unionization. Another assumption was that home work was an old-fashioned form of production, associated with nineteenth-century industry and levels of poverty that would become irrelevant as society progressed. It was assumed that home work would make up no part of modern industry and that it would cease to exist.

This has, however, not happened. Even at times when home work was little publicized, it has persisted. In the United Kingdom, for example, during the Second World War, women assembled aircraft parts in their homes and garage workshops (Allen and Wolkowitz, 1987, p. 13). After the War, it was noted by the unions concerned that large numbers of homeworkers were still employed and were on the increase in the boot and shoe industry and also in the clothing industry (Pennington and Westover, 1989, pp. 156-157). However, at grass-roots level, there was also experience of working with homeworkers as union members, for example, in the Union of Boot, Shoe and Slipper Operatives.

More recently, in the 1970s and 1980s, home work, far from decreasing, has been shown to be expanding in both industrial and developing countries. In its Expert Meeting on homeworking, held in October 1990, the ILO noted that the increase of home work is associated with the growth of subcontracting, both internationally between countries and within specific countries (ILO, 1990). A Council of Europe report, published in 1989, also noted the spread of home work throughout most European countries and the fact that it was undertaken mainly outside any forms of regulation (Council of Europe, 1989).

Reasons for an increase in home work

Research into the clothing industry has shown the underlying patterns which have led to an increase in homeworking (Mitter, 1986). The industry has been restructuring in a way that decentralizes production. In the seventies, much of the mass production of clothing was exported from the industrialized countries to Third World countries, such as the Philippines or Bangladesh, mainly to take advantage of low wage costs in these countries. More recently, a just-in-time model of production has encouraged the use of subcontracting and the consequent employment of homeworkers nearer home. The classic case has been that of Benetton, which uses the latest technology to monitor sales in its retail outlets throughout the world and responds "just in time" to avoid holding stocks (Conroy Jackson, 1990).

These more recent developments have led to a restructuring of the workforce in line with the new management of production. In a general way, this can be seen as the division between the "core", a minority of the workforce employed in relatively stable and well-paid jobs, and the "periphery", who are a flexible workforce only employed when the demand is there. This periphery includes many workers, in free trade zones, for example, as well as homeworkers in the industrialized, as well as developing countries.

The above patterns of production and their implications for the workforce have been most intensively researched in the clothing industry. What has been observed is also applicable to other industries, including motor vehicles and electronics. Similar patterns can be seen in the service industries, where in retail trade, for example, there is a growth in part-time and temporary work. In Europe, many surveys have shown that whereas traditional manufacturing jobs are in decline, the growth in employment is occurring in the service sector, in jobs often seen as women's jobs because they are part time and low paid.

The trade union response

The restructuring of the economies of industrialized countries has meant a disastrous decline in union membership drawn from large workplaces, and has led to some re-assessment by the unions of their role, methods of work and traditional areas of operation. Many of them have, in particular, re-examined their policies and practices in relation to women members and have developed policies on equal pay and the wider participation of women in their organizations.

At the same time, the issue of home work has been re-examined by the international trade union movement, mainly as a result of the work of women organizers in developing countries, particularly the Self-Employed Women's Association (SEWA) and the Working Women's Forum (WWF) in India. SEWA and the WWF have challenged the old idea that homeworkers are impossible to organize by developing more flexible methods of organizing women in the informal sector.

Groups outside the official trade unions have also developed work with homeworkers, usually around ideas developed by the women's movement working on a community basis. In the United Kingdom, for example, since the early 1980s, the National Group on Homeworking has loosely coordinated a number of groups and individuals around the country campaigning for better conditions for homeworkers. The trade unions have moved away from their call for a ban on home work and now hold official positions advocating the organization of homeworkers.

In Italy, a similar shift has taken place in the attitude of the trade unions. In the 1950s, legislation on home work was advocated with the aim of essentially abolishing it. However, by the 1970s, the trade unions were acknowledging that home work could not be abolished. Therefore they advocated new legislation with the aim of improving the terms and conditions of employment for homeworkers (Conroy Jackson, 1990).

The growth of home work in recent years has, therefore, forced the trade unions to re-examine the issue in general. This is taking place in a context where a substantial proportion of employment is being restructured to create a more flexible workforce, of which home work is simply one example. Concern over the new "flexible" patterns of work, or casualization of employment in general, has increasingly become a central issue for many unions because of the growing participation of women in their organizations.

The trade unions in industrialized countries have, on the whole, little recent experience of working with the informal sector. This contrasts sharply with the experience of working people in developing countries who have often been forced, by necessity, to organize outside official structures. The last 20 years have in particular seen the growth of many different forms of women's organization which combine traditional trade union issues, such as relating to paid employment, with other aspects of women's lives (Mitter, 1989).

Home work: Legal or illegal?

It is sometimes assumed that most home work in industrialized countries is illegal and undertaken "on the side". This is often cited as one of the reasons why homeworkers are so difficult to organize. In reality, however, home work is not necessarily illegal. The status of this work usually depends on the particular laws in each country.

At one extreme, home work is a "normal" and regulated form of employment. Homeworkers are employed, in some instances, on similar terms as workers within a factory; they are treated as employees, with deductions made for social security and tax payments and their employment is registered and regulated by law. Furthermore, the homeworkers can be unionized. In some countries, they are likely to have been employed by the same company inside the factory and their employment simply continues when the worker moves to work at home, usually because of family responsibilities. Expenses for electricity, insurance or materials may also be paid.

There are examples of this "formal employment" of homeworkers in the United Kingdom (Yorkshire and Humberside Low Pay Unit, 1991). In Denmark, a trade unionist reported that homeworkers in her industry were treated as part of the regular workforce.[1] In Italy too, homeworkers are sometimes treated this way (Conroy Jackson, 1990). It is estimated, however, that homeworkers working under such conditions make up a small minority of the total number of workers in this category.

The majority of homeworkers can be described accurately as working in informal employment, in the sense that their employment rarely comes within official regulations or is registered officially. This situation should not be seen as implying illegality, although this may be the case depending on national legislation. In the Netherlands and the United Kingdom, for example, most homeworkers work unofficially "off the books"; payments are in cash without tax and social security deductions, and without any official registration. They are not covered by legislation and are therefore in legal limbo rather than illegal. In some cases in the United Kingdom, the illegality may be on the part of the employer, who may not be paying "legal" wages, and not on the part of the homeworker.

Similarly, there are cases where the illegality connected with home work is in relation to laws other than employment laws, for example immigration and social security legislation, but the employment relationship itself is not illegal. In other cases, the employment relationship is illegal. For example, in Australia before the change in legislation, a homeworker was supposed to have a permit to work at home. In such cases, where a permit had not been obtained, the employment relationship was illegal.

[1] Report back from European Health and Safety Conference, held in Sheffield, United Kingdom, 1992.

* * *

This part of the book looks at the experience of three trade unions in Australia, Canada and the Netherlands, which are tackling the issue of home work. In a general way, this can be seen as working with women in the informal sector since many of the homeworkers are women. It describes the strategies adopted and the results achieved.

6

Australia[1]

Jane Tate

Background

The Clothing and Allied Trades Union of Australia (CATU) launched a campaign in 1986 to organize outworkers in response to changes in the Australian clothing industry. In a report entitled *Outwork in the Australian clothing industry*, the union outlined the changes in the industry which were the backdrop to their outwork campaign (CATU, 1987). These changes meant that, at that point in time, the union estimated that there were more outworkers in the industry than workers in factories.

The changing pattern of clothing production in Australia is similar to that in other industrialized countries. In 1973 the Government began a process of cutting protection for the domestic clothing industry. In 1973 tariffs were cut by 25 per cent. From 1977 quotas were introduced, but from 1982 import quotas on clothing were successively liberalized. It had been anticipated by some that the removal of protection would make the domestic industry more efficient. However, the union pointed out that this "efficiency" has been achieved, in most sectors of the industry, by a strategy of moving production from factories to outworkers and "by making outworkers carry the burden of production costs, including electricity, delivery, machinery, rent and other overheads such as cotton and trims" (CATU, 1987, p. 1).

The union launched its campaign in 1986 in anticipation of a further decentralization of the industry. It distinguished between separate developments in different sectors of the industry. In the production of jeans and overalls, for example, it was appropriate to introduce expensive new equipment as a way of improving efficiency. In these sectors, outwork was not an important factor. The sector of the clothing industry where most outwork was performed was the women's fashion sector. Here it was practical to put out the labour-intensive work of machining, mainly performed on a flat-bed sewing machine.

The growth of outwork in this sector of the industry was also linked to increasing concentration and competition on the retail side, and the need for flexibility and quick response by manufacturing to consumer demand, which was closely monitored with the introduction of computerized systems in the retail trade.

The clothing industry in Australia is highly concentrated, with 90 per cent of

[1] Information on the campaign in Australia is based on a number of different sources, mainly three reports from the Clothing and Allied Trades Union of Australia (CATU, 1987, 1990; Laverty, 1988). The written material has been supplemented by discussions with Sylvia Carbone, who was employed by the union to work with outworkers in Melbourne, from 1986 to 1990.

the industry being in only two locations: New South Wales (35 per cent) and Victoria (55 per cent). The union reckoned that the majority of outwork was also based in these areas, in either metropolitan or decentralized industrial regions. In the absence of accurate statistics, it estimated that there could be between 30,000 and 60,000 outworkers in the industry, as many as in the known workforce (CATU, 1987, pp. 5-6).

The union identified that the motive for increasing outwork in the industry was the desire to compete with growing imports by cutting costs. Outwork also allowed for the cutting of wage costs in various ways: the reduction of hourly rates and associated costs such as holidays and sick pay, as well as social security and tax payments; the cutting of overheads such as electricity and rent; the increase of the intensity of labour by eliminating breaks and through piece-work payments; and ensuring flexibility in numbers employed by laying off outworkers when no work is available.

The union noted that outwork had always been part of the industry but that, between 1977 and 1987, it had grown substantially. A large part of this growth was clearly in the informal sector.

The outworkers

In the factory workforce in the Australian clothing industry, 95 per cent of the employees were reported to be women and the majority were "migrant" women. The union assumed that this would also be true of the outworkers. Furthermore, they linked the employment of outworkers of particular communities with firms owned by people of the same community: "Outwork bosses often engage women of their own ethnic community in certain geographic communities. This reflects the tendency of ethnic groups to live in the same locality, the trust between people of the same ethnic origin and the need to facilitate pick-up and delivery of work" (CATU, 1987, p. 5).

The union identified close community links and familiarity with a common culture as one important element leading to outwork. In some cases, outworkers were newly arrived migrants or refugees who encountered racism outside the home and lacked the language and confidence to work outside the home. In others, the women had had experience of factory work but preferred to work at home because of many negative aspects of factory work, including sexual harassment, authoritarianism and paternalism of management. Other factors identified were lack of appropriate training and education, child-care facilities and public transport.

The overall situation was that few women felt that they had any choice. Outwork was their only alternative, and wages were kept down by the competition for work with an oversupply of labour. The social security system failed to provide an adequate level of income, thereby encouraging work "on the side". Outworkers were isolated and vulnerable to intimidation and harassment by employers. The union also identified the fact that the existing law stipulated the need for a permit to work at home and that the lack of such a permit criminalized outworkers and made it more difficult for them to come forward.

The union summarized the position of outworkers in the industry as follows:

Outworkers were cruelly exploited. They earn below award wages, work long hours, do not receive the benefit of industrial awards or legislation and face major expenses for equipment and overhead costs.

Outworkers are isolated from mainstream workers. They are employed as a clandestine workforce and their employers avoid their responsibilities, and costs, under employment law. The effect of this isolation is that outworkers have become disenfranchised within the labour movement. Their de-unionization ensures that they suffer gross injustices and inequalities compared to other mainstream workers in Australia (CATU, 1987, p. 1).

Union strategy

The union adopted a dual strategy, combining a legal approach with the organization of outworkers. The campaign could roughly be divided into the four stages corresponding to the four years when the union focused on outwork. In the first year, the aim was to reach outworkers, find out about their pay and conditions and publicize the results. Part of the aim of this was to win public support, both nationally and within the communities concerned, for legal protection of outworkers. In the second year, cases were taken forward as new regulations on outwork could be established through legal precedents at both state and federal levels. In the third year, the union was successful in winning new legal rights for outworkers and worked closely with a tripartite working party made up of unions, government and employers. In the fourth year, the emphasis was on ensuring that the new awards were in fact implemented. Numerous claims were fought by the union on behalf of outworkers as a way to recruit them into the union.

The union's above-mentioned strategy combined a number of different ways of working on different fronts, both legally, within the community and through joint national work. At the same time, from the outset of the campaign, there was a recognition by the unions of the crucial importance of organizing outworkers, without which new legal rights for these workers would be ineffective.

The law

Regulation of the clothing industry is covered by both Federal and separate State Clothing Trades Awards. The Federal Award regulates the wages and conditions of workers employed by respondents to the award. The State Awards apply to all other employers not covered by the Federal Award. The union had mixed results in pushing for all the protection that they advocated. Although they had success in some states, similar measures in other states were thought not practical in the light of a general move towards deregulation. In a report written in 1990, the union concluded:

The approach for common legislation, i.e. deeming provisions, was abandoned by the union when it was judged difficult to obtain [it] across all states in Australia ... The experience of the union in New South Wales, where such legislation did exist, demonstrated that the union and outworkers were only marginally better off because, in the end, any campaign to enforce the award — such as it was — would only shift the problem to other States where the deeming provision was not available (CATU, 1990, p. 2).

Although it was only partially successful, the union's strategy in relation to legal reform is worth looking at in some detail as it contained several points particularly important for outworkers.

The fundamental basis for the legal campaign by the union was the overturning of earlier judgements that outworkers were "independent contractors". An important judgement established that outworkers could not be called "independent contractors" simply because the employer said so, or because their work was not in the factory. The judgement argued that outworkers were an integral part of the production process, worked as part of a team (even if they were not aware of this themselves) and were subject to control by the employer. This judgement laid the basis for many claims subsequently taken up by the union. The union also argued for the following changes:

— The burden of proof should be on the employer, not the outworker. The outworker should be treated as an employee unless the employer could prove otherwise.
— The permit and ratio system should be removed. The permit system made outwork illegal unless the outworker had a permit. Permits were granted if the homeworkers had a particular reason, for example a disability, for working at home. Similarly, employers were restricted to a fixed ratio of outworkers to factory workers.
— By winning employee status for outworkers, they automatically came under the clothing award as far as wages were concerned.
— Hours of work were limited by restricting the amount of work that could be delivered over weekends or holidays. A limited amount of work was permitted if overtime rates were paid.
— Outworkers had to be employed for a fixed number of hours. Full-time workers were employed for 38 hours and those who worked fewer hours were treated as part time. The number of hours was calculated through the piece-work rates. If work was not available for the contracted hours, payment still had to be made.
— Records of outworkers had to be kept by employers, and the union, as well as government inspectors, had the right to see these.

The success in winning legal rights for outworkers then became the basis for a major information campaign among outworkers, as well as their recruitment to the union as discussed below.

The union campaign

As part of its campaign for legal change, the union did extensive publicity and information work in order to build public support and to reach outworkers directly. In March 1988, it also published a report of a visit to Europe where they had discussed, with people in the United Kingdom, Italy and Switzerland, different strategies adopted in relation to homeworking (Laverty, 1988).

The union launched a major publicity campaign in 1986 when it first set out to vary the Federal Clothing Trades Award in order to make changes for outworkers. This campaign aimed to expose the exploitation of homeworkers and win support for their legal protection. The campaign was judged successful, "because the constituents for which the union was seeking the variation were women and migrants and were able to be seen as exploited workers in the Australian context" (CATU, 1990, p. 3).

At the same time, a campaign was launched specifically aimed at outworkers and the communities involved in outworking. The union was concerned to let outworkers know directly about the union's policies on outwork. They used the "ethnic media", both newspapers and radio, as a way of reaching outworkers and establishing links with community workers. In one state, Victoria, the state government set up a multilingual hotline for advice and help to outworkers. The union collaborated with the state government and produced thousands of leaflets in 14 different languages, and employed a project worker to deal with inquiries from outworkers. In a period of about one year, over 6,000 outworkers contacted the union for advice. The union commented on the importance of this by stating that, "prior to this information campaign being implemented, the union scarcely heard from any outworkers" (CATU, 1990, p. 4).

Once the move to establish legal rights had been successful, the information campaign went into a second stage to publicize the rights that outworkers now had. The same methods were used to reach outworkers, including community networks and media. The union employed two outreach workers, in Victoria and New South Wales, the two areas where outwork was concentrated. The new element of the campaign at this stage was the ability of the union to take claims forward for outworkers based on the new award. The union assessed the success of this effort in the following way: "there has been a considerable increase in the number of claims made by outworkers regarding their wages and conditions, and in the number of outworkers who are now members of the union" (CATU, 1990, p. 5).

Compared with many other countries, the union was in a strong position at this point to represent outworkers. In order for an outworker to make a claim for wages, she had to be a member of the union. This gave outworkers a direct benefit from union membership. The union also had considerable powers in relation to employers. The project workers could, for example, require employers to give them information, such as the names and addresses of outworkers. Furthermore, the union successfully pursued many claims for outworkers and at the same time recruited them into their membership. Most of these claims, however, were only taken up once an outworker had come into conflict with an employer or already finished her employment. The problem of ensuring continued employment for outworkers while enforcing their new legal rights proved to be more difficult.

The commitment of the union to its campaign to organize outworkers is well illustrated by an issue of *Ragmag*, the union journal, in April 1988. This issue focused on "Outwork: New rights for workers, new rules for employers". The details of the new award, with samples of written contracts and records of work, were printed in 12 languages.

At this time, the union also employed a variety of methods to reach outworkers. It:

— held meetings for outworkers, either by language group or location;
— developed networks with community workers, especially migrant community organizations;

— maintained information updates on ethnic radio through announcements and interviews;
— helped outworkers in their contacts with the union and assisted the union in processing claims made by outworkers (CATU, 1990, pp. 4-5).

The union also employed project workers to liaise with outworkers in areas where they knew that was a concentration of outwork.

The main difficulty faced by the union was keeping up links with the outworkers, particularly maintaining membership and developing ways of organizing them in an ongoing way. The traditional union structures were based on workers coming together in a factory and could not incorporate the dispersed workforce of homeworkers. As long as project workers were employed, the contact with the outworkers was maintained; but the union did not find a way to make this continuous, once the project worker left.

Results

In 1990, the union's assessment of the success of its information campaign was that it had managed to reach many outworkers, who were now informed about their rights under the law. In terms of the success of regulating the industry, the union states that many employers are now complying with the award, or have switched back to employment within the factory. In the following observation the union recognized that there was a problem about continuing illegal employment: "There are, however, many employers who operate on a 'backyard' basis, who are very difficult to locate. The union — especially in New South Wales — is testing out a system for tracing these employers" (CATU, 1990, p. 5).

In its general conclusions about its work, the union saw the important turning-point as being a change from the policies which, to some extent, blamed outworkers themselves for their work which was often illegal. This approach was changed with the campaign, in the late eighties, of legal reform and active organization in order to "legitimize outwork and free [workers] from the burdens of illegality" (CATU, 1990, p. 7).

The union made important progress in establishing legal rights for outworkers and organizing them, but it did not claim to have been totally successful or to have found all the answers to the problems associated with this work. In particular, the problem of ongoing organization for outworkers remained a difficulty. Although numbers of outworkers joined the union, especially when they wanted to pursue a claim for back pay, the numbers of members were never more than a small minority of the thousands of outworkers. After the major campaign from 1986 to 1990, the union saw itself as stepping back and adopting a policy of "mainstreaming" the issue of outwork. The argument was that, since outwork was now legitimized, any future policies or strategies would include outworkers as part of the workforce. The work of contacting and developing work with outworkers was therefore reduced:

> As far as the ongoing contact with outworkers is concerned, and the support required by them to overcome the effects of their isolation in the workforce, the union now believes that this can

best be achieved through community-based organizations. The union, over the last three years, has sought to provide this service to outworkers. The experience has shown that because it is not a regular function of unions, we are unable to be both consistent and available (CATU, 1990, p. 6).

At the same time, the union made a commitment to work with unions in other industries, apart from clothing, to develop a strategy on outwork. A national meeting was planned with the Australian Council of Trade Unions (ACTU) to develop a strategy based on the clothing industry experience. In this connection, the following observation was made: "We believe that this approach will help to create an environment which will allow outworkers to 'come out' and be seen and see themselves, as legitimate workers in the workforce" (CATU, 1990, p. 7).

The Australian outwork campaign is an important example of a union tackling the issue of outwork and changing its position from one that essentially blamed the outworkers themselves to one that attempted to "legitimize" and work with the outworkers. The union successfully adopted a variety of new methods of working in order to reach outworkers in the numerous minority communities where they were based. At the same time, it managed to win important legal precedents which established employment rights for outworkers. Furthermore, the union recognized at the start of its campaign that organization would be the key to implementing rights for outworkers. This was a problem that the union did not manage to solve in the long term although it clearly was able to take initial steps to reach outworkers. The union's analysis was that the basic contact and information work would have to be taken up by community-based organizations. Tackling the issues involved, as well as outwork in other industrial sectors in Australia, will be important areas of work for the future.

7

Canada [1]

Jane Tate

One of the most recent examples of a trade union that has developed work with homeworkers is the Ontario District Council of the International Ladies' Garment Workers' Union (ILGWU) in Toronto. In 1991, in response to changes in the local garment industry, the union started research into the pay and working conditions of homeworkers. The following year they set up a homeworkers' association and, in November 1992, held a conference on homeworking together with other unions and organizations.

Background

There are many similarities between the changes in the garment industry in Toronto and the situation faced by the clothing union in Australia, and indeed in many industrialized countries of the North. This industry in Ontario accounted for 30 per cent of Canadian garment production, with 60 per cent being found in Quebec and 10 per cent elsewhere. The period 1987-92 has seen a dramatic reduction in the numbers of officially recorded clothing workers, from a total of 13,000 to 6,500, of whom about 2,000 are unionized. The industry is still facing closures and the numbers are expected to decline still further. Some of this decline has been due to a rise in imports, which account for 40 per cent of clothing in retail stores. There has also been fragmentation of production. The union estimates that 77 per cent of current production in Ontario is being carried out in workplaces with fewer than 20 workers, and that there are at least 2,000-3,000 homeworkers in Toronto, although this number may well be an underestimate.

The union describes this as a "hollowing-out" of the production process. At the top of the pyramid are the big retailers, where ownership and control are increasingly concentrated. Production is being transferred from factories, many of them unionized, to subcontractors, with homeworkers at the bottom of the pyramid. This new structure is linked to the retailers' demands for a quick response strategy which relies on "just-in-time" production, with the stores introducing electronic equipment to monitor sales.

In examining the union's response to these changes it is useful to outline some ILGWU history. The "International" in the union's title refers to the fact that it

[1] This account of organizing in Canada is based on documents from the ILGWU and discussions with union staff in Toronto in November 1992.

organizes in both the United States and Canada. Set up early this century in the United States, with the Toronto branch being established soon after, the union has a long history of organizing in the garment industry, particularly in the sector of women's fashions. In Toronto, another union covers other clothing sectors. The union's membership, at least among the majority of its women machinists, has always reflected patterns of migration so that there has been a history of organizing in different communities and, inter alia, adapting to different cultures and demands of the membership (Pesotta, 1987). In the early part of this century, this meant that many of the members of the Canadian branches of the union were Jewish and later Italian. Now many of those entering the garment industry are of Chinese origin, from Hong Kong, China or Viet Nam.

The union has also recently adopted a broader approach to organizing than is traditional in many unions. This is reflected, for example, in the ILGWU's American "Campaign for Justice" which was launched with a strategy of working closely with community organizations (ILGWU, 1990). The union recognized that it needed to work in alliance with other groups, particularly those based in minority communities, in order to unionize and regulate the clothing industry. It studies a particular clothing chain from top to bottom, tries to use consumer pressure on retailers and uses a union label to encourage good employment practice and recognition of the union. More recently, the union has recognized the importance of working with another group of "precarious" workers in the campaign to organize among flower-sellers (Lipsig-Mumme, 1987).

In both the United States and Canada, the right of the union to engage in collective bargaining for groups of workers has a legal basis, where they are union members. While giving a strong bargaining right where membership is established, this makes it more difficult for the union to represent other groups outside. The ILGWU has, therefore, developed an Associate Membership Programme as a basis for organizing workers in situations where the union does not have the legal right to collective bargaining.

On the negative side, the ILGWU has had a long-standing policy of advocating a legal ban on home work, which is viewed as inherently exploitative for the workers involved and also as undermining collective organization at the workplace. Under the Reagan Administration, home work was partly deregulated in the United States and the union's submissions on this were firmly opposed to the measure.

In the United States, the union still maintains a policy of calling for a strengthening of the ban on home work. Until this is changed, it will be difficult to organize homeworkers.

In Canada, the legal situation is different. Compared to other countries, there are relatively detailed regulations for home work. The ILGWU has found, however, that most home work falls outside this regulation and is hence informal but not illegal. The union's policy of attempting to ban home work rather than organize homeworkers has, however, prevailed until recently.[2]

[2] See account of the strike in Montreal in Lipsig-Mumme (1987).

The homeworkers

The first step taken by the ILGWU was to commission research on homeworkers. From its knowledge of the clothing industry, the union knew that there were many Chinese clothing homeworkers. It applied for outside funding and carried out in-depth interviews with homeworkers. The results of this research were presented to the state government in December 1991 (ILGWU, 1991).

Average earnings were found to be below the legal minimum wage. A few women earned above the minimum and some earned well below. Out of 30 homeworkers interviewed, only one received holiday pay. Average weekly hours of work were 46, although in rush periods some women worked as many as 100 hours a week. No overtime rates were paid and no social security contributions were made by employers. Homeworkers bore the cost of overheads, such as sewing-machines, and encountered serious health and safety problems.

Although many of the women were seen as "immigrant" and lacked English language skills, the majority had lived in Canada for many years and all but six were Canadian citizens. The single most important reason for working at home was child care. Many had previously worked outside in a garment factory and left because of pregnancy. Twenty-seven out of 30 stated that they would prefer to work outside, but felt that they had no alternative but home work.

The research revealed that there were two problems relating to the law for homeworkers. First, the provisions that do exist were simply not being implemented. For example, homeworkers are defined as employees under the Employment Standards Act. Second, in some areas homeworkers are excluded from protection, for example, on maximum hours of work, overtime pay and statutory holidays. Thus, the union identified early on that a double approach was needed which consisted both of finding ways to ensure that the law is implemented and of strengthening the law itself.

Union strategy

In 1992 the ILGWU developed its work with homeworkers in a number of different ways. It set up a homeworkers' association, as a local (branch) of the union, with a membership of 22 Chinese garment homeworkers. At the same time, it worked with a number of different groups in a "Coalition for Fair Wages and Working Conditions for Homeworkers" (the Coalition, for short). In November 1992, a conference was organized to bring together the organizations from the Coalition, the ILGWU and the Public Service Alliance of Canada (PSAC), which was concerned with the introduction of home work for white-collar workers in government employment. The conference also brought together people from other countries working with homeworkers or garment workers. Simultaneously with the conference, the Coalition launched its "Clean Clothes Campaign", with the aim of bringing consumer pressure to bear on the big retailers (see below).

In a workshop held at the conference, Alex Dagg, Manager of the Ontario District Council of the ILGWU, outlined some of the thinking behind these activities:

A common theme to this kind of organizing is that it is a long-term approach. Traditional union organizing campaigns focus their strategy around a target that may last several months. Organizing in non-traditional areas where unions have little stronghold means that the union must commit to an extremely long-term and patient approach. Campaigns focus around years of work rather than months. Another common thread is that some of the most creative organizing is not coming from traditional trade unions but from grass-roots women's organizing outside . . .

One of the biggest challenges to organizing homeworkers is to locate them and understand the underground network of contracting and homeworking . . . If the union is to take on such a campaign, it is imperative that the union work within the community. We have in particular targeted the Chinese and Vietnamese community in Toronto since it is by far the largest community doing garment homework in the city. Organizers must be a member of this community and be able to speak and work with community members . . . (Dagg, 1992a).

At the conference, speakers from the ILGWU outlined how they had set up a homeworkers' association and a clothing homeworker herself outlined her pay and conditions.

The union employed a woman to work with homeworkers. Over a period of several months, she organized various activities and invited homeworkers to attend. These met with varying success until some bus trips were organized over the summer, which proved popular. She continues to organize "social teas", as a chance for homeworkers to get together and break out of the isolation of working at home. She is currently organizing English language classes in response to requests from homeworkers. The union has also had an advice line that homeworkers can ring for help on many different questions, including their work.

As a result of the above, the homeworkers' local was set up:

The Homeworkers' Association [HWA] is a chartered local of the ILGWU, Ontario District Council, and is affiliated with the international union's Associate Membership Program. This local functions as a union local but the union does not have the right to negotiate a collective agreement for the members of the association since there is no formal recognition from the Labour Board. The association functions as a pre-union, which can provide services, legal advocacy, lobbying and other political work . . .

A crucial part of the functioning of this local has been that programs and services and events be centred out of the union office. This means that the members of the association routinely hold meetings, arrange the pick-up point for outings and trips and generally congregate there. The union then functions not simply as an administrative office . . . but also as a drop-in centre where workers in the *community* become used to dropping in for help of any sort (Dagg, 1992a, p. 3).

The union organizers stressed the need to be able to respond flexibly to the demands of homeworkers, the importance of personal contact and word-of-mouth information within the community, and a long-term approach to the work. Alex Dagg adds that:

What has become clear is that like most organizing work, there is no one magic wand or one magic technique that will work to organize workers in such a sector. A variety of creative techniques must be developed and tried and re-tried . . . Our goal is eventually to be in a position when we can organize some of the HWA members into becoming full-fledged union members with a formal bargaining relationship . . . (Dagg, 1992a, p. 5).

In the summer of 1992, the union organized a conference to bring members from the factories together with the homeworkers and to discuss their strategy with organizers and researchers from the unions. This was, for most of those who took part, the first opportunity for them to meet each other. It was an important opportunity for the union to develop educational work about the trends in the industry, increase the understanding of its members and, in particular, ensure — through a common unity — that homeworkers were not seen as outsiders, undercutting union labour.

The union has raised funding from outside its own organization for both the research work and the setting up of the homeworkers' association. It also employs its own researcher and raised additional money for a worker to organize the conference. At the same time, a number of other organizations have contributed to the campaign on homeworking.

The different groups who make up the Coalition show the range of this support: Centre for Research on Work and Society; Chinese Workers' Association; Coalition of Visible Minority Women; Ecumenical Council for Economic Justice; ILGWU; Labour Council of Metro Toronto and York Region; Mujer a Mujer; National Action Committee on the Status of Women; NDP Spadina Trinity Riding Association; Ontario Coalition for Better Childcare; Parkdale Community Legal Services Clinic; School Sisters of Notre Dame; and Workers' Information and Action Centre of Toronto.

The broad range of organizations has enabled the homeworking campaign to develop on a number of different fronts at the same time. While the union has focused on organizing the association, it also takes part in the Coalition which mobilizes a range of bodies and skills in support of the campaign. The conference involved others, particularly the PSAC and the international aspect of the work. The result has been a high level of support and publicity around the issue of homeworking and considerable interest from the Ontario, New Democratic Party government.

Considerable progress has been made in a detailed examination of the law on homeworking and of practical ways of ensuring implementation. For example, the union is looking into the possibility of joint liability legislation, whereby those at the top of the pyramid (usually a retailer) have responsibility for conditions all down the subcontracting chain. Another possibility being explored is that of reviving an old union practice of hiring halls. This idea would mean that an employer who wanted to take on a homeworker would have to take the next on the list and the union would monitor pay and conditions.

At this stage, the homeworking campaign has already made considerable progress. The association has been set up and has provided an organization for homeworkers, enabling them to break out of their isolation through a number of social activities. A number of cases have been taken up for homeworkers who are owed money for work they have completed. These are being dealt with through outside legal advice and the results are not yet known. At the same time, a broad basis has been built, both through the alliance and through publicity for the wider campaign for legal reforms and consumer support.

Conference: "From the double day to the endless day"

"From the double day to the endless day" was the title of the Conference held in November 1992 in Toronto, which brought two broader elements into the campaign on home working. The conference brought together homeworkers and organizers from the garment industry and members of the PSAC, who were concerned about recent government moves to introduce home work. The concern of this union about the spread of home work — or telework — was outlined in a document included in the conference information pack:

> In the federal Government, teleworking is a new concept whereby an employee, with the approval of management, works at home from one to five days per week. All terms and conditions of the employees' collective agreement remain in effect, as do departmental policies and procedures. What does change is the place in which the work is done and the employee's report to work process . . .
>
> PSAC members have been performing telework informally for a number of years . . .
>
> The [PSAC] is researching the extent and consequences of home work in the federal public service. A goal of the research project is to examine the conditions under which home work may be an acceptable option . . . Another goal of the project is to develop suitable contract language to address the problems articulated by PSAC members . . .
>
> The PSAC is co-sponsoring the Homeworking Conference with the International Ladies' Garment Workers' Union, the Coalition for Fair Wages and Working Conditions for Homeworkers, and the Centre for Research on Work and Society. By joining hands, sharing experiences and ideas, we build solidarity and support each other in working towards gaining better working conditions for all homeworkers (Dagg, 1992b).

During the conference, the difference between the two groups of workers — garment workers and teleworkers — was acknowledged. With the garment workers, the issue was how to bring them into membership of the union and to regulate their work. With the teleworkers, the issue was more how to protect existing pay and conditions, and maintain the unity of the workforce that faced the possibility of fragmentation.

The other broader aspect of the conference was the participation of international speakers — both on home work and the garment trade — from Nicaragua and Mexico. Mujer a Mujer, a women's collective network operating in Canada, the United States and Mexico, was on the organizing committee of the conference and brought a wider international perspective to it. One particular focus was the discussion of the free trade agreement already concluded between Canada and the United States, and the proposal for this to be extended to include Mexico. A common concern was how to protect jobs and working conditions in the face of this agreement, working in solidarity with each other rather than in competition for jobs. The conference illustrated well the strategy of the ILGWU to combine developing flexible ways of organizing homeworkers with building the broadest alliances possible.

Another element in the union's strategy was developed simultaneously with the conference. A "Clean Clothes Campaign" was launched with a rally outside a major shopping centre to draw in consumers. Publicity from the campaign gave examples of the terms and conditions of garment homeworkers and encouraged consumers to make this an issue. The focus is on putting pressure on the big retailers to take responsibility for terms and conditions of employment down the subcontracting chain. The use of the union label is seen as one way for consumers to insist on good employment practice.

Wider issues

The ILGWU's initiative on home work can be seen as a direct response to the changes in the garment industry and loss of membership from the organized factories. At the same time, the union has drawn on experience from elsewhere in looking at the issue and also sees the experience of working with homeworkers in Toronto as being more relevant to wider questions than the changes in the garment industry. Furthermore, Alex Dagg acknowledges the importance of the experience of other groups of women organizing:

> There are some encouraging trends in organizing, however. There have been some excellent and creative examples of women organizing precarious workers in various parts of the world that the Canadian labour movement can learn from. For example, there have been some interesting examples of union organizing in Mexico with the 19th September Garment Union which involves leadership training of the women activists. They routinely include assertiveness training as a key component of their union organizing. In England, there are numerous homeworking projects going on in many sectors, using a form of organizing that we have used in the HWA in Ontario . . . (Dagg, 1992, p. 2).

But she also points out that the particular experience of the garment union is relevant to others in Canada:

> We feel that our experiences over the past few years may easily in the next five years be felt in many other sectors of the economy, both public and private. The garment industry has been described as the DEW (Distant Early Warning) line for other sectors . . .
>
> I think that no sector is immune from the homeworking phenomenon and that this may be the fundamental challenge for the labour movement in Canada and other countries in the months and years ahead (Dagg, 1992a, p. 1).

The lessons from the ILGWU's work with homeworkers are relevant to others, as are the problems. While the union considers that its work has been difficult but exciting, the main problem identified is the need for extra resources. It is impossible for a union to fund the intensive work necessary to organize homeworkers out of the membership dues, let alone from the dues raised from homeworkers alone, particularly in the early stages. While short-term funding can be raised for this work, the problem of a more stable funding base remains to be solved.

One of the issues discussed at the conference was ways in which the ILGWU experience could be taken forward into the broader labour movement. One idea was that of forming a central (national) union committee that could pool financial resources, with a well-defined system for bringing in new members and allocating them to particular unions. In addition, the experience of working with homeworkers in the

Netherlands was discussed: "There was also a general discussion about the need to form a Working Women's Association which could be the backbone of a pre-union for many women who cannot easily form a traditional trade union . . ." (Dagg, 1992a, p. 6).

Although many of the ideas and strategies discussed were specifically addressed to the situation in Toronto, they could equally well have been about how to tackle the "flexibilization" or "casualization" of the workforce, whatever form it is taking throughout the industrialized world.

Conclusion

The experience of organizing homeworkers in Toronto has in some ways been a defensive response to the loss of union membership in the factories. By tackling the issue of home work in a positive way, the union has managed to incorporate a number of different approaches into its work and develop a new pattern of working which is moving ahead fast. Central to the strategy is the organization of homeworkers themselves, and this is still at an early stage. As was pointed out at the Conference organized in Toronto in November 1992, it is crucial that unions demonstrate that they can defend "precarious" workers, such as homeworkers, and the ILGWU has moved to meet this challenge.

8

The Netherlands[1]

Jane Tate

Work that has been done with homeworkers in the Netherlands is very different from that in Australia. This is partly because of the nature of the Women's Union itself and partly because the work has concentrated not only on the clothing industry but also on the broad range of home work in the Netherlands.

The Women's Union is one of the 19 unions affiliated to the Netherlands Trade Union Confederation (FNV). It is not an industrial union but a general organization for all women, whether in paid employment or not. Homeworkers can at the same time have dual membership of the Women's Union and an industrial union. The Women's Union does not have negotiating rights and does not engage in collective bargaining for its membership. It campaigns on women's interests generally within the FNV and with the Women's Committee of the FNV. A recent document states: "We devote ourselves to the protection of the interests of specific groups left out by the other unions: homeworkers, domestic helpers, women re-entering the labour market, domestic workers (staff), voluntary workers, housewives, etc." (FNV, 1990).

The Women's Union took up the issue of home work in 1979. As part of a union education project it had sent a questionnaire to the membership which included a question about home work. The results showed that, among its members, there were over 100 different kinds of home work being done. Following this, it carried out more investigation with the members and campaigned for improvement in the homeworkers' pay and working conditions. As part of this work, the Women's Union supported homeworking projects in the Netherlands and carried out a range of work, both local and national. This included advising and giving support to homeworkers, as well as carrying out interviews to compile material on home work. These homeworking projects were not solely managed by the union but were independent projects similar to those in the United Kingdom (see "Introduction", Part III of this book).

Background

An important part of the brief of the National Home Work Support Centre (HSC), in Hengelo, was to carry out research on the extent and nature of home work.

[1] The information on the Netherlands is mainly based on contacts between the Dutch Home Work Support Centres and the West Yorkshire Homeworking Unit over the last four years. The Women's Union provided a background paper for a group who visited the Netherlands in September 1990 (FNV, 1990).

Before this centre was wound up in 1992, four booklets had been published giving the detailed findings of the research (HSC, 1992a, b, c and d). They showed that home work was widespread in many different industries in the Netherlands. In a paper published in 1991, the following industries are listed: food; leather and shoes; wood and furniture; paper and paper articles; graphics and printing; chemicals; building materials, earthenware and glass; metal products; electronics and electrical products; transport products; wholesale; services; textiles and garments (Heumakers, 1991).[2] The type of work done by homeworkers in these different industries was varied, but generally labour-intensive. Some homeworkers use machinery, such as sewing-machines, simple engineering machines or computers, while others work by hand. The HSC estimated that there were 166,000 homeworkers in the whole of the country, constituting about 3 per cent of the female population.

The majority of homeworkers are women (97 per cent). In clothing and textiles, the HSC estimated that the proportion of migrant homeworkers was 4 per cent in textiles, and 8 per cent in clothing. With non-Dutch nationals making up 6.6 per cent of the population in general, the HSC estimated that a greater proportion of migrant women than Dutch women do home work, but have no figures for this. Although many of the non-Dutch homeworkers are from Morocco or Turkey, women from 12 other countries were also found doing home work.

Other research in the Netherlands has shown that similar trends are operating there within some sectors of the clothing industry, as in other European countries and Australia. The restructuring of the clothing industry in recent years has led to much work being outsourced to developing countries, but with another trend for work to be subcontracted within the Netherlands. This process of subcontracting within the country has led to the growth of an informal sector, based on small workshops and the use of homeworkers. Many of these workers are Turkish women (van Geuns, 1992). However, the approach of the Women's Union and the HSC has been to deal with home work as a whole, rather than focus on it in one particular industrial sector.

Who are the homeworkers?

As in other countries, the majority of homeworkers are women whose reasons for working at home are linked to their family responsabilities. Their reasons for taking up home work are their need for additional family income, lack of education or training, and the difficulty of finding a job outside the home. The need to be at home with young children is one factor among many and does not seem to be the main reason why women take up home work, as has often been found to be the case in other countries. The HSC stresses, too, that the income from home work is too low to support a single parent and that the majority of homeworkers are married women, with another income coming into the family (Heumakers, 1991, p. 6).

The HSC further points out that for Turkish homeworkers, the situation is even more difficult: "While a number of Dutch homeworkers choose home work in

[2] This picture closely reflects what is known about some other European countries such as Germany, France and the United Kingdom. In all these countries, although home work is prevalent in the clothing industry, it is also spread throughout different industries.

order to be able to care for children and family, hardly any Turkish homeworker chooses to work at home voluntarily, but nobody found a regular job outside the home . . . Working at home increases the triple discrimination of these women: they are women, migrant women and on top of all that homeworkers" (Heumakers, 1991, p. 7).

Home work and the law

The HSC points out that although most home work in the Netherlands is informal and outside the purview of regulation or the law, only a small proportion is illegal. Even then, the illegality often arises from people claiming benefits while working rather than from the employment relationship itself. For the majority of homeworkers with whom the HSC had contact, their work was completely legal. The informality arises from the fact that homeworkers are often outside the law and have few employment rights. This was summarized as follows: "In most of the cases the labour laws, which are applied to all employees, are not applicable to homeworkers. This means that homeworkers cannot claim the *minimum* wages for their work, they are not covered by the *minimum* wages and the *minimum* holiday allowance laws. They work for a very low piece-rate. They have no employment contracts. They are not protected by law in case of dismissal. They do not benefit from social security. They have to wait and see whether they get work or not and how much they have to work. They do not get extra payment for overtime or working at weekends. Sometimes they have to provide their own tools, machines and even materials . . . They are not informed about their rights, if any, about health hazards, about anything at all" (Heumakers, 1991, p. 4).

In the Netherlands the Home Work Law had been passed in 1933. However, it had largely been ignored and before the Women's Union uncovered the extent of home work and initiated action around the issue, there was not even a general awareness of the extent and importance of home work in the country.

Union strategy

Following the results of the 1979 survey, the Women's Union carried out more investigation and lobbying round home work. In 1981 it published a pamphlet, *Home work: In your place ten other workers*, which argued for recognition of the importance of home work. After extensive lobbying and pressure on political parties and discussions with other unions, the profile of home work and the problems associated with it were raised publicly. The Women's Union carried on investigating the extent of home work and visited the United Kingdom to find out what was being done for homeworkers there. On the basis of this, in 1985 it set up the first HSC, which acted as the National Centre. Others were established in Amsterdam and The Hague, and another independent centre was set up in Tilburg.

Funding for the support centres came from the national Government. The HSCs were independent of the Women's Union, although it and other unions were involved in running the projects through their governing boards. Alongside the HSCs, the Women's Union carried on lobbying and developing work with the other unions, and formed a close working relationship with the Women's Secretariat of the FNV. For example, in 1987 a working group with the FNV was set up to compose a policy report and action programme on home work. This programme was then used to lobby for further action. The work was also discussed by the five policy councils of the FNV and a final programme was drawn up. One aspect of the programme that has been taken up by other unions has been the need to include homeworkers in collective bargaining by the unions and to draw up collective agreements which specifically include them.

The HSCs were not permanently funded by the Government. After six years of funding, the National Centre at Hengelo has now been closed because the research has been completed. Local centres continue to provide an advice service for homeworkers, although their future is not guaranteed. In 1992 the Women's Union itself appointed three workers to work with homeworkers directly, this time under the direct control of the Women's Union.

The Women's Union and the HSCs consistently advocated legislation as the main way to improve conditions for homeworkers. They saw the main problem faced by homeworkers as being that they are outside legal regulation. Their analysis was that the key regulation needed was for homeworkers to be defined as employees in order to bring them under legal protection. On this central point, they have not yet been successful although some legislation has been introduced relevant to home work. A recent health and safety law, for example, specifically covered homeworkers. In terms of inclusion of homeworkers in collective agreements, the legal status of homeworkers continues to be an obstacle, as only employees can be covered by such agreements in Dutch law.

In terms of union membership, the HSCs were successful in bringing a minority of homeworkers into union membership. This was done by making special provisions for legal services to homeworkers outside the normal rules of the union, enabling those who faced a particular problem, where legal help was needed, to obtain assistance. Concrete benefit was also provided by union membership. Membership dues to the Women's Union were low enough to be accessible to homeworkers. Less progress was made in terms of membership of the industrial unions, since their normal dues were too high in general for homeworkers.

Home Work Support Centres

The HSCs served a double purpose. On the one hand, they provided an advice and support service to homeworkers. Through their contact with homeworkers, they were able to collect information and develop policy about home work in the Netherlands. Bringing home work out into the open was important:

> Visualising homework was very important, because until that time homework was a blind spot in the Dutch economy. One acknowledged that there has been homework in the nineteenth and the beginning of the twentieth centuries, but one did not believe that there would be homeworking in the Netherlands on a big scale nowadays . . . At most, there would be an illegal circuit in which homework was done and that mainly by migrants (Heumakers, 1991, p. 3).

The Hengelo Centre was set up in an area where manufacturing industry – textiles, clothing and engineering – was in decline and home work was known to exist. The centre had a staff of four, two consultants, a policy worker and an information worker. One of the consultants was Turkish. The main tasks of the centre were as follows:

- to give information, advice and support to homeworkers concerning the relationship to their employers, payment, working conditions, social benefits and taxes, materials, tools, machines, and so on;
- to bring homeworkers into contact with each other so as to work together to improve the position of homeworkers;
- to collect data about home work, the number of homeworkers and businesses which make use of home work, the problems arising from home work, and so on;
- to distribute information about home work;
- to cooperate with all kinds of organizations and institutions, such as local and national government, women's organizations, legal aid organizations, the employment inspectorate, trade unions and others in order to exchange experiences, improve services to homeworkers, and formulate policies about home work for the Government;
- to stimulate, in cooperation with homeworkers, trade unions, employers' organizations and the Government to initiate better legal regulations for homeworkers; and
- to initiate jurisprudence about home work (Heumakers, 1991, p. 3).

The office for the project was in the busy part of the town centre and the project aimed to provide both a telephone and a drop-in advice service. Inquiries were treated in strict confidence and were often followed up by home visits when required. Regular meetings were organized at the centre on a range of subjects, usually relating to legal rights and benefits, but with some social events on special occasions such as the anniversary of the Centre.

Through such contacts with homeworkers, data were collected systematically to compile an information base on home work. The project also focused its research on specific areas of industry at different times in order to build up a more complete picture of the industry as a whole and the place that home work played within it.

The National Centre liaised with relevant trade unions where possible, in order to build contacts between homeworkers, the organized workforce within the factory and the relevant trade union. Such attempts were partially successful. It identified the homeworkers' uncertain legal status as one of the main problems in attempting this kind of liaison and negotiation on behalf of these workers. On the basis of its contact with homeworkers and the research undertaken, the Centre was able to work with trade unions to make them more aware of homeworkers and to persuade them to adapt some of their practices to encourage homeworkers to join unions, for example by having some flexibility in membership dues. It was also able to develop a wide range of policies on the basis of thorough research.

The policies of the HSCs were to promote the regulation of home work in order to bring homeworkers under the protection of employment law. Until this was done, it was considered difficult to improve the position of homeworkers. It was also argued that it was up to the support centres to continue their work. While considerable progress has been made in making trade unions more aware of the issue of home work at policy level, they still find it difficult to devote the resources necessary to organizing homeworkers. The Women's Union could develop the work further in some ways. However, it is difficult to perceive how they could maintain contacts with homeworkers throughout the country.

Results

The Women's Union in the Netherlands, not being an industrial union, has worked in a different way and in a different context. Up to 1992, it acted as a bridge between independent HSCs and the trade union movement in general, as well as political parties.

Until recently, the Women's Union has not carried out the work on home work directly but has worked indirectly through the HSCs. This work has been crucial in building up a body of research and policies on home work and in making homeworkers visible; it has made the Netherlands one of the few countries in Europe where such information is available. It now seems that in the future the Women's Union will be carrying out work with homeworkers more directly with the general aim of "mainstreaming" them in the general unions at the end of three years. The goal of introducing new laws has still not been achieved, although within the trade union movement there is now more awareness of the issues involved. The experience of the Netherlands has constituted an important contribution to a working group organized by the European Commission.

The work done in the Netherlands has made visible the widespread nature of home work in almost all industries in the country. Work focusing on the garment industry has sometimes been interpreted as evidence that home work is particular to one industry, or one group of women, who are usually "migrant" women. The work of the Women's Union has shown that home work is a prevalent feature of the economy, with many of the homeworkers being Dutch women.

Conclusions to Part III

Jane Tate

The experience of the three unions in Australia, Canada and the Netherlands shows that it may be difficult, but not impossible, to reach homeworkers and even to organize them. At the end of the twentieth century, it is clear that home work, far from dying out, is once again on the increase; and the challenge posed by home work to the unions is important for their future.

In both Australia and Canada, this challenge has been taken up by a clothing union and many parallels can be drawn between the experience in these two countries. Externally, the changes in the industry, particularly in the sector of women's fashions, threatened to destroy or undermine the organized sector of the industry. Within the unions, a change in attitude to homeworkers probably reflected changing attitudes and priorities regarding women in the unions. Homeworkers had traditionally been seen as outlaws or scab labour by the unions, which had supported a legal ban on this form of work. At one level, this policy had to be changed because of its ineffectiveness. At another level, however, a fundamental shift took place when instead of blaming homeworkers for the increasing use of home work, the unions instead tried to understand the reasons for women taking up home work and undertook to work with these women rather than against them. This shift was no doubt influenced by changing values within the unions, away from a male-dominated union structure. Furthermore, in both Australia and Canada, the majority of homeworkers are women of minority communities and the unions' shift to working with homeworkers has therefore represented a move away from a movement which reflected the needs of a predominantly White workforce.

The Women's Union, in the Netherlands, is a different kind of union which has represented the interests of women not organized within other unions. This union has itself undergone a transformation since its origin. It was not accidental that it was this kind of union that in the Netherlands first pinpointed the continuing importance of home work to the women themselves, and in a wide range of industries.

At a wider level, all three unions have been working in an international context in which there has been a realization of the growing significance of home work, linked to the growth of subcontracting both within countries and between different countries. At the same time, organizations such as the Self-Employed Women's Association (SEWA), of Ahmedabad, India, have worked for many years within the international trade union movement to raise awareness of home work and the possibilities of organizing homeworkers. By the end of the seventies, the long-term campaigning by SEWA was beginning to be reflected in official conferences and resolutions which called on the unions in different countries to tackle the issue.

In practical terms, the unions that have made a commitment to collaborate with homeworkers have had to learn new methods of working, as their more traditional methods were not relevant to a workforce that was scattered, usually invisible and highly precarious. As the workforce was also in many cases made up of women, with a high proportion from minority communities, they have had to draw on the experience of women's groups and community organizations.

There have been many informal, bilateral contacts between the unions concerned with home work and other groups working with homeworkers. The experience of SEWA, for example, has often been quoted and studied to demonstrate that homeworkers can be organized. The Women's Union and Home Work Support Centres in the Netherlands have had many contacts with homeworking groups in the United Kingdom and the methods used by the HSCs are similar to those of the British groups. Similarly, CATU, from Australia, studied the experience in Italy, Switzerland and the United Kingdom as part of the development of their work. In Canada, Alex Dagg refers to the method used by the 19th September Garment Union in Mexico, as well as the homeworking groups in United Kingdom, as examples of creative organizing from which the unions have to learn.

The particular patterns of organizing must be developed in relation to the actual conditions in each country and the needs of homeworkers themselves. While there is no "magic wand", a number of common methods can be seen in the work done in Australia, Canada and the Netherlands:

- The first step was to establish contact with homeworkers. This is not as easy or obvious as it may seem because most homeworkers are working in the informal sector and their work is scattered and highly precarious. Contact has to be made by working intensively in particular communities, establishing contacts with community organizations, employing workers who could work in these communities, and so on. One important method was establishing a hot line, or free inquiry line, so that homeworkers had a contact point where they could come for advice. Generally, confidentiality and personal contact were important. In the case of Australia and Canada, these were ensured by setting up special projects and employing project workers. In the Netherlands, the Women's Union supported the setting up of the independent centres, although they have recently started their own project.
- Once contact has been established, the union can then collect information about homeworking. Since most home work is invisible, information can only be collected through contacts with homeworkers themselves. The information can then be publicized to generate support for activities to improve the situation of homeworkers, including advocating reforms in the law or generating funds for further work.
- In all three countries, an important element in the homeworking campaign has been advocating legal reform, although the exact situation in each country is different. In Australia, the initial step taken was to advocate the "legalization" of home work by campaigning for the permit system to be changed to enable homeworkers to come forward. It was then followed by a major campaign for employment rights for homeworkers, which achieved substantial success. This then

formed the basis for fighting numerous claims on behalf of homeworkers. In the Netherlands, a major focus of the Women's Union and HSCs has been the need for new laws to cover homeworkers. An old law dating back to 1933 had fallen into disuse. The Women's Union sees legal reform as a precondition for improving the situation of homeworkers. By 1992, a law had been passed on health and safety for homeworkers, and the Women's Union continues to advocate legal reform at both national and European level. In Canada, relatively good laws already exist in Ontario which should theoretically give homeworkers protection. These include defining homeworkers as employees and also entitling them to minimum wages. Most homeworkers, however, operate outside this regulation and the laws are not effectively implemented. The union therefore advocates the strengthening of the law, as well as its enforcement.

In all three countries, there has been recognition of the fact that, however successful the campaign to bring about strong legislation, the question of the organization of homeworkers is still crucial. The experience is more varied here.

In the Netherlands, the Women's Union has acted as a bridge between the HSCs and the traditional unions. The HSCs have organized low-key activities for homeworkers, such as social events and in some cases factory visits and links with unions. A minority of homeworkers have joined the Women's Union, which has membership dues low enough for homeworkers. There has been less success recruiting homeworkers to the traditional unions, whose dues are still relatively high. The industrial unions also face a legal obstacle in negotiating agreements which include homeworkers until they are classified as employees. There are likely to be changes in the Netherlands, as the Women's Union has recently launched its own project on homeworking.

In Australia, the union launched a four-year campaign from 1986 to 1990 on the issue of home work. In the initial stages of this campaign, extensive publicity and contacts were used within community organizations to make contact with homeworkers and to promote change. The union also employed project workers specifically to work with homeworkers. The campaign was largely successful in winning support for change and a shift in attitude to homeworkers. However, at the end of the period the union concluded that it could not undertake the community-based work with homeworkers, as this was not part of its brief. In terms of membership, a minority of homeworkers had joined the union but many in the informal sector were still unorganized.

In Canada, the union has tackled directly the issue of organizing homeworkers through the setting up of an association, under its associate membership scheme. The union has consciously employed non-traditional methods to work with homeworkers, as well as working with a broad alliance of other organizations in its campaign. The work in Toronto is the most recent. Although it is in its early stages, it has so far been successful both in reaching homeworkers and winning broad support for them.

An obvious problem for all three unions has been that of resources. No union is able to fund the intensive, long-term work needed to work with homeworkers from its own resources, drawn mainly from the membership. In the three countries studied, the unions have been able to draw on some short-term funding for specific periods, but the long-term funding for the work remains a difficulty.

Resources are also needed for a more systematic and consistent exchange of experience around work with homeworkers. The contacts that have taken place have been important in passing on experience between different homeworking groups and those working with other groups of women, particularly in developing countries. A properly funded and resourced network for this would clearly be valuable.

At the 1990 ILO Meeting of Experts on the Social Protection of Homeworkers, some of the union representatives present spoke of the need to regulate home work and to organize homeworkers. They acknowledged, however, that this would be an impossible task for the unions to tackle alone. The experiences of the three unions demonstrate the realities behind this statement. However, the experiences also show clearly that work can be done with homeworkers; their work can be made visible and, with non-traditional union methods, they can be organized. Some unions in other countries, such as Denmark or Italy, have been successful in organizing a minority of homeworkers who work within the regulated or relatively formal sector. The challenge that has been taken one step further by the three unions studied in this report is to tackle working within the informal sector. Not surprisingly, this is an area where traditional Western unions have little experience.

Two of the unions studied have confronted the dramatic changes in the clothing industry, particularly the women's fashion sector. The work by the Women's Union and HSCs in the Netherlands has uncovered home work in almost all industries, not only the garment industry. Both the Australian and Canadian unions have recognized that the issues raised by their work in the clothing industry are relevant for the wider trade union movement.

Patterns of production within the clothing industry have often been seen as specific to this sector only and the problems of homeworking are also associated with the particular problems faced by immigrant women, and in some cases minority businesses. What the unions have shown in their work is that the spread of home work is part of a fundamental restructuring of the industry which is particularly sharp in the clothing industry but far from unique to it. The patterns of decentralization of production, just-in-time production and increasing use of subcontracting are found in the car industry in different parts of the world. There is little research on homeworking in this industry, but a growing number of anecdotal reports of women assembling parts for cars in Germany, Italy, Japan, the United States and the United Kingdom. Other reports show that home work in the electronics and electrical industry is also on the increase.

The experience of working with homeworkers in the clothing industry is relevant then to the future of unions in a wide range of industries. It can also be linked to other forms of flexible work that are posing a threat to traditional union methods of organizing. The lessons from the pioneering work done by the three unions studied here contain many valuable lessons for all those trying to organize homeworkers and other precarious workers in the 1990s.

Bibliography

Allen, S.; Wolkowitz, C. 1987. *Homeworking: Myths and realities* (London, Macmillan).

Clothing and Allied Trades Union of Australia (CATU). 1987. *Outwork in the Australian clothing industry* (Sydney, New South Wales).

———. 1990. *National Outwork Campaign 1986-90* (Sydney, New South Wales).

Conroy Jackson, P. 1990. *Beyond Benetton*, Newsletter No. 10, July (Yorkshire and Humberside Low Pay Unit).

Council of Europe. 1989. *The protection of persons working at home* (Strasbourg).

Dagg, A. 1992a. *Organising homeworkers into trade unions*, paper presented at the Conference on Homeworking, Nov. 1992, Toronto. (Also published in *Yorkshire and Humberside Low Pay Unit Newsletter* (Batley, Yorkshire), No. 15, Feb. 1993).

———. 1992b. *Homeworking (telework) for federal public workers*, Toronto, Conference document, Nov.

Geuns, van, R. 1992. "An aspect of informalisation of women's work in a high-tech age: Turkish sweatshops in the Netherlands", in S. Mitter (ed.): *Computer-aided manufacturing and women's employment* (Berlin, Springer-Verlag).

Heumakers, H. 1991. *Homework and the Homeworker Support Centres in the Netherlands*, Paper for the Subregional Workshop on Home-Based Work, Manila.

International Labour Office. 1990. *Social protection of homeworkers*, Documents of the Meeting of Experts on the Social Protection of Homeworkers (Geneva).

International Ladies' Garment Workers' Union (ILGWU). 1990. *Campaign for justice* (New York).

———. 1991. *Working conditions of Chinese-speaking homeworkers in the Toronto garment industry* (Toronto).

Johnson, L.; Johnson, R. *The seam allowance* (London, Women's Press, 1982).

Laverty, S. 1988. *A report on strategies to organize and regulate outwork in United Kingdom, Italy and Switzerland* (Surry Wales, New South Wales, CATU).

Lipsig-Mumme, C. 1987. "Homework and the 1983 garment strike in Canada", in *Studies in Political Economy*, 22, Spring.

Mitter, S. 1986. "Industrial restructuring and manufacturing homework: Immigrant women in the UK clothing industry", in *Capital and Class* (London), No. 27, Winter, pp. 37-80.

———. 1989. *On organizing workers in the informal sector* (Brussels, ICFTU).

National Homework Support Centre (HSC). 1992a. *Bereop: Thuiswerker* [Profession: Homeworker] (Hengelo, Steunpunt Thuiswerk).

———. 1992b. *Balans van Thuiswerk* [Home work: An assessment] (Hengelo, Steunpunt Thuiswerk).

———. 1992c. *Thuiswerk in Twente* [Home work in Twente] (Hengelo, Steunpunt Thuiswerk).

———. 1992d. *Bij Gebrek aan Beter* [For want of something better] (Hengelo, Steunpunt Thuiswerk).

Netherlands Trade Union Confederation (FNV). 1990. *The Women's Union FNV and homework* (Amsterdam).

Pennington, S.; Westover, B. 1989. *A hidden workforce* (London, Macmillan).

Pesotta, R. 1987. *Bread upon the waters* (ILR Press).

Yorkshire and Humberside Low Pay Unit. 1991. *A survey of homeworking in Calderdale* (Batley, Yorkshire).

Part IV

Organizing women in the rural sector

Introduction to Part IV

Margaret Hosmer Martens

A singular trait which characterizes women in casualized employment is the entire lack of uniformity of each situation. This naturally makes organizing that much more of a challenge. Nevertheless, there are certain approaches which have been shown to work in some areas and workers' education has been quite effective for women in the rural sector.

The three chapters which follow are based on case studies of ILO workers' education projects for women in the rural sector in Africa, Asia, and Central America and the Dominican Republic. Although rural women workers often have informal links with rural workers' organizations (RWOs), usually through their families, they themselves have rarely been active. Through these projects, workers' education has been used to sensitize the women to the importance of organizing and has made it possible for them to empower themselves as active participants in their unions, members of their communities, and in small self-help projects.

The first two projects, in Africa and Asia, were designed with a similar approach and carried out by coordinators who are themselves members of the International Federation of Plantation, Agricultural and Allied Workers (IFPAAW). The Latin American project was based on a carefully constructed methodology which the women employed in their RWOs to try to improve conditions for their members and their communities. Through these approaches women become more active in their union and, eventually, move up to leadership positions, thereby encouraging more women to join.

Several points emerge which are worth noting:

— The need for active participation is becoming more widely accepted in workers' education, but this has proved indispensable for women in the rural sector.

— The use of drama is important in Africa, where oral literature is the main medium of education among the traditional communities (this has also been observed in the Caribbean, the Pacific and elsewhere). Beyond their appropriateness for training, drama troupes have proved a big success in the unions and rural communities, as in the case of Uganda.

— The need for developing socio-economic activities became obvious in small communities where the people are desperately poor and there is little hope of outside income. However, this was not always identified as the biggest priority in cases where unions felt that it would detract from the more political involvement of women's participation in union activity.

— It was believed that points of friction which emerged in relations with the leadership would be greatly reduced through the introduction of gender sensitization for trade union leaders. This is an important point and is developed further in the case studies.

9

Workers' education for women members of rural workers' organizations in Africa

Kathini Maloba-Caines *

Background

Although women have long played an important role in agriculture, it was only in the mid-1980s that their near-invisibility in the leadership of their rural workers' organizations (RWOs) was recognized. This was the situation for rural women workers throughout the world, and especially in Africa. Their predicament became evident from reports given at the Fifth Congress of the International Federation of Plantation, Agricultural and Allied Workers (IFPAAW) in 1982. It was decided that the way ahead was to encourage the IFPAAW affiliates to involve women in their unions' activities. A measure to this effect was adopted and the affiliates agreed to take deliberate measures to encourage the participation of women.

Later in the year IFPAAW representatives met during a regional seminar organized for the leaders of RWOs in East and Southern Africa. It was decided that the most effective means to involve women more actively in RWOs in Africa was by involving the women themselves in deciding what must be done. Accordingly, women representatives met for a week-long regional seminar in 1984 to study the most appropriate approach to the situation in Africa. An intensive women-only workers' education programme was designed and the pilot project was begun in March 1986.

Workers' education assistance to rural women workers

The project was funded by the Norwegian Government, with the ILO responsible for execution in cooperation with IFPAAW (similar to the arrangements made for the DANIDA/ILO/IFPAAW project in Asia, which started slightly later). RWOs from Ghana, Kenya and Zimbabwe participated during the pilot phase. At the end of this phase Kenya was omitted and Uganda took its place, retaining the representativeness of the East, South and West African subregions.

The pilot phase began in March 1986. During preliminary visits to participating unions, the leaders enthusiastically welcomed the programme; they assured IFPAAW and the ILO of their total cooperation and support.

* Former regional women's activities coordinator for the International Federation of Plantation, Agricultural and Allied Workers, and now a consultant for the ILO and other organizations.

Project objectives

The project's immediate objective was to create a corps of women worker specialists who would be equipped to improve women's participation in RWOs in selected countries in Africa, as well as a cadre of women to further this work at the local level. The development objective called for the full participation of rural women in the affairs of their self-chosen workers' organization.

Implementation of the programme

The Project Coordinator met with representatives of the participating workers' organizations to arrange for the first series of two-week seminars. These were conducted from May to July 1986, with 25 women attending each seminar. At this point the national coordinators were selected by their trade unions and took up their positions in each country. The second round of two-week seminars was held from September to November 1986, paying attention to topics of particular importance to women working on plantations and in rural areas.

Twenty-five of the most promising participants from the two-week seminars were selected to attend an eight-week trainers' course held at the College of Adult and Distance Education of the University of Nairobi. The course concentrated on women's leadership roles, health and family education, the development of organization-based services, and self-help activities for women members.

Following the pilot project, Phase I began in July 1989 with further briefings for the leaders of participating unions and orientation sessions in some unions where the leadership had changed. These were followed by project evaluation and planning seminars in Ghana and Zimbabwe and a two-week orientation course held for Uganda, which was new to the programme.

The project's second eight-week training of trainers' course was held in Harare with 37 participants. Observers from four RWOs in Africa and one observer from India attended. Fifty local seminars were conducted following the trainers' course.

The project's immediate objective has been achieved in that 1,850 women have undergone orientation courses since the programme commenced. Of these, 43 have been trained as specialists for women workers' concerns in the unions. Over 75 per cent of these have been retained by the unions and are furthering the work of consciousness-raising and training of more women in the countries concerned.

The need for flexibility depending on local circumstances was seen in Zimbabwe where the participating union, the General Agricultural and Plantation Workers' Union of Zimbabwe (GAPWUZ), was a newly developed RWO. Prior to independence, women members had not benefited from basic workers' education. To prepare the women from Zimbabwe more adequately for the second two-week course, four weekend courses were conducted by the GAPWUZ national coordinator to help equip the women better.

The curriculum

The curriculum was designed by the Project Coordinator to produce women trade unionists capable of:

— representing women members in their unions;
— running a trade union education programme; and
— running a trade union organization.

Particular attention was given to subjects designed to kindle the women's desire to participate in the socio-economic and political affairs of their countries. The trainers' courses included the following:

— trade union administration including organization building, education, representation, and financial management of union funds;
— labour law and national laws relating to women such as inheritance and succession, and marriage and divorce;
— international labour standards — ILO Conventions and Recommendations relevant to women workers and rural workers, as well as the process of adoption and ratification, were discussed in detail;
— appropriate technology was covered in order to create awareness and provide the women with information which could be used to assist their members in reducing their work burden;
— theatre skills were developed among the women worker specialists. Theatre was identified as a very effective method of adult learning — particularly in Africa, where oral literature is the main medium of education among the traditional communities.

Topics discussed in the two-week seminars concerned matters of immediate relevance to the women: women's participation in trade union activities; social security and its implications for women; support services for working parents; changing social attitudes towards women; sexual harassment; occupational health and safety; the proper use of hazardous chemicals; income-generating possibilities for rural women; child and maternal care (including the importance of breastfeeding) and hygiene.

Participatory methods of adult learning were emphasized, and techniques taught at the specialists' courses (role-play; group discussions; taking minutes of group sessions and reporting to plenary, as well as chairing and moderating sessions; storytelling and drama production) were used to help the women articulate their interests, concerns and problems in their workplaces and in society at large.

Formation of women's committees

Women's committees were seen as an important means to achieve the immediate as well as the development objectives of the programme. They would be able to keep up the pace of the work begun during the seminars, continue to educate themselves and clarify their needs in the workplace as well as in the unions. They would act as an advisory organ to represent matters concerning women members which the union could take up as issues in their collective negotiations.

Women's committees were formed in all the participating unions and are monitored by the women's departments set up by the unions in response to the programme. The national and local coordinators were to serve as Women in Development (WID) Officers at the union headquarters and provincial levels.

The local coordinators kept in touch with the women's committees and reported on progress to the national coordinators. In addition to discussions of problems and concerns around the workplace, women in some places set up income-generating activities such as raising chickens, knitting and crocheting. Others initiated activities such as nursery schools, adult literacy classes, music, drama and dance. The committee leaders have all received trade union education. In fact, the majority of the local coordinators came from the leadership of such committees. The committees are in place in most areas and should serve as the target for future training activities. In the long run, these are the women who will sustain the development objectives of the programme.

Socio-economic activities

The income-generating aspect of the programme created a problem when some union leaders decided that these activities could involve the women to the extent that they could be marginalized from the mainstream of the union. Although the income-generating activities are continuing, their objectives and role in the programme had to be redefined, especially to the trade union leaders. The activities have been used to encourage more women to meet regularly. It is during the process of dealing with income-generating activities at their meetings that the women discuss problems at the workplace and possible solutions.

Civic responsibilities for women

Conscious of the objective for the women to make their own contribution to national development, subjects were included in the curriculum which would help the participants to understand their civic responsibilities.

As a result, the women's consciousness was raised as to their potential to contribute to national development and to participate in the decision-making bodies of their local and national public authorities. Some later campaigned for and won election in their local assemblies in Ghana and Uganda. The local coordinator for the programme in northern Ghana was elected by her community to represent them in the district assembly. A local coordinator in Uganda ran for a post on the Resistance Council No. V of her area and won. Others have contested positions at the community level in Uganda.

Drama as an important medium for rural workers' education

After a while it became clear that new approaches to adult learning needed to be explored to meet the needs of the women. Based on the experience and widespread practice of oral traditions in Africa, it was decided to use theatre as a medium. During the training of trainers' course in Harare, Zimbabwe, in 1990, eight days were set aside for training in theatre skills. To assess the level of adoption of the skills and techniques, course participants were divided into three groups, and each group was assigned to produce a play. The three themes were "the problems of plantation workers", "the problems of women workers" and "the problems of women in society".

While Uganda's National Union of Plantation and Allied Workers (NUPAW) had already been using drama as a medium, the team lacked a theoretical base in drama production. Their plays were purely for entertainment. However, since their training the group has markedly improved on the techniques and concepts. It now produces plays on such issues as occupational health and safety in the plantations, working and living conditions in the plantations, and the negotiation process at company headquarters.[1]

Drama has therefore been adopted as the new approach to workers' education in Africa. It can deal with any subject-matter, the financial requirement is minimal, it makes it possible to reach many workers and the larger plantation community in the shortest time. It is as entertaining as it is educational; it helps recruit more union members. For the long-term objective of self-reliance, the unions in developing countries and in particular RWOs in Africa should consider the use of drama for their members' education. Combined with video recording to provide feedback, the method should have a far-reaching effect in a relatively short period of time.

Achievements

The project's development objective seems to have taken root. Of the five unions which have participated, none had women in their executive at the beginning of the programme in 1986. Today there are women on the national executive councils in three of the five participating unions. In Uganda five women were elected, while in Ghana there are also five, four elected by women on special tickets and one elected at the congress. In Kenya one woman was elected to the national executive council of the Kenya Plantation and Agricultural Workers' Union (KPAWU), which only participated in the project for one year. In Zimbabwe, although there are no women in the executive, the participation of women in the union cannot be doubted. As explained above, the union was at the initial stages of organization and project-trained women have played a key role in recruiting members to the union. The women have also been involved in handling grievances for their members. These examples and others clearly indicate the participation of women in their self-chosen RWOs.

[1] Ed. note: This group is very well known in Uganda and has also developed songs and skits on important social issues such as national unity and the problem of AIDs. The troupe is the pride of the union.

Participation in the national labour movement

During the various evaluation activities of the programme, both internal and external, there was evidence of cooperation and sharing of experiences between the RWOs and the other unions affiliated to relevant national centres. Thus experiences gained through the programme became useful when the women's committees of the national centres were being formed.

For example, the head of the Women's Council of the Zimbabwe Congress of Trade Unions (ZCTU) informed the final evaluation mission that the Zimbabwean women from the GAPWUZ trained in the project took the leadership of ZCTU women's committees in virtually every province. They were the first to attend meetings and seminars called or organized by the ZCTU Women's Council. In Ghana both the principal of the Labour College and the head of the GAWU told the evaluation team that the women participating in the programme always stood out from the others and made definite contributions to the union.

Regional and international cross-cultural experiences

Rather than run separate training of trainers' courses in each of the three countries, the programmes were designed for the maximum interaction among the women from the three different African subregions. This facilitated the sharing of experiences among the women of different countries, while broadening their perspective of situations prevailing among the working people of Africa and beyond.

Sharing experiences through country reports and storytelling during drama helped the women participants to have a clearer understanding of the concerns and problems of workers throughout the African continent. It also helped them determine the similarities and differences in dealing with specific country problems affecting workers. The interaction thus built a new confidence in the women and a broad perspective of dealing with workers' issues nationally. In addition to the interaction encouraged at the African level, the Project Coordinator made an attempt to create a south-south dialogue among the rural workers by inviting two women from Asia, IFPAAW's coordinator for its very similar Asian project, and the coordinator for the South India portion of that project. Both the African and Asian women shared their common experience and diversities in the world of agricultural and plantation workers and their related communities. The Project Coordinator stressed the importance of these interactions particularly for rural women workers who rarely have the opportunity to leave their countries to represent their unions abroad.

Conclusion

The approach of women-only programmes has worked marvellously in increasing the participation of women in their chosen RWOs and endowing them with confidence to accept their civic challenges. One of the major contributing factors for the success of the programme is the fact that a community-based approach was applied throughout. The community itself could range from the African region as a whole to the shop floor. The decisions on how and what should be taught were discussed between the Project Coordinator and the national coordinators at all stages. Training needs assessments were established for all seminars. In conducting such a programme it must be assumed that the union members are not homogeneous and therefore their approach to learning differs from country to country, region to region and even crop to crop. Study materials, if used, must therefore be very carefully selected.

The project has definitely had an impact on African RWOs, both nationally and regionally. However, more needs to be done to enhance what has already been achieved. Gender sensitization for the union leaders and IFPAAW representatives is clearly needed. The women beneficiaries of the programme have discussed and to a large extent overcome the cultural attitudes which have kept them from emerging as leaders in their organizations, whereas their male counterparts in the unions are still subscribing to the societal attitudes that contribute so adversely to the advancement of women in the unions and in society at large.

In training the unions' male members on gender issues, the IFPAAW and the ILO must address the sustainability of women who are moving up to senior offices in their unions. The present situation gives reason for concern. One wonders whether the unions are ready to accept women among their senior officials. The assumptions made at the beginning of the programme were sufficient at the time. However, a fresh look at ways to sustain the women who have gained experience in their unions is needed. This should take up the major proportion of any assessment for future programmes to help women succeed in the RWOs. More orientation for union leaders and officials might perhaps ensure not only sustainability but also acceptance and tolerance of the women who are now assertive and have achieved self-esteem. This and other new approaches need to be identified in ensuring total integration of the women in RWOs.

10

Workers' education for women members of rural workers' organizations in Asia

Neena Hari-Correa *

Conditions of rural women workers in Asia

Rural workers, whether wage earners or self-employed, constitute the vast majority of workers in developing countries. In some Asian countries a substantial proportion of the total rural workforce is made up of women. They carry the major burden of the work as family breadwinners, as well as the full responsibility of running a home.

During the last decade, the participation of women in the labour force in most Asian countries has increased substantially. Several governments and most trade unions have introduced measures to reduce discrimination and unequal treatment of women workers. Yet little progress has been made in practice. Women continue to be discriminated against because of persisting obstacles which limit their access to education, productive assets, decision-making and better conditions of work and remuneration.

Statistics count mainly women in paid formal employment and grossly underestimate their real economic contribution. Women carry out a multitude of essential economic activities as unpaid family workers, and in the informal sector and agriculture, which are usually unrecorded in statistics. Women's work is especially unrecognized in rural areas. Typically, the rural woman's working day is 14 to 16 hours long and filled with a multiplicity of arduous tasks: subsistence food production; food processing and preparation; fetching wood; drawing water; handicrafts; marketing; and child care.

Women workers in the rural areas of the Philippines are mostly self-employed smallholders or members of households which often receive their income from a combination of rural and industrial work. In India, two-thirds of the agricultural workforce own small plots of land, half of them less than 1 hectare which barely provides enough to survive. Caught in an endless cycle of indebtedness, most are dependent on the landlords for employment in order to subsist. About 40 per cent of this workforce are women.

Women's participation in the activities of RWOs is proportionately extremely low, and the number of trade union activities for women even lower. Partly because of this, the services of RWOs seldom cater specifically for the special needs and concerns of women workers.

* Former project coordinator for an ILO/IFPAAW/DANIDA project in Asia.

Workers' education assistance to rural women workers

To help promote women's active participation in their RWOs in Asia, a joint ILO-IFPAAW (International Federation of Plantation, Agricultural and Allied Workers) project was funded by DANIDA and conducted over a five-year period, beginning in 1987.

In many respects the objectives followed the model of the ILO-IFPAAW project in Africa. However, as great care was taken to organize the programmes according to the needs of the target groups, the course content and execution of each project varied considerably, not only between Asia and Africa but often among the individual countries and regions themselves. The two-phase Asian project was aimed at women members of RWOs and potential members of IFPAAW-affiliated organizations in three countries — India, the Philippines and Sri Lanka. Because of its vast size and complex nature, for administrative purposes India was treated as two separate components: India (North) and India (South).

Project design

The project was designed to build and strengthen a corps of women trade unionists as specialists who would then work together to improve women's participation in RWOs. To achieve this objective the Project Coordinator developed a systematic workers' education programme which combined a variety of techniques including in-depth eight-week seminars, short community-based workshops, international cross-cultural exchanges, community surveys, organizational and socio-economic projects, and special services.

Following their training, these women trade union specialists became the project's liaison officers serving under a national coordinator. All the national coordinators reported to the Project Coordinator, herself a member of IFPAAW, based in Manila.[1]

In its entirety the project was intended to:

- strengthen RWOs through greater participation of their women membership;
- encourage a sense of cooperation and self-reliance amongst women, both in their organizations and in everyday life;
- develop the personalities and leadership qualities of women workers in RWOs; and
- lay the foundation for the organized development of women workers' education activities within IFPAAW affiliates.

[1] The project was designed to have a national coordinator in India (North), India (South), the Philippines and Sri Lanka. Because of unforeseen events this was not always possible and for different periods the Project Coordinator was obliged to cover India (North), the Philippines and Sri Lanka from Manila.

The strategy for training women

The programme was implemented in two phases: selection and training of women from among the participating trade unions; and organizing, training and assisting rural women to join together and participate more actively in their communities and RWOs.

Phase I

(a) The participating unions nominated women to take part in a series of two-week national workshops on "Leadership training for rural women". These women were trained to serve as resource persons/organizers working with the rural women. The workshops focused on leadership training, understanding the problems of the rural/plantation workers and the role of the trade union, general labour laws and laws relating specifically to women workers, health, hygiene and general family welfare and, most important, organizing techniques. Finally, each participant drew up an action plan to be implemented upon return to her union.

(b) Outstanding participants were chosen for further training at an eight-week subregional seminar. Those who successfully completed this seminar became the liaison officers responsible for the day-to-day administration of the project in their regions. National coordinators were also chosen from the group.

The curriculum for the eight-week course was divided into the following modules:

— **the situation and organization of rural women workers:** their needs and how to organize them;
— **union administration:** principles of democratic leadership and how women can be integrated into trade union activities;
— **development of a local education programme:** needs assessments; training methodologies; planning and preparation of education programmes; teaching demonstrations; and evaluation and follow-up;
— **special services for RWOs:** the union's role in special service programmes; designing socio-economic projects; a study of the cooperative movement and how it functions; cooperative management; field visits to rural projects; sources and financing of projects; and preparation and presentation of individual projects.

One of the key features of the subregional seminar was the surveys which the participants were trained to conduct in the rural areas. These served as important information-gathering devices, as well as providing an excellent introduction to the women, their families and day-to-day life in their communities. The trainees recorded information on the women's lives, their socio-economic condition and the problems they faced. Once the data was gathered, the liaison officers set about developing different approaches to assist the women.

Phase II

(a) As a first step towards working in a community, one-day workshops were offered to reach a large number of women at once. General leadership principles were introduced, as well as the concept of strength through solidarity and the union. If the women were not members of a local organization, they were urged to join or form one. These workshops also helped to identify promising women for further training at three-day orientation courses.

(b) The orientation courses were usually conducted at the union's headquarters. Participants, drawn from the one-day workshops, were often leading figures in their villages or organizations. These women activists eventually served as the link between the community and the liaison officer and, thereby, the union. They were taught more about trade union structure and their rights as workers which the unions were ready to defend. Depending on their needs, they were introduced to a variety of other subjects ranging from sanitation and personal hygiene, child care, nutrition, adult education, literacy training, and skills training for income-generating activities. The women activists were encouraged to teach their new skills to their neighbours and often formed cooperatives.

(c) As part of their follow-up work, the liaison officers visited the villages regularly and worked with the women activists to introduce a variety of self-help projects and activities in the communities. One particularly beneficial service was the assistance which liaison officers were able to provide in serving as links between the rural community and the government bureaucracy. This helped the women by providing legal advice when necessary and teaching them how to take advantage of government schemes. This was particularly important in India where rural people are often unaware of existing government programmes from which they might benefit.

All educational activities implemented through the one- and three-day basic workshops focused either on leadership or on specialized topics in response to the women's needs, with the following objectives:

— to impart practical concepts and practices of trade unionism to rural women;
— to stimulate awareness of rural women towards involvement in trade unions or rural activities by analysing specific measures to help them overcome existing obstacles to women's active participation;
— to assist rural women to determine and develop a programme of action to enhance group activity as a means to alleviate severe conditions in the rural areas;
— to enhance the women's personalities and build self-confidence;
— to develop positive attitudes and values.

Socio-economic activities

Following the project's Phase I and in preparation for Phase II, the Project Coordinator met with the national coordinators and liaison officers in an evaluation and planning workshop. It was concluded that, although the workshops and general education activities were of prime importance for the project's success, more training was strongly recommended for the rural women on skills aimed at income-generating and socio-economic activities and cooperatives. This decision was made because it was evident that the financial status of the women had to be improved in order to gain the respect of the men in the villages and the male trade union leaders.

As a result, emphasis was shifted slightly in Phase II and a consultant on socio-economic activities was engaged for one year to advise the liaison officers and conduct training. Workshops were held on "Income-generating project development for rural women" and "Rural women and rural transformation". Thus, while conceived as a means of improving the immediate living standards of the participating women, the welfare-oriented and income-generating activities were soon perceived as a tactical vehicle for breaking the ground for women's increased participation.

During Phase II more than 150 socio-economic/income-generating schemes were developed. In India these included projects on rope making, tailoring, rabbit breeding, basket weaving, *bidi* leaf collection, honey collection, livestock rearing for dairy products, reforestation and spinning. In the Philippines basket weaving, pig raising, poultry keeping, knitting, vegetable gardening, fisheries and papier mâché products were popular. In Sri Lanka there were projects on sewing, cattle raising and poultry keeping.

Developing audiovisual materials

A two-week Regional Workshop on Assessment and Planning of Women's Training Programmes was organized as follow-up training for Phase I liaison officers to promote their skills in preparing and conducting workers' education programmes. The focus was on the development of study materials and teaching aids and included a module on producing audiovisual materials. In particular, the women were shown in detail how to take pictures and prepare slides for formal presentations.

Each participating liaison officer was provided with a production kit consisting of a camera, slide viewer, light board and slide projector. The liaison officers produced their own slide shows to be used as background material during their educational activities. These materials are now being used by the unions during seminars and workshops.

Cross-cultural learning

An important aspect of the liaison officers' training was cross-cultural exchange. The Project Coordinator very carefully developed this approach in the subregional seminar, highlighting the backgrounds of the Filipino, Indian and Sri Lankan participants to broaden their awareness of the variety of problems that rural women face. Just as the participants were taught to introduce the concept of solidarity to the rural women, they observed how much they were able to learn from each other's experiences during the eight-week seminar.

In Phase II the cycle was begun again and a new group of women were nominated by their unions for training as women worker specialists. Whereas the eight-week subregional seminar in Phase I was conducted in Manila and in Bacolod in the Philippines, in Phase II it was conducted in two parts, with the first three weeks held at the IFPAAW Workers' Education Centre in South India and the remaining five weeks conducted in the Philippines. In between the two sessions there was a four-week period where the women returned to their regions for practical training. In this way participants experienced first hand the situations in both countries and could use the intervening period to test their new skills.

Conclusion

The key to the project's success was the careful preparation of the women worker specialists and the highly practical approach to training. Each topic introduced had to be seen by the participants as something potentially beneficial which they could personally put into practice. This approach was continuously adapted in response to the needs of the rural target group.

The training strategy and the target audience were very well coordinated. The liaison officers themselves were representative of the rural women and through the project were able to find their voices and the strength to attempt to bring about change. These are very committed women. The unions have given them the means to help themselves and others, and they are excellent spokeswomen for the labour movement. Given the liaison officers' experience and training, they have been able to convince the rural women of the responsibilities and benefits of union membership.

During the five years (1987-92) of the project's duration, it is clear that much change has taken place. A corps of 53 women worker specialists has been formed to fulfil an important role in training other women at the grass-roots level in an awareness of their rights as women and as members of their own organizations. Through their specialized training and their work as liaison officers, the women worker specialists have developed leadership qualities. Many have reached the decision-making level of their unions.

Understandably any large-scale change of this nature threatens traditional power structures, and as such has also created tensions, misunderstandings and some unfortunate situations. Some problems have been solved or alleviated through timely interventions of the cooperating partners, but in other instances some of the women have chosen to withdraw from the project.

The project staff were sensitive to the necessity of a good working relationship between liaison officers and their organizations, even though this did not always work as well as could have been hoped. During Phase I, participants for the eight-week seminar were chosen by the Project Coordinator in consultation with officials from the participating unions. This was adjusted in Phase II so that the unions alone were responsible for nominating the women representing their organizations. This was done to involve the unions more in the liaison officers' training, thus attempting to create a stronger link early on.

In spite of difficulties, there have been extremely positive outcomes. All the women who have been trained have shown increased awareness of their rights and responsibilities; there has been a multiplier effect in reaching rural women at the grass-roots level; unions have instituted structures such as women's committees at local, branch and national level; and constitutions have been amended to include some representation of women on executive committees. Although every union is autonomous in its decisions, most have made considerable progress in promoting women's participation at some level within their organizations.

Annex

Countries and organizations participating in the project

Name of the affiliate	Category
India (North)	
Agricultural Labour Association (ALA)	Rural/agricultural
Hind Khet Mazdoor Sabha (HKMS)	Rural/agricultural
Indian National Rural Labour Federation (INRLF)	Rural/agricultural
Labour Organization of the Rural Poor (LORP)	Rural
National Union of Plantation Workers (NUPW)	Plantation
West Bengal Tea Plantation and Allied Workers (WBTPAW)	Plantation
India (South)	
Andhra Pradesh Vyvasaya Abhudhaya Seva Sangam (APVASS)	Agricultural
Hind Khet Mazdoor Sabha (HKMS)	Rural/agricultural
Indian National Plantation Workers Federation (INPWF)	Plantation
Indian National Rural Workers Federation (INRLF)	Rural/agricultural
Karnataka Industrial and Plantation Workers' Union (KIPLU)	Plantation
National Union of Fishermen (NUF)	Rural
National Union of Working Women (NUWW)	Rural
Neelamalai Plantation Workers' Union (NPWU)	Plantation
Nilgiris District Estate Workers' Union (NDEWU)	Plantation
Rural Workers' Organization (RWO)	Agricultural
United Front for Repatriated Workers (UNIFRONT)	Agricultural
Philippines	
Associated Labour Unions (ALU)	General workers
Association of Trade Unions (ATU)	
Farmer's Growers Organization (FGO)	Agricultural
Federation of Agrarian and Industrial Toiling Hands (FAITH)	Agricultural
Lakas Ng Magsasakang Pilipino (LMP)	
National Congress of Unions in the Sugar Industry of the Philippines (NACUSIP)	Sugar/plantation
Pambasang Kilusan Ng Paggawa (KILUSAN)	Agricultural
Workers' Alliance of Trade Unions (WATU)	Agricultural
Sri Lanka	
Ceylon Workers' Congress (CWC)	Plantation
Lanka Agriculturists' Association (LAA)	Agricultural
Lanka Jathika Estate Workers' Union (LJEWU)	Plantation

11

Workers' education for women members of rural workers' organizations in Central America and the Dominican Republic

Maritza Delgado González *

Socio-economic background

The economies of Central America and the Dominican Republic have traditionally been based almost entirely on agriculture and its accompanying industries and services. People working in this sector are usually: (a) employed in subsistence agriculture; (b) workers on banana, sugarcane and pineapple plantations; (c) subcontracted or seasonally employed in the cultivation of bananas, coffee, sugarcane, pineapple, citrus fruits and melons; (d) employed as agricultural labourers but also grow their own subsistence crops.

Some of these crops are no longer lucrative because of new technologies or crop substitutes such as sugar beet, which in some areas have replaced sugarcane. New patterns of consumption in industrialized countries have meant dwindling employment possibilities, and this has in turn led to rural-urban migration. In spite of this, exports continue to contain a high proportion of agricultural produce and governments are trying to introduce new methods of farming for export crops which require less manual labour. However, this will not benefit most rural workers because it is almost impossible for them to acquire the land, capital and machinery necessary for these new methods of production.

Other common problems confronting rural workers in Central America and the Dominican Republic can be summed up as follows:

— at the place of employment: low wages; poor working conditions; arbitrary dismissals; long working hours; no guaranteed remuneration for days off; no paid leave; lack of safety and hygiene; no medical services; lack of technical training; no right to benefits; sexual harassment and discrimination;

— at the social level: unemployment; illiteracy; violence in the home; problems of health and access to education; lack of crèches; lack of access to the land; precarious drinking-water supplies;

— at the economic level: lack of credit; lack of crop insurance; extreme poverty;

— at the organizational level: lack of workers' participation in trade union posts; little trade union power;

* Project Coordinator for the Instituto Centroamericano de Asesoría Laboral; specialist in the field of women's trade union organization in Central America.

— at the family level: for women, heavy family responsibilities; high cost of living; male chauvinism, marginalization and self-marginalization;
— at the political level: agrarian legislation which does not correspond to the needs of the sector; exclusion of workers (especially women) from political posts; political repression; no specific programmes for women; failure to reform the labour code; contempt for human rights; lack of sanctions against those who infringe such rights and collective agreements relating to the agricultural sector; lack of government support; lack of will to improve the quality of life of agricultural workers.[1]

Although the foregoing problems are among those which are holding back the rural sector, within it exists a large group which is even more oppressed not only by economic hardship but also by cultural factors which aggravate the situation to a still greater degree. We refer to rural women workers.

The women's situation

As the economic situation worsens, more and more women from both urban and rural areas are joining the labour force. For women in urban areas this has often meant work as a domestic servant in people's homes or employment in industries in export processing zones. Although neither of these jobs is particularly rewarding, rural women workers have fared even worse. They are faced with seasonal employment and task work, little job security, wages below the legal minimum wage (and usually lower than men's wages), unhealthy working conditions, long hours and no overtime pay. Rural women are found harvesting seasonal crops, clearing and preparing the land, and cleaning, sorting and packing on banana and tobacco plantations. They rarely have access to permanent jobs.

Rural workers' organizations (RWOs), which are usually closely linked with trade unions, could provide an important vehicle to assist and defend rural workers, men and women alike. However, women's participation has been limited because of various cultural factors. Women have rarely had a voice in decision-making bodies and workers' education programmes have been attended by far more men than women. This is because meetings and seminars are organized and timed without respect to women's domestic responsibilities. The same is true of women's participation in trade union activities as a whole. The few women in managerial positions in RWOs are usually found in traditionally "female" jobs such as taking minutes at meetings, the secretary for women's affairs or responsible for social activities.

In spite of the foregoing, the RWOs[2] have begun to understand the necessity for a female contribution. This realization has created numerous openings for women in the RWOs, which they are now trying to consolidate. The ILO workers' education

[1] Taken from the ILO document *Instrumento de investigación para construir un perfil de las OTR contrapartes del proyecto* [Inquiry instrument for the delineation of a profile of the RWOs taking part in the project]; in Spanish only. Project OIT/RLA/89/MOI/DAN (Feb. 1992).

[2] The RWOs taking part in this project are listed in the annex.

project described in this chapter has had an important impact on the possibilities for these women.

This chapter provides an explanation of the membership system within the RWOs, followed by an outline of the structures for women members in these organizations today. It then gives a description of phases I and II of the project and the methodology which has made it so successful.

Membership of RWOs

In most cases, would-be members join the RWOs directly. The only ones to use the "indirect" system are FECCC and FEDELAC; this means that subscriptions are collected on a family basis, so that wives and children become indirect members. Indirect membership is not the only kind available to women, who can equally well become direct members. Nevertheless, in these two RWOs the indirect membership of women does occasion problems for them inasmuch as they play no part in decision-making and do not have access to positions of responsibility.

The majority of RWOs taking part in the project are mixed, grouping men and women indiscriminately. Only two of them, CONAMUCA and CODIMCA, consist exclusively of women.

The biggest RWO is ATC, which has 70,000 members. In descending order of size follow FENAZUCAR with 65,000, FEDELAC with 61,460 and ANACH with 56,000. The membership of the others varies between 24,000 and 4,319. As would be expected, the mixed organizations have larger memberships than the exclusively female ones, as evidenced by CODIMCA's (5,000) and CONAMUCA's (4,319) membership.

With respect to female membership, ATC and FEDELAC have the highest concentration of women, the first with 22,400 and the second with 11,535, representing 32 and 18.7 per cent of the total membership respectively. Among the other mixed organizations, ANACH has the highest proportion, with 14.2 per cent (8,000 women), and SITRACHILCO the lowest, with 6 per cent (274 women).

An important fact to remember is that the total membership of the organizations in question is 325,679, of which women account for only 34 per cent.

Women's structures within the RWOs

A point worth noting is that within the RWOs organs have been set up to fight for equality of opportunity and remuneration between men and women workers. They have a well-defined structure which enables them to carry on their work and to help women to play a more active part in the workplace, in the RWO itself and in society as a whole.

Among the RWOs, two (CONAMUCA and CODIMCA) consist entirely of women. Five (ANACH, ATC, FEDELAC, FENAZUCAR and FESIAN) have a secretary for Women's Affairs at executive level; and of these ATC, FEDELAC and FENAZUCAR also possess a Department of Women's Affairs, which functions as a permanent support organization for women's activities. In the case of FENAZUCAR this Department was established quite recently.

The two banana unions, SITRATERCO and SITRACHILCO, each have a Central Committee for Women's Affairs. FECCC has had a Provisional Committee for Women's Affairs since 1991, the purpose of which is to promote conditions for the establishment of a permanent women's structure.

At regional level, only seven of the mixed RWOs have any sections concerned with women. In the case of plantation workers, these take the form of subcommittees in the packing stations or sugar-mills. ANACH, FECCC and FEDELAC have regional promotional teams. ATC has Secretaries for Women's Affairs for each production sector at the level of each Federation and in all regional structures.

On account of their organizational structure, CONAMUCA and CODIMCA possess regional federations. ATC excepted, the remaining eight RWOs with regional structures have yet to set up any offices specifically dealing with women's interests.[3]

Apart from the post of Secretary for Women's Affairs, women officers in the nine mixed RWOs hold posts such as Secretary for Minutes or Secretary for Social Assistance — in other words posts normally held by women in this kind of organization, so that posts of greater importance are all occupied by men.

Workers' education assistance for rural women workers

To help to promote women's active participation in their RWOs, a DANIDA-sponsored ILO project on Workers' Education Assistance for Rural Women Workers in Central American Countries and the Dominican Republic was begun in 1987 and is still continuing today in a later phase. This project followed two earlier programmes which provided a training process and advisory assistance to women workers.[4] Whereas urban unionized women workers were the main target group of the first programmes, the later project was designed specifically for rural women.

Two essential considerations in the design and implementation of this project were the distinctive characteristics of the rural sector in these countries, and especially the circumstances specific to rural women workers. This is most evident in the methodology which was the keystone of the programme and one of the project's most essential contributions.

The first phase of the project and its methodology

The methodology was specifically developed for the women's use in their own communities and RWOs. At the beginning of the project an on-site analysis was conducted of conditions in each participating RWO. This analysis helped to establish

[3] ILO: *Workers' education assistance for rural women workers in Central America and the Dominican Republic*, Interim evaluation report, May 1991-June 1992 (San José, 1992; RLA/89/MO1/DAN).

[4] The earlier project was instrumental in the formation of the International Committee of Women Trade Unionists of Central America and the Dominican Republic.

a profile of the needs of women trade union leaders in the rural sector. Based on this assessment, the method was elaborated and introduced at the project's first regional seminar, a ten-day workshop held in November 1987.

The workshop brought together 20 women representatives from the RWOs which took part. A highly participatory approach enabled the women to work through the four objectives of the seminar:

— the identification of the main problems affecting rural women workers, through an analysis of their situation in the rural sector;
— the identification of strategies and actions currently promoted by the RWOs to help rural women workers confront these problems;
— the identification and examination of important theoretical and practical issues to be considered in developing a process to enable the full integration of rural women workers in their RWOs;
— the establishment of a preliminary strategy to further such an operation, as well as possibilities for ILO support.

An important portion of the seminar was a presentation on investigative methodology for rural women workers based on systematizing data compiled on the subregion. The women then worked in small groups organized by country to verify each country's indicators and complete a project worksheet detailing fundamental characteristics of: the rural population; the agrarian structure; basic social services of the rural sector; the rural labour market; the work performed by rural women workers; and institutional programmes and projects oriented towards them. The work groups used posters to present their results.

Following the seminar, two- to three-day workshops were held for women members at each of the participating RWOs. The project staff developed the overall strategy for the series and the local coordinators designed, conducted and evaluated their own workshops based on the subject-matter covered at the seminar and according to the needs of their individual RWOs.

It was during this phase that special services or demonstrative intervention projects (DIPs) were researched and developed according to the particular needs of each RWO. These DIPs were intended to provide an opportunity to implement the project's methodology in an assessment of the conditions and needs of the RWOs, and to simultaneously serve the rural community. Although the same methodology was used in all the RWOs, it was found to be equally applicable under very different circumstances. In each case, five different studies were carried out:

— a needs assessment;
— a market survey;
— a technical study;
— a financial study; and
— a sociopolitical study.

The second phase of the project

During the second phase work continues in three primary areas: organizational, educational and productive. Efforts are going on to consolidate the integration of a work team at national level in order to promote the dissemination of the DIP methodology through the establishment and/or training of regional teams within the RWOs. Women members of the work teams have been developing educational programmes at the national, regional and grass-roots levels to train others to apply the methods and techniques diagnosing, formulating, carrying out and evaluating projects which provide services to the community and/or are income generating.

In addition, work has begun on the production of study materials for rural working women. The material consists of a set of self-instruction booklets for the use of the grass-roots group members who will be participating in the training programme on the DIP methodology, and a series of manuals to guide grass-roots educators and provide teaching aids.

Actions taken to meet the needs of women members

Within the RWOs various steps have been taken to raise the level of women's participation in their organizations and their sectors and, by the same token, to raise and maintain their rights. These steps can be broken down by area as follows:

— **organization:** organization of women into basic groups as a means of promoting the participation of women in their own RWOs and involving them in activities oriented towards improving the living standards of members;

— **dissemination of information** (publications, broadcasts): only two RWOs actually report that they have this means of communication, although it is possible that others may possess at least one such medium;

— **claims:** this is the area which seems to receive most emphasis in the RWOs. Such activities have two elements, namely negotiations with employers regarding conditions of work, and actions concerned with improving the living standards of members;

— **education:** the RWOs carry out many activities ranging from trade union training to literacy courses and the development of skills through income-generating projects.

The activities related to organization, claims and education are the ones which most interest the RWOs on account of their continuing growth and increased importance owing to the current economic and social crisis.

Another line of action, aimed at helping families increase their incomes, has been to provide technical training courses in, for example, manual skills. In this respect the ATC is a special case in that it trains women in skills which are not traditionally "female" such as home electrical repairs, the repair of home appliances, wickerwork, carpentry and elementary bookkeeping. It also provides courses in subjects such as collective agreements, sexual education and AIDs, teaching techniques, cultural self-improvement, law and home medicine. Another outstanding case is

CONAMUCA, which runs educational workshops on agrarian reform, the feminist movement and neoliberalism.

Finally, it is to be noted that, while not all RWOs carry out all the activities, they nevertheless agree on the essentials. Some of the main areas of action are described below.

Many efforts are being made to provide women with better links with the employment market. The ATC is implementing a training programme in non-traditional skills for women in Nicaragua which not only gives them access to sources of employment but also helps them to enter sectors from which they have hitherto been excluded. This shows the interest of this organization in promoting equality of opportunity and remuneration.

The ATC also has 29 projects under way, of which 14 are run by women. Although they do not generate income for their beneficiaries, other projects reduce family costs for health care by offering their own medical services both to members and to non-members. For this purpose, the ATC has three gynaecological clinics and is in the process of setting up a medical advice office in Matagalpa. In addition, it gives support to women workers via the Rural Child Services and the Legal Advice Bureau.

Other RWOs also carry out major income-generating activities as in the case of ANACH, which implements programmes on agricultural production, livestock raising and crafts; and CODIMCA, which has 100 agricultural projects under way involving, among other things, plant nurseries, coffee, maize and red beans, all by means of revolving funds. Some RWOs run productive projects such as mills, dairies, dressmaking shops and craft workshops.

Inasmuch as their membership consists of wage earners, RWOs such as SITRATERCO, SITRACHILCO and FENAZUCAR do not directly run income-generating activities, but they do offer services to their members in fields such as health, finance, family support (crèches, gynaecological care) and retail shops. CONAMUCA also provides such services as a health centre.

FEDELAC and UNAC carry on activities such as crop farming, livestock farming and craftwork, while FESIAN implements projects concerned with agriculture, plant nurseries and crèches. As yet, FECCC has no projects of this kind because it has only recently set up a Provisional Committee for Women's Affairs and has not had time to develop economic activities of this type.

Relations with the national confederations

The nine RWOs affiliated to national confederations maintain relations with the confederations' women's affairs departments, notably for advice on approaches to organization (five cases) and participation in the educational activities which they organize at national level. In other cases, because of various problems with the women's structure of one confederation, or relations between the confederation and the RWO, the bond is not as close.

With regard to the type of financial support received from the confederations, it should be pointed out that, as a rule, the resources available to the confederations' women's departments are too limited to enable them to give specific attention to the needs of the RWOs.

Achievements of the RWOs

Beginning with the second phase of the ILO project in 1991, the RWOs mentioned in this study have succeeded in establishing or strengthening various organizations in order to carry out the training programmes proposed by the project. Thus UNAC has set up a Women's Secretariat, and FENAZUCAR and FENELAC, FECCC, ATC and FESIAN have succeeded in founding and reinforcing base-level associations, organizations and groups in their own territories. ATC stands out as having organized 400 unemployed women members into 20 working groups for the benefit of unemployed women. SITRACHILCO has founded the Changuinola Working Women's Branch in order to strengthen organization among women.

Apart from the foregoing, the banana organizations SITRATERCO and SITRACHILCO are restructuring their Central Committee for Women's Affairs. Since its fusion with FENTAP, FENAZUCAR has succeeded in consolidating its Women's Secretariat and strengthening the women's union structure in the workshops.

Finally, FECCC has a Women's Commission with the goals of strengthening the participation of women in trade unions and coordinating the work at regional and national level. SITRACHILCO succeeded in having a member elected to the Social Assistance Secretariat.

Another aspect which shows the progress of the women's movement in these RWOs is the development of various projects oriented towards satisfying the educational, economic and service requirements of their members. This represents a success both for the RWOs themselves and for the sector as a whole.

Conclusion

The project's strategy emphasized the importance of focusing on the needs of the individual RWOs in each country. The methodological approach helped to give the women a profound knowledge of their situation inside and outside their organizations so that they were able to identify, plan and carry out projects to improve their working and living conditions.

The strategy ensured that women leaders would be able to apply what they learned in the DIPs, which in turn helped to teach other women. As a result of the project, women leaders developed more self-confidence and were both more committed and more active in their RWOs. The women developed a clear social and political awareness based upon the understanding of their own condition and the actions they should undertake in order to modify this reality. This enabled them to play a more essential role in their organizations.

The project's methodology supported the women in adopting a leading role in issues of their direct concern. This helped them to negotiate with the regional and national bodies of their organizations and with governmental agencies, where they had in the past "maintained a petitioner's attitude".

The methodology provided to be both effective and efficient and its use is recommended in other projects, not only those linked to RWOs but all those with both women and men as target groups. The project's strategy has not only strengthened the women's position in their RWOs but has also benefited the communities where the demonstration projects take place.

Annex

Countries and organizations participating in the project (percentage of women members in brackets)

Costa Rica

FECCC	Christian Agricultural Workers' Federation of Costa Rica (16.8)
FESIAN	National Agricultural Trade Union Federation (12)

Dominican Republic

CONAMUCA	National Confederation of Women Agricultural Workers (100)
FEDELAC	Dominican Federation of Christian Workers' Leagues (18.7)
FENAZUCAR	National Federation of Sugar, Agricultural and Allied Workers (10)
FENTAP	National Federation of Sugar and Plantation Workers (10)

(The above two organizations were merged in 1993.)

UNAC	National Agricultural Workers' Union (20)

Honduras

ANACH	National Association of Honduran Agricultural Workers (14.2)
CODIMCA	Council for the Integrated Development of Women Agricultural Workers (100)
SITRATERCO	Tela Railroad Company Workers' Union (44)

Nicaragua

ATC	Farmworkers' Association (32)

Panama

SITRACHILCO	Chiriqui Land Company Workers' Union (6)

Total: 34 per cent women members in participating RWOs.

Part V

Organizing self-employed and informal sector women workers

12

Experience in organizing women in the informal sector in India

Margaret Hosmer Martens

India has long taken the lead in organizing women in the informal sector. There are several organizations working with self-employed women and they have been very successful in lifting women out of the most abject poverty and painful living conditions. The case study of the Working Women's Forum (WWF) in Chapter 13 describes the organization's objectives and grass-roots structure. Of particular interest is the Forum's approach to leadership training and consciousness raising, which is closely linked with the goals of the organization.

The Self-Employed Women's Association (SEWA) is also well known for the breakthroughs it has achieved in organizing impoverished and lower-caste women and, in particular, lobbying the Indian Government on their behalf. SEWA worked hard in the early 1970s to achieve recognition of these women and their right to organize for fair wages and decent working conditions. The Government at first refused to recognize the union on the grounds that its members had no identifiable employer. SEWA was supported in this fight by the Textile Labour Association of which it was originally a member. In 1972 the union was finally recognized, the first of many of SEWA's accomplishments.

SEWA is today an independent union affiliated to several international trade secretariats and open to all self-employed women above the age of 15. Its members are petty traders or small-scale sellers, home-based producers, and casual labourers and service workers. It seeks to help them through obtaining recognition for their work, improving their working conditions, and promoting equitable shares and partnership. From its inception in 1972, SEWA helped the women to obtain small loans and eventually formed its own Cooperative Bank.

In addition to its work for self-employed women in India, SEWA has been instrumental in raising awareness within the international trade union movement concerning home work and the possibilities of organizing homeworkers. This has gradually paid off in drawing attention to these workers, who have long been considered not only impossible to organize but a direct threat to organized labour.

Although SEWA's history has already been widely documented,[1] it is useful to compare two areas of its experience in organizing women with those noted in the study of the WWF.

1. It is interesting to observe the different needs which women express as their situations gradually improve. When SEWA started its first training programme

[1] See, for example, S. Selliah: *The Self-Employed Women's Association, Ahmedabad, India* (Geneva, ILO, 1989).

for its members, literacy training was initially its focus. However, it soon became evident that the women wanted skills training which would improve their income-generating possibilities. Once they had learned to improve their products and increase their earnings, then they were ready for basic literacy courses.

The account of reasons for joining the WWF is illustrative of how a woman's outlook evolves as she begins to emerge from a bare subsistence level. An older member is heard to say that she joined for the training and that the need for credit was secondary, then admits that the circumstances were such in her family that she did not hesitate to join immediately. The lesson which the author points out is that once the member's life has slightly improved, then her perception of the possibilities offered by the Forum begins to expand.

2. Although many are aware that these women face great hardships, some of the experiences in organizing rural women are a reminder of the absolute bondage in which the women live and how essential is the work of these organizations. The WWF study notes that Dr. Nandini Azad has shown that approximately 75 per cent of the Forum leaders have successfully survived emotional crises, usually involving their husbands. Claire Bangasser reports that the last resort in trying to collect an overdue loan is to send the member a card showing the status of her account and how much she has repaid. The Forum does not like to have to use this procedure because there is the risk that the husband might find the card and realize how much money his wife has saved. The following account from SEWA's experience illustrates the male population's reaction to its work in the rural areas. It also shows how anxious the Forum women have reason to be for fear that their husbands will learn of their attempts at independence:

> The efforts to organize rural women disturbed the traditional relationship between men and women. That women should learn new roles as organizers, trainers and group leaders was not easily accepted by the men in the villages, who, in fact, resisted the organization of women. In the poorest families, any extra income was welcome to the males and to that extent they supported the union's activities. But at the community level, the men found it very difficult to accept equal status for women. When women persisted, the men might even become unbalanced and assault them. Over the years, the situation has improved considerably and a better understanding has been established.[2]

Both the WWF and SEWA focus on liberating their members from the tyranny of the moneylenders. In addition to their husband's wrath, women particularly fear the moneylenders to whom they can be indebted for an entire lifetime. In the WWF study the poorest members are described as responsible for feeding their children and living on the edge of starvation. It is only by pawning their few jewels and cooking utensils that these women manage to obtain a meagre loan on which their families can exist. When a woman cannot pay the interest on time, the moneylender comes and insults her loudly in front of the door of her hut.

One woman with a good deal of experience organizing the tribal women in the forests explained that entire families could be indentured servants to local moneylenders, who wield immense power over the rural poor. A priority for the union was to organize the women to help free them from the moneylenders' grasp. One of the

[2] ibid., p. 21.

major reasons for debts was the need to pay for family weddings and the union was able to convince some villagers to organize several simplified weddings together as a way to save money. Shortly afterwards some of the members' houses were reportedly set on fire in revenge for trying to go against the system.[3]

Finally, SEWA, continuing its struggle to open up communication and understanding between the poor and the legal system, has tried a two-pronged approach to touch both lawyers and its members. In collaboration with the legal aid committee of Gujarat High Court, SEWA brought the two groups together twice yearly in an effort to encourage social awareness in lawyers and increase rural women's knowledge of how the law has an impact on their lives.[4] Again we see how these women gradually understand how some formerly obscure decision-making process far removed from them can affect their lives and their ability to do business. Most important, they are learning that together they have the potential to voice their opinion and work for change.

[3] Christine Nathan, formerly with the Hind Mazdoor Sabha Trade Union Confederation and now with the International Federation of Building and Woodworkers. Personal interview, Caracas, March 1992.

[4] Selliah, op. cit., p. 20

13

The Working Women's Forum: A case study of leadership development in India

*Claire L. Bangasser**

The history of the Working Women's Forum

The Working Women's Forum (WWF) was first created as an experiment in Madras following a flood in 1978. Mrs. Jaya Arunachalam, a well-known political activist and social worker, found that instead of free rice and free blankets poor women in the slums actually wanted access to credit. She thus helped some 30 of these women to obtain a loan to start or expand small businesses. Today the Forum owns its own cooperative bank and has more than 225,000 members in nine branches across the three southern states in India of Tamil Nadu, Andhra Pradesh and Karnataka.

The WWF is a non-political grass-roots organization, run by poor women for poor women, which aims at "participation, self-reliance and sustainability" (Arunachalam, 1991, p. 2). The Forum helps women, often illiterate and usually living below the poverty level, to obtain credit, develop leadership skills and discover solidarity and courage, as well as a sense of their own dignity. The Forum is seen by its members as a unique path to economic, social and political empowerment.

The Forum, or *"Sangam"* as its members call it, can be considered simultaneously as a trade union,[1] a women's cooperative and credit association for low-caste women in the informal sector, a self-help group, a powerful women's lobby and a popular non-violence movement.

As most Forum members like to explain, their life in the Forum is about "boldness": the boldness to face their daily existence and their community, to confront the fear of injustice and oppression, to balance the conflicting expectations of their society's traditions and their own human needs, to overcome cowardice in themselves and others, and to change a system which exploits and oppresses them. This is made possible through the loans which they are able to receive through the Forum and two qualities they develop over time through their participation in meetings and workshops: solidarity and boldness.

* Postgraduate researcher on developing leadership in women; has been working for the ILO Special Adviser for Women Workers' Questions.

[1] The Forum is affiliated to the International Federation of Plantation, Agricultural and Allied Workers (IFPAAW).

Objectives

To develop this new spirit, the Forum's objectives are:

(1) to provide visibility to the valuable economic role played by poor women workers,
(2) to devise a grass-roots delivery system and organizational structure so as to effectively reach large numbers of poor women,
(3) to develop an effective credit and employment strategy to address the critical needs of the poor women,
(4) to implement an intensive health and family welfare program to strengthen women's productive roles,
(5) to provide support services to the poor women,
(6) to help the women perceive the discrimination, exploitation, and harassment inherent in their living and working environment,
(7) to create awareness concerning their basic rights and also to provide them with the leadership skills, confidence and courage required to fight for these rights,
(8) to make them realize their state of powerlessness as well as the scope and power of their empowerment,
(9) to make them understand the need for the strength of collective action among them so as to overcome the gender, class and caste oppressions,
(10) to provide them with the skills, experience, and knowledge that can provide alternative employment opportunities, increase and regularize their incomes, improve their living and working conditions as well as social state and . . . facilitate investments in productive assets, and
(11) to enable these women ultimately to help themselves in improving their overall quality of life.

(Arunachalam, 1991, pp. 12-13).

The aim of the Forum is to empower its members through access to credit, training, awareness and solidarity — or to make them "bold" *(dhairiyam)*, to use a word familiar to the women themselves. A Forum member, then, can be said to be bold when she has:

— the economic strength to provide for the basic needs of her children and herself;
— the awareness of her self-worth; and
— the solidarity of group members when her immediate environment tries to exploit her and to deny this self-worth.

A holistic approach

In order to achieve these objectives, the Forum follows a "holistic approach" and offers a series of programmes which, apart from credit assistance, include:

— consciousness-raising workshops;
— appropriate technology for *idli* (pancake) sellers, washerwomen, etc.;
— marketing for the lace workers in the rural branch of Narasapur;
— legal cells to pay lawyers' fees for evicted vendors;

— registration of common-law weddings;
— inter-caste weddings;
— non-violent demonstrations against the dowry system;
— a petition for civic amenities;
— the provision of day-care centres;
— centres for child workers, where children are taught and fed in the evenings;
— nutrition presentations;
— family planning information;
— consciousness raising on hygiene and environmental sanitation;
— free distribution of contraceptives;
— children's immunization (Arunachalam, 1991, pp. 5-7).

Thus, the WWF's approach is holistic in that it takes up a whole range of seemingly separate issues, although each important in its members' lives, and places these issues in the context of equity and choice.

A psychological contract

The growing empowerment which a Forum member experiences over a period of a couple of years leads to a strong psychological contract[2] between the Forum and its members:

— first, the organization helps to release and channel the women's energy and motivation through economic, political, and social empowerment;
— then, in return, the women are motivated through their newly discovered sense of satisfaction and pride, as well as the desire for financial independence, to achieve the Forum goals of high repayment rate, increased awareness and continued expansion.

For the members, the success of their *"Sangam"* means not only their own success, but that of many women. All they can see is the multitude of women who need the Forum. Hence, whether they can express it themselves or not, many members are looking forward to the uplifting of their gender and class through their organization.

Structure

Without outside institutional help, poor women could not obtain bank loans and had to resort to moneylenders and their high interest rates. The Forum, therefore, began by helping poor women gain access to small loans of Rs.200 each from nation-

[2] "The notion of a psychological contract implies that there is an *unwritten set of expectations* operating at all times between every member of an organization and the various managers and others in that organization." See H. Schein, 1988.

alized banks through a structure of neighbourhood loan groups (NLGs), group leaders, area organizers and Forum staff.

At the Forum, a woman's loan collateral was and still is her own work and the group itself. In the early days a group could count up to 20 members. Today the average group includes about ten women. The group leader[3] is generally elected by her members, who recognize in her a responsible, honest and vocal woman, willing and able to speak up for their needs. Sometimes her leadership skills are noticed by an area organizer who appoints her as a group leader, as long as she is able to form a group of ten women.

Each small group, therefore, gains access to credit while benefiting from the Forum's organizational network and social services. The members learn to identify and articulate their problems, while developing a sense of solidarity which helps them tackle their daily life with more boldness.

The groups spread far and wide through word of mouth. Thus a woman living in another state may hear through a relative or a friend of this organization which helps women free themselves from the moneylenders. She often takes it upon herself to come to the Madras office to ask for help. Two Forum organizers then travel to check out the new environment and ensure that the potential members are willing and able to repay the loans.

Membership today

Counting over 225,000 members spread over the three southern Indian States of Tamil Nadu, Karnataka and Andhra Pradesh, today the Forum includes: urban petty traders in and around Madras; fisherwomen in Adiramapattinam; landless women labourers in Bidar; weavers and ropemakers in East Godavari District; women workers in the rural markets of the Dindigul area; lace artisans in Narasapur; incense-stick *(agarbathis)* makers in Bangalore; cigar *(bidi)* rollers in Vellore; and women weavers in Kancheepuram. Thirty-five per cent of these women are urban, while 65 per cent are rural. Their ages range from 22 to 50 years old. Fifty-six per cent of the members are illiterate, particularly among the older age group (Working Women's Forum, 1992, p. 13).

The landless women in the Dindigul area were first helped to rear cattle for milk. When a drought set in, they were also given loans to be able to sell at local fairs. Fisherwomen in Adiramapattinam were able to escape the hold of the middlemen and wholesalers through credit loans. Lace artisans in Narasapur obtained higher wages from lace exporters. Marketing and production centres were added in a second stage of development. By becoming organized, incense-stick makers in Bangalore and cigar rollers in Vellore were also able to obtain higher wages from the suppliers and middlemen. In all cases, each woman had to face her own lack of consciousness and ensuing economic exploitation and lack of access to credit, before she could improve the conditions in her life (Arunachalam, 1991, pp. 6-7).

Recently, the WWF has also extended its operations in Lucknow, Northern

[3] A group leader's role is akin to that of a shop steward in a traditional trade union.

India, where it has organized *chikan* embroidery workers as well as migrant workers and children in the Kanpur industrial belt of Uttar Pradesh (Arunachalam, 1991, p. 11).

Reasons for joining

One often finds a difference between recent and older members in their explanation for joining the Forum. An older member says nearly in the same breath that "credit is secondary" and that training was her real reason for joining a group. When asked whether she gave much thought to joining, she replies: "I joined immediately, as the circumstances were such in my family." Her circumstances, of course, were that of intense poverty.

However, once a member has been out of abject poverty for some time (and the eradication of extreme poverty is often positively related to her growing boldness, i.e. about two years), she realizes that there is more to the Forum than the loans. She then moves on to another plateau where awareness and boldness bring her self-respect and power.

Obtaining a loan

Usually, a new Forum member comes to the organization to obtain a loan. To do this she must first join a neighbourhood group. While the loan is to the individual, the responsibility for the total loans rests with the leader, whose task it is to collect and bring the monthly instalments to the Forum by a specific date. *It is this loan procedure which binds the women together.*

Members like the conditions of credit offered by the Forum for the following reasons:

(1) the processing costs, particularly the psychological costs, are low (bank employees usually treated them in an insulting manner);
(2) the layers of supervision are tight with a short span of control (members, group leaders, area organizers), thus creating a safe "collection" environment; and
(3) neighbourhood loan groups have created an environment conducive to effective, positive, and empowering group dynamics (Arunachalam, 1991, p. 21).

Each new group member is entitled to a first loan of Rs.200 (US$6.70 in October 1992), repayable in ten monthly decreasing payments. To receive this loan, the new member incurs certain expenses for a photograph, a passbook and so on. She is required to pay a small entrance fee and to contribute Rs.20 for a share in the Cooperative Society.

A Forum member is expected to save at least Rs.5 a month and some save up to Rs.200 a month. She can also take a life insurance for Rs.3.25 a year, which will ensure a paid funeral and an amount of Rs.1,000 given to her family at her death.

The second loan is usually between Rs.400 and Rs.800 depending on the increase in trade volume and the individual member's ability to pay. The maximum loan that the society offers is Rs.3,000. Loans between Rs.200 and Rs.2,000 are repayable in ten monthly instalments, while those above Rs.2,000 are repayable within 20 months (Arunachalam, 1991, p. 23).

The Cooperative Society charges interest at the prevailing market rates, i.e. 15 per cent per annum. However, in reality, the interest rate works out to 8.25 per cent as it is computed on the decreasing capital (Arunachalam, 1991, p. 28).

Nevertheless, this credit structure is a lure for the underlying goals of the Forum, namely: economic and caste emancipation; emancipation from male oppression; physical strength; and breaking out of a closed world through awareness and confidence (Chambers, 1986).

A high repayment rate

The Forum's high repayment rate of 92-95 per cent is one of its many claims to fame.[4] This high rate can be explained by the tight layers of supervision the organization provides, as embodied in:

— the leader's constant concern;
— the organizer's monthly check-up on her groups' repayment schedule;
— the vigilance of the Forum's staff; and
— the peer pressure applied both within and among the groups through the organization's grapevine.

The financial control is tight and the procedure systematic. A list is kept of all the repayment dates. Every Saturday, during the weekly organizers' meeting, the organizers are told of the groups' delays. One finds that some groups are always more difficult to deal with than others and that a few leaders are bound to default, i.e. to keep their members' repayments, because of family problems. The default leaders are usually accepted back, however, within two or three years, once they have repaid the loans completely.

When a group leader fails to repay her group loans and a "default" takes place, the procedure is as follows:

— the first month that she fails to repay the loans, the area organizer goes to check the situation and talks with the leader and her members. If the organizer finds that the leader has a genuine reason for not repaying, such as sickness in the family, she gives the leader one more month;
— when the group leader fails to repay the loans for a second month, she is automatically out. A representative from the Forum office visits the area, appoints another leader and asks the group to place greater pressure on the default leader for her to pay back what she owes;
— the third month, as a last resort, a card is sent to each member, giving her the status of her account and how much she has repaid. The Forum does not like to use

[4] "In all the WWCs, the loan repayment rates are uniformly high: Madras 95.7 per cent, Bangalore 95.4 per cent, Dindigul 97.8 per cent, Adiramapattinam 96.5 per cent, Vellore 95 per cent, Narasapur 99.9 per cent, Bidar 94.9 per cent and Kancheepuram 96.7 per cent." See Working Women's Forum, 1991, p. 15.

Portrait of a member

"Money and a good husband are very necessary for a woman". Thus speaks Hamsa, a 39-year-old Forum member, mother of four grown children and living in a South Madras slum. Every Forum member would agree with her. Money and husbands are important, but hard to come by. Poor unskilled men can only expect low, unreliable daily wages. Traditionally, "coolie" male workers give just a few rupees to their wife out of their daily income. Poor men often spend their money at the liquor shop. Finally, they may have "favourite ladies", as if sex were a compensation for poverty.

Indian society is a patriarchal one where man is seen as the all-powerful head of the household — and the breadwinner, whether he does the earning or not. A poor Indian woman, therefore, faces two seemingly incompatible duties: to stay at home, raise her family and attend to age-old rituals as her society requires; and to find a job so as to feed her children when her husband does not give her enough to support their family.

The average Forum member's age is 32 to 35 years old. As a young unaware woman in her early twenties, she gave birth to children and was busy with household chores. In her late twenties, however, she came to realize that her husband could not support their family: she had to find means to step in financially and replace him.

Of the 70 per cent of Forum members who are married, few can rely on their husbands for financial support. Many have known physical abuse at one point or another. Divorce is not really a solution, since a woman who leaves her husband is called "deserted" and finds herself rejected by her community. The other 30 per cent are heading households, whether as widows or as deserted women. As such, they usually stand pretty much on their own, destitute and harassed, unless they find a man willing to spend a couple of nights a week with them as a sign of protection.

Often a Forum member will explain that, until she joined the Forum, she "suffered too much". The word "suffered" means that she was starving: she had been living on water for several days, or on gruel (rice and water) once a day for weeks on end. The poorest member is the head of household, with no other income than her own to feed and to educate her children. She and her family live on the edge of starvation. The vessels in which she cooks, the few jewels she wears, often go the way of the pawnbroker. If she cannot pay the interest on time, usually every evening, he comes in front of her hut and insults her loudly. Deeply ashamed, she hides behind her mud walls.

The potential Forum member, therefore, is, like Hamsa, a woman who belongs to the informal sector (both rural and urban). She usually has poor health, a low level of education and skills, and a poor self-image. She is exploited by family, employer and society. Traditionally humiliated for her caste and class origins and seen as a second-class citizen because of her sex, she is refused access to key inputs, such as credit, training and markets. While protected *de jure* by social legislation, she experiences daily *de facto* discrimination. As she belongs to the "vast pools of underemployed labour" forever scratching for a living, she is exploited as a worker. She does not benefit from minimum wages. In fact, to feed her family she must compensate for decreasing wages by working longer hours. She does not receive workers' benefits and does not know job security or safety on the job. She cannot join workers' education programmes.

Finally, this woman is not only officially invisible; she is also voiceless — as if she had neither thoughts nor feelings, neither hope nor despair. By joining the Forum, however, a woman at last will be seen and heard.

this procedure: the member's husband may find the card, discover how much money his wife has saved and make trouble. Finally, the members of the group will not be able to obtain a new loan until their previous loan has been repaid.

Thanks to this systematic approach, 30 per cent of the arrears are recovered within a period of three months, 50 per cent within three to six months and only 17 per cent beyond six months. In all, only 1.25 per cent of the WWF members default on loans (Arunachalam, 1991, pp. 23-24). This group consists mainly of members who move away from the area following natural calamities such as floods or fire, or family difficulties.

Leadership training

Following a survey of 400 families who had received loans, the Forum decided that some type of further training was necessary for the women. The families were seen to have made little if any progress. It was decided to focus on two main areas in the training: (a) leadership and/or awareness raising; and (b) family planning.

The Food and Agriculture Organization of the United Nations (FAO) was then conducting the Bay of Bengal Scheme in southern Tamil Nadu. The programme lent money to poor rural people. Not only did the project get a low rate of return, but it ran into many instances of graft *(benami)*.[5] In the final analysis, the target group hardly benefited from the project. In 1981, therefore, FAO approached the Forum asking whether it would take over the project and offered to sponsor a leadership training programme for those women receiving the loans.

Developing their own training programme

While preparing the leadership training programme for the Bay of Bengal Scheme, Dr. Nandini Azad examined the literature available on leadership programmes. She soon realized that there was no known approach which answered the women's needs. Too many members, for instance, were illiterate: the training had to be tailored differently.

Dr. Azad decided to involve three remarkable Forum leaders to pool their knowledge and experience to help her to develop the curriculum through a series of brainstorming sessions. In the next six months they identified and developed together the main themes of the training, such as the need for women's solidarity, the dangers of superstition, sexual discrimination, the vicious circle brought about by

[5] In this case a rich person will use a poor person's name to borrow money at a low interest rate. This often occurred in the days of the Differential Rate of Interest Scheme (DRI) offered by the Bank of India in the early 1970s. The repayment rate then usually averaged around 65 per cent.

child marriages,[6] and the need to educate daughters and abolish the dowry system.

More women came to Madras from the Forum branches to look at the material prepared and helped polish each point of the programme. They rehearsed and practised until everyone felt that their creation was finally ready. As a final touch, the themes perceived by the women were drawn by an artist especially brought in. These are the "charts" still used today for all new members coming for their first three loans.

An indigenous group process

The first leadership training course took place in Adiramapattinam, the Bay of Bengal Scheme's headquarters, and lasted five days. The day the programme started, the participants arrived very frightened. Never before had they left their "four walls" just to spend time talking with women. But the course offered them a novel, while familiar and safe, environment with fisherwomen just like themselves, who all sat cross-legged on the floor and tucked their sarees under their knees.

On the second morning of the course, one of the husbands, who happened to be an important man in the village, decided that his wife would stay at home that day. All the other women marched to their house and helped him change his mind. "This was the first instance of boldness in the Forum", said Rajeshwari, first organizer in Adiramapattinam.

The charts, the drawings and the trainers' presentations took the women on an inner journey which led them to reflect on their lives, possibly for the first time. They were surrounded by trainers from the Forum, poor women too, but women who somehow stood out as role models and talked bravely of their misery, of their difficulties and of the unfairness of their lives.

During these five days, the group analysed and questioned their daily life. While listening to other women sharing their existence, they came to see their own in another light. For once, they did not feel alone, rejected or humiliated. Out of the experience, they gained strength, faith in themselves, and a new sense of solidarity and dignity.

For the past three years, the five-day training course has become a one-day course. This shorter training is seen as a better use of time for those new members who will be receiving their first three loans. For interested and motivated members who have been part of the Forum for the past five to ten years, the five-day IFPAAW training is offered from time to time to groups of 16 to 30 women.

In Madras, the one-day leadership course is offered ten times a month, which means that between 300 and 350 women are being trained monthly. Seven trainers work in Madras, while the eight other branches employ only four trainers each.

[6] This begins when a child bride of 13 gives birth. By the time she is 20, she has four children. Her husband leaves her for another girl. She is rejected by her family and her community. She must find a job to feed her children. Unskilled, she can only manage to get a very low wage and must have her own small children work if they all are to survive.

Training objective: Self-awareness

"The training does not teach you to disrespect people, but to fight injustice" (Tamilselvi, aged 24, WWF leader).

The one-day leadership training course is a door which opens up the path to boldness. Women do not become bold in one day. Maybe four or five participants may truly understand what is going on during one day of training. In the long run, however, it will change the lives of these women who until then had felt inferior, isolated, and at the mercy of their families and communities.

The process can be described as follows:

— women discover their many roles, and with them a new sense of self-worth;
— women realize they all face the same problems, and develop a new sense of solidarity;
— women teach one another, and through the process realize their collective strength.[7]

The Forum leader

Dr. Nandini Azad has shown that 75 per cent of the Forum leaders have successfully overcome emotional crises, usually related to their husband (Azad, 1988, p. 258; see also Azad, 1986). One could say that, having undergone a psychological tearing and a kind of cultural divorce from their traditions, these women feel willing and ready to help other women break free from "the shackles of powerlessness".

A member, however, may want to become a leader for several reasons: to receive a bigger loan; to improve her status in the community; or, quite often, to be able to help her family, friends and neighbours receive loans.

To become a leader, a woman has to be recognized by her peers as someone who:

— is a good representative of their needs;
— is known for her regularity in repaying loans and thus is seen as responsible and honest (she "doesn't eat the members' money");
— knows the Forum rules;
— attends the Forum meetings;
— can take the time to do the job; and
— is not a trouble-maker.

The leader's immediate role is relatively time-consuming. It consists of collecting and bringing the monthly repayments to the Forum office by the 15th of each month; and creating an atmosphere of "peer pressure" so that no member will dare default on her loans. The leader also acts as an organizational activist: she talks to potential members; checks their business potential (will the new member be able to re-

[7] Explained in a conversation in October 1991 by the late Mrs. Kalavathy, then Head of Training and the Forum's General Secretary, a woman from the informal sector herself.

pay?); identifies possible loans; visits defaulting members; passes messages about meetings; asks a member to take a petition with her to the Municipal Corporation (e.g. to ask for a sewer or a bus route); calls her members to join in a non-violent demonstration; and helps form a new group when her own is growing too big. "In fact, the best leaders will be those whose groups have a high rate of loan repayment and whose level of social consciousness has substantially risen" (Azad, 1988, p. 258). To ensure a high loan repayment rate, therefore, leaders must identify good, responsible members who will pay back on time. They also must recognize those members who "want to change" and who will be willing to attend meetings.

The group leader thus plays a "pivotal role" between the members and the organization. She is not only responsible for assisting in loan processing and recovery. Above all she is a *role model*, a "catalyst helping members perceive the exploitation and denial of rights and services at the local level" (Arunachalam, 1991, p. 15).

A successful Forum leader often shows dynamism, organizational skills, patience and selflessness, and has an eye out for women who are in trouble or who could use some help. Her interest goes beyond her immediate needs and she tries to encompass the good of her members, the community and the organization.

Good leaders are those who identify, foster and nurture leadership within their group. As they detect potential leaders among their members, they help their members start new groups. Some will be at the origin of 40 to 60 new groups and thus become an area organizer.

The main problem faced by a Forum leader is when one member is unable or unwilling to repay her loan. As a first step, the leader goes to the defaulting member and talks with her. As she understands the situation, she will then choose one of three courses of action: (a) she will advise her organizer and do what she is told to do; (b) she will talk with her other members and together they will decide on an appropriate course of action; or (c) she will talk to the member and solve the problem on her own.

Quite often, the leader ends up paying one or two instalments out of her own pocket until her defaulting member can once again assume her responsibilities.

Forum members and leaders have a great understanding of and compassion for the hardships facing women in their community. They do not easily reject an insolvent woman or a bad leader who has eaten her members' money. No one likes the idea of getting rid of a bad leader. They know too well that life sometimes is so crushing as to turn sudden temptations into irresistible opportunities.

"Networking in sisterhood"

Since 1990, the WWF has expanded its action to a global network, known as GROOTS.[8] It now publishes a newsletter, sponsored by a grant from the United Nations' Development Fund for Women (UNIFEM). It strives to share the experience and knowledge the Forum members have gained, while learning from others. It also hopes to help poor grass-roots women, both in the developing and developed world,

[8] For "Grassroot Organization Operating in Sisterhood"; see Working Women's Forum, 1992, p. 22.

to understand and to apply successful development models in their own lives and communities so that they too may experience awareness, solidarity and boldness.[9]

Conclusion

For the past 14 years, the WWF has shown a remarkable talent for fostering and nurturing a culture of leadership through:

- **"leadership from below"** (Chambers, 1986, p. 18), participative and non-hierarchical, where members know that, their wisdom being recognized, they have direct access to decision-making;
- a **path to leadership** open to all by leadership training tailored to the milieu in which it is offered, with a system whereby leaders are automatically elected or appointed for every ten members they can gather;
- a newly born **"Networking in Sisterhood"**, whereby the Forum is now sharing its experience and successes with kindred organizations all around the world.

Today, the Forum is still built on the highly participatory structure of its early days. It is based on neighbourhood loan groups which form the pillars of the organization. As has been shown, each group is headed by a leader and supervised by an area organizer (who can be responsible for up to 600 members). Both the leader and the organizer come from the same socio-economic background and geographic area: they know the problems faced by their members because of having had to cope with them themselves.

The unique leadership style of the Forum means that it is the Forum's rank and file, namely the neighbourhood loan groups and their leaders, who tell the area organizers and Forum staff what needs to be placed on the Forum's social agenda. Both members and leaders alike have a say in the direction they want the Forum to take, be it health services, night classes, day care, training courses or housing schemes. This very responsive attitude to the needs of the grass-roots explains the high level of trust towards the Forum staff encountered among the membership and the widening success of the organization.

A Forum member often does not take long to become a leader; she sees another group's success, forms her own group, and joins the Forum as a leader right away. The Forum, however, offers a process which helps the new member or leader not only to understand the meaning of leadership but also to look consciously at her life, usually for the first time. It awakens an awareness of her life, her situation and what she can do about it.

The "contagious" attraction of the Forum's leadership style for the grass-roots women of the informal sector is because it is so easily replicable and both participatory and dynamic. It catches the attention of poor women because, thanks to its simple organizational structure, it brings them rapidly both money and status, while breaking down their walls of loneliness and self-contempt.

[9] The WWF is funded through its membership fees, development assistance from the Government of the Netherlands and various private contributions. It also runs a health project in conjunction with the Government of India, the ILO and the United Nations Fund for Population Activities (UNFPA).

Bibliography

Arunachalam, Jaya. 1991. *Credit needs of women workers in the informal sector. Case study of Working Women's Forum (India)*, Paper presented at the Asian and Pacific Development Centre, Kuala Lumpur, Malaysia. September 1991.

———. 1992. *NGO – Cooperation for Enterprise Development: The empowerment of women.* Paper presented at the Society for International Development Conference, "Development with Equity and Ecological Security: Strategies and Institutions for the 21st Century", Rome, Italy, 11-12 September 1992.

Azad, Dr. Nandini. 1986. *Empowering women workers: The WWF experiment in Indian cities* (Mylapore, WWF).

———. 1988. *Creating bases of women's solidarity: A study of the grassroots of the Working Women's Forum in India* (Ann Arbor, Michigan, University of Michigan Press).

Burns, James MacGregor. 1978. *Leadership* (New York, Harper and Row).

Chambers, Robert. 1986. *The Working Women's Forum: A counter-culture by poor women* (Brighton, University of Sussex, Institute of Development Studies).

ILO. 1991. *The dilemma of the informal sector*, Report of the Director-General, International Labour Conference, 78th Session, Geneva.

Schein, Edgar H. 1988. *Organizational psychology* (Englewood-Cliffs, New Jersey, Prentice-Hall, 3rd ed.).

Working Women's Forum (India). 1992. *Reaching out to poor women through grass-roots initiatives: An Indian experiment* (Madras).

14

Trade unions and workers in the informal sector in Burkina Faso

Mamounata Cissé *

Background

Burkina Faso, a landlocked country in the heart of West Africa, is increasingly faced with the problems of unemployment, underemployment and poverty, phenomena which cloud the outlook for development and make structural adjustment policies both necessary and difficult for the population. If one analyses the various studies on the socio-economic situation of Burkina Faso, one finds that the informal sector accounts for about 20 per cent of gross domestic product and provides a living for some 80 per cent of the economically active urban population.[1] It offers an alternative to employment as such. The predominance of women in this sector is even more striking. It is also noticeable that these studies are in general agreement as to the heavy burden of women's work and its unfortunate effect on the day-to-day lives of the women concerned.

The trade union movement needs to investigate the composition of the informal sector workforce, which contains many potential members.

The present report sets out the experience of the National Organization of Free Trade Unions (ONSL) in the informal sector. The purpose of this organization is to seek solutions to the problems of underdevelopment in Burkina Faso. Such solutions must inevitably take account of the contribution of women to any development programme. The Cissin-Natenga Women's Association and the group of women merchants in the markets of Ouagadougou are affiliated to the ONSL. Their history will help the reader to understand the ONSL's policy of intervention on behalf of women in the informal sector.

The first part of the report places the workers of the informal sector in their socio-economic context by type of activity, while the second deals with the trade union organization of women in the informal sector.

* Administrator of Financial Services and Chairperson, Women's Committee, ONSL; President, Women's Committee, ICFTU.

[1] *Colloque sur l'acquisition des qualifications et l'emploi dans le secteur non-structuré urbain d'Afrique francophone*, Final report, Ouagadougou, July 1990.

The informal sector in Burkina Faso

Burkina Faso is a country where agriculture is still the driving force of the national economy and the main provider of employment and income. About 85 per cent of the economically active population is employed in rural areas. Both the modern and rural sectors are undergoing difficulty in achieving growth owing to climatic hazards and problems associated with financing and competitiveness, thus favouring runaway expansion in the informal sector, which accounts for some 60.6 per cent of total urban employment. Women represent 47.77 per cent of the economically active population; they are occupied chiefly in agriculture.

A breakdown by type of activity of the active population employed in the informal sector will give an idea of their nature and the relative importance of each (table 1).

Table 1. Type of activity in the informal sector by sex, Burkina Faso (percentages)

Type of activity	Male	Female	Combined
Agriculture	91.2	93.5	92.3
Commerce	1.9	3.7	2.8
Crafts	2.4	1.1	2.8
Total informal sector	87.6	74.1	80.4

Note: Totals may not add up exactly, owing to rounding.

Source: National Institute for Statistics and Population (INSD).

An inquiry into the informal sector in Burkina Faso was carried out in 1987 by the National Office for the Promotion of Employment (ONPE) in the five major cities of Ouagadougou, Bobo-Dioulasso, Koudougou, Ouahigouya and Banfora.

The inquiry covered a population sample of 796,329 inhabitants. Altogether it identified 83,109 informal sector workers, of whom 40,390 were women and 42,718 men. The capital city of Ouagadougou alone accounted for 25,404 female and 24,651 male workers, respectively 30.57 per cent and 29.66 per cent of the total. The two major centres, Ouagadougou and Bobo-Dioulasso, made up 87.53 per cent of the whole. This concentration of activity in the urban zones undoubtedly has unfortunate implications with regard to working conditions and levels of remuneration.

The scale of the informal sector keeps pace with the level of socio-economic development of the cities in Burkina Faso, and is notable for its diversity. The breakdown of such workers by type of activity (table 2) shows the importance of commerce, which represents 69.67 per cent of the informal sector total. It is estimated that women in commerce represent 41.96 per cent of all workers in the informal sector in these cities, or 86.33 of female workers. Retailing business tends to be seasonal, occasional and irregular; it can be taken up freely and calls for no particular training or investment.

The informal sector is largely made up of independent workers who rarely engage assistants when business is going well. They possess no social security what-

Table 2. Type of activity in the informal sector of major cities by sex, Burkina Faso, 1987

Type of activity	No.		%		Overall %
	Female	Male	Female	Male	
Manufacturing crafts	3 308	6 596	3.92	7.93	11.92
Artistic crafts	116	929	0.14	1.12	1.26
Services	1 513	6 440	1.82	7.75	9.57
Building	29	2 005	0.03	2.41	2.44
Transport	56	2 135	0.07	2.57	2.64
Commerce	34 871	23 029	41.96	27.71	69.67
Miscellaneous	497	1 585	0.60	1.90	2.50
Total	40 390	42 719	48.60	51.40	100.00

Source: ONPE: Direct inquiry among informal-sector workers, 1987.

soever. Lack of machinery, shortage of raw materials and other needed products, chaotic channels of distribution and a low level of education all detract from the competitiveness of the goods they produce, often forcing them to carry on several different trades at the same time. They have access neither to capital nor to guarantees, so that it is difficult for them to obtain credit. The variety and high rates of taxation cause many of them to remain hidden. The inquiry revealed the number of workers in the informal sector to be at least 116,401, as opposed to 83,109 declared by employers.

The discrepancy implied that 33,292 workers did not come forward to be counted in the census because they feared the possibility of taxation of their profits. At the present time the number of unidentified workers in the big cities has grown much larger. They are to be found everywhere, increasingly on the public highways, in reserves or on the fringes of populated areas, and they evade any form of fiscal registration.

More research needs to be carried out regarding the informal sector, the activities of which should tend towards the organized sector of the economy, whereas in fact the opposite trend is to be observed.

While it is true that both men and women work in the informal sector, the fact remains that their conditions differ in many respects, for example hours and type of work, remuneration, length of working life and family responsibilities. To this must be added constraints of a social and cultural kind which prevent women from leaving home and working outside the framework of the family. Very often their spouses, whose permission is final, are polygamous, and the activities of the wives are controlled by the husbands. The economic survival of women, and especially poor women who form the majority and who carry on their little businesses from their homes, often depends entirely on the informal sector.

The trade union and its members

Traditionally, trade unions are organizations of formal sector workers. For a long time the trade union movement as a whole preferred to ignore the question of workers in the informal sector. This was due to the fact that the unions already had enough trouble trying to mobilize those in the structured part of the economy. Nevertheless, in a mainly agricultural country such as Burkina Faso, where 85 per cent of the population was illiterate, the movement could hardly go on ignoring them, or the informal sector where most of them made their living.

Whereas the traditional task of the unions has been to promote the material and moral interests of wage earners, nowadays they attempt, by playing a part in the socio-economic development of States, to broaden their scope to cover all those who constitute a real social force.

The ONSL is affiliated to the International Confederation of Free Trade Unions (ICFTU). In Burkina Faso there are six national federations and a multitude of independent unions. This multiplicity has existed ever since independence. For a long time there was a congress grouping all the federations. As differences of opinion appeared between the federations the congress dissolved, but the federations and some of the independent unions still meet regularly to discuss common problems.

The ONSL has an Executive Board with 37 members, five of whom are women. In 1991 it set up a number of technical committees. A women's committee of three members, who are members of the Board, was also constituted. The latter committee helps the department responsible for women's affairs in working out policy for the promotion and representation of women in trade union activities; it has established local committees in each of the movement's six provincial sections. The federation employs numerous managers and instructors, but there are very few women instructors. The committee looks after training, and the organization and implementation of socio-economic projects relating to women.

Increasingly, the ONSL approaches existing women's associations with a view to persuading them to join unions, and maintains friendly relations with them. The best means of attracting women into the trade union movement is by the training of militants. It is through training that they succeed in making their presence felt, in assuming higher responsibilities and in altering the male-dominated image of Burkina Faso trade unionism. Since its last congress in 1990, the ONSL has organized five seminars with an average of 30 participants for the benefit of women workers. Thanks to the increasing importance which the international organizations and NGOs accord to women worldwide, the federation's male members have begun to realize the need for training women workers, and the Executive Board now welcomes projects and programmes in their favour.

Trade union activity in Burkina Faso is regulated by Act 62/AN of 7 July 1962. The text of this law is no longer adapted to existing conditions, and trade union members are often subject to injustice and sanctions at the workplace. The grievances of men and women workers are set out each year in a memorandum and presented to the Government jointly by the unions. Those relating to women's working conditions are very badly expressed and attract little attention. The reason for this state of affairs is that women play no part in the drawing up of the texts. In 1992, as an exception, women representatives of five federations and about ten independent unions took part in the preparation of the memorandum.

Intervention by the ONSL in the informal sector

Since its foundation, the ONSL has represented workers of both sexes from the informal sector.

The most important groups of informal sector women affiliated to the ONSL are the market women's association, the Cissin-Natenga Association of Women Workers and the Friendly Society of Alumnae of the Gounghin Crafts Centre. The first two groups are described in detail below.

The market women's association

The first informal sector workers to affiliate to the ONSL were the butchers and small traders from the Ouagadougou markets. They belong to a trade union whose Secretary-General is a member of the ONSL's National Executive Board. Women constitute 40 per cent of the membership. The union's annual subscription is 600 CFA-francs. In its turn, the union pays an annual contribution to the ONSL National Office. As shown in table 2, commercial activities are extremely important in the informal sector, and the dynamism of the women traders in the main market of Ouagadougou is highly impressive.

We take as an example the women selling fruit and vegetables in the city of Ouagadougou (12,270 in 1985). They set up their stalls in the markets, in front of the big stores, on the thronged main roads and in kiosks erected by the Chamber of Commerce throughout the city. So far, in Burkina Faso, women have a monopoly of this particular trade. Not all these women are ONSL members, since there are two unions in the market which are not affiliated to it.

There is in fact no specific organization of women fruit and vegetable vendors; rather, they have teamed up with women selling other kinds of goods and have established a system adapted to the milieu. There is an office where they meet once a month. Their president is a fruit and vegetable seller in the main market of Ouagadougou. In the course of an interview concerning their organization and the problems which hinder their trading in the market, she explained how, in general, their social lives influence their business activities. There are financial problems and social constraints such as attendance at marriages, christenings and funerals. "We organize tontine funds in the market and in the districts where we live. These are traditional moral obligations of our society, ruled by the rights of seniority, whether of age or length of presence in the market. We set great store by this kind of social structure", she said, implying that it constituted a bond of solidarity, of moral support and mutual aid. In the context of the family:

> . . . our lives are just as overloaded as those of women who live out in the country. Setting aside part of our stock to feed our families cuts into our profits and our ability to save. All this reduces

the prosperity of our businesses to such a degree that some women lose their working capital and are forced to borrow from shady businessmen. Then there is taxation and assessment for the rental of our market stalls, which is very high. The trade regulations cause a lot of difficulty on account of our lack of education, the majority of women being illiterate like myself. As compared with those in other sectors, the State does not provide workers in our type of activity with adequate incentives.

These women are well aware of the need for a structured organization for their trade, but are worried about the dilution of their financial and personal interests in a group. Thus, some of them would prefer a trade union which would strengthen solidarity within the informal sector, promote their activities and, finally, give them access to information and education.

The federation is not unaware of these difficulties. In 1989, the ONSL Women's Committee established a Market Women's Committee which has 28 members. In 1991, ONSL organized a seminar for persons responsible for the work of women in various trades in the informal sector.

The Small Traders' Union

The Small Traders' Union is a commercial member of the Burkina Chamber of Commerce and Crafts; a member of the Ouagadougou Commercial Zone Organization Commission (known as ZACA); and a member of the Commercial Bureau of the Burkina Market Management (SOGEMAB). Of its five affiliates, two are composed of women. It played an active part in the project to set up a Revolutionary Economic and Social Council, and has applied for membership (ONSL is a member already). The Union defends the interests of its members within the context of all these bodies.

Since the renovation of the main marketplace, the Small Traders' Union has made representations to the SOGEMAB for the reduction of rents. As a consequence, rents which formerly stood at 10,000 CFA-francs and 4,000 CFA-francs have now fallen to 9,000 and 2,000 CFA-francs respectively. The majority of women rent stalls at 2,000 CFA-francs, and have thus benefited from a reduction of 50 per cent.

The Cissin-Natenga Women's Association

It all began with a group of Catholic women attending a literacy course about 4 kilometres from where they lived. In 1984 they asked the parish priest to open a literacy centre in their own district. They formed a group of 25 women and set up an office, then asked two teachers to give them lessons at the house of the group's president. Classes were held three afternoons a week. The teachers were paid 200 CFA-francs per session. The monthly subscription was 100 CFA-francs, and the money thus collected was also used for the purchase of supplies and for the end-of-year ceremony.

After a year, it became apparent that more and more women were coming to the course. They therefore decided to open it to all women, whatever their ethnic origin or religious persuasion, and contacted ONSL's Assistant Secretary for Workers' Education to ask for help. His advice was to found a women's association with well-defined objectives, and thus the Cissin-Natenga Women's Association came into being. The Secretary-General of ONSL was asked to look into the possibility of helping and organizing these women.

The person responsible for youth-related matters and the author, responsible for women's affairs, were designated to provide guidance to the new association. In April 1985 it became officially affiliated to ONSL. Its members subscribe 900 CFA-francs per year to the Federation. The latter's first contribution was to provide them with learning materials and two lamps so that they could also hold courses at night.

By 1986 the Federation included a number of women with literacy diplomas. It was therefore decided to make the instruction a permanent activity and the ONSL decided to apply for a site on which to build a craft and literacy centre for its female members. In 1987 a committee consisting of two women from the association, two teachers and the author took active steps to obtain such a site from the communal and provincial authorities. Two years later a site of 3,030 m^2 was allocated to District 17 of the city of Ouagadougou; the previous year the Association had already received aid in the form of weaving machinery and soap-manufacturing plant thanks to its contacts with UNICEF.

A savings account was opened for the receipt of subscriptions and money received from the sale of the association's products. UNICEF also assumed the cost of having two of the Association's members trained in soap manufacture and vegetable drying.

The weaving looms enabled the women to produce cotton garments which they sold either in the market or at the former Faso Dan Fani, a public body for the promotion of Burkina apparel. However, the lack of ONSL-owned premises was an

Portrait of a member

Ms Madeleine has been a ONSL militant since 1984. She is one of the members who played a part in setting up the Cissin-Natenga Women's Association. Married into a polygamous family, the mother of eight children, Ms Madeleine started in business by crocheting babies' bonnets which she sold in the main market of Ouagadougou. With the proceeds from these sales she bought groundnuts to sell in front of her house. This did not prevent her from following literacy courses for three years, at the end of which she received a diploma. A few years later, she decided to give up crocheting and take up weaving. She bought a traditional loom and began weaving cotton garments which she sold to dealers in the market. By instalments she then went on to buy a modern loom which enabled her to improve both quality and output. During this time she took part in several trade union training courses. In 1987, when the State organized a competition to pick out the best women weavers in Ouagadougou, she was one of the 30 women selected. So that she could step up her output the ONSL gave her an extra loom. Her cloth was put on show in large boutiques and in the exhibitions mounted by the former Faso Dan Fani. Nowadays she dresses several well-known personalities in Burkina Faso and other countries, earning her family's living and paying her children's school fees.

obstacle to the development of their activities. The ONSL therefore submitted a project for the building of a women's artisanal and literacy centre to the ICFTU; this was adopted by its Women's Committee. The ICFTU then launched a solidarity campaign among its affiliated bodies on behalf of literacy among the women workers of Burkina Faso.

The construction of this building, which contains three classrooms, a storeroom and toilet facilities, was completed in June 1992 thanks to the aid of the Belgian General Federation of Labour (FGTB) via the intermediary of Socialist Solidarity, a Belgian NGO installed in Burkina Faso. The ICFTU and its affiliates are financing the roofing and equipment of the centre in time for the beginning of the school year in November 1992.

The centre will be open to all women members of the organization and will thus supplement and relieve pressure on the literacy, weaving and soap-manufacturing activities which have been carried out with the women of Cissin-Natenga since 1985. The guidance given to these women by the ONSL has enabled hundreds of them to become literate and to learn a trade. They have received courses on trade unionism in the same way as the Ouagadougou market women. The training and education of workers are priorities in the ONSL's women's programme inasmuch as they represent the most suitable method of sensitizing, informing and educating union militants. They also facilitate the recruitment of members, most of whom have no idea of what a trade union is and what it does.

The ONSL promotes the sale of cloth, bracelets and tablecloths produced by women of the informal sector at inter-African and European conferences. However, much remains to be done in view of the very low earnings of these women and their social conditions in a world where the first objective is to survive.

Conclusion

In Burkina Faso, it is the organized or formal modern sector which is supposed to generate economic growth and stimulate economic and social progress. In principle, the traditional or informal sector should be destined to disappear. Yet our experience is that when many modern sector workers lose their jobs they end up in the informal sector, notably in the case of women.

The ONSL's contribution to the trade union organization of market women and the Cissin-Natenga Women's Association has been a long struggle. The Union has practically no financial resources and receives no state subsidies. Members rarely pay their subscriptions. Nevertheless, with its limited means, it has trained thousands of workers and built nine literacy centres which enrol workers from every sector. In some districts it has also provided young farmers with equipment.

All that has been possible thanks to international trade union solidarity and to the ICFTU. However, the problems faced by the workers are undiminished. Trade union action needs to reach as many workers as possible in a world where increasing numbers of them are turning away from the unions.

Trade union policy must be designed to attract unorganized workers. This will not be an easy task. With the establishment of a State that respects the rule of law, all kinds of workers' associations and friendly societies are springing up with almost the same objectives as those of trade unions. However, in spite of all the constraints, the aim of the ONSL is to found cooperatives or similar groupings in favour of workers in the informal sector.

The ONSL considers that workers in the organized sector can best preserve their security and dignity by reducing the vulnerability of those in the informal sector, particularly women. The challenge is to find ways of rendering the informal sector more formal. This calls for the participation of all trade unions in a much more scientific organization better adapted to the political and socio-economic context of Burkina Faso. A revitalization of union activities is required at national and international level by the integration of women and by facilitating their access to the taking of decisions on a basis of equality. Special programmes need to be worked out in favour of women workers and to encourage women in the informal sector to form cooperatives or agricultural or craft groupings.

In order to succeed, the trade unions must strive to obtain equal protection for all workers, whether men or women, and to heed the concerns of women, such as child care, feeding their families and the sharing of domestic tasks. Without any doubt, such a change would be of strategic importance in achieving a breakthrough in the informal sector.

15

Trade unions and women workers in the rural and informal sectors in Côte d'Ivoire: The case of SYNAFSI

Mahan Gahe Basile *

The informal sector in Côte d'Ivoire

In Côte d'Ivoire, the activities of the informal and formal sectors are practically one and the same. Only the actual working conditions are different. Jobs include:

— for men: cobblers, mechanics, sellers of spare parts, itinerant tailoring, car-washing, itinerant sellers of food and cloth, road repairs, laundry, small traders (selling artefacts, textiles, shoes, charcoal, drinks, watches and belts), taxi services, pottery, portering, electrical repairs, garbage collection, local watchmen;

— for women: food sellers in markets, home laundering, hairdressing, home delivery of food products, tending cooked food stalls, itinerant sellers of beauty products and cloth, fish cleaners, potters, dressmakers.

Those who work in the informal sector report that they have to cope with an enormous amount of competition resulting from the informality of the work itself. As the effects of the current economic crisis become more far-reaching, these workers have to accept lower and lower compensation if they are to find customers. Moreover, since they are illiterate, they are too often the prey of swindlers who, pretending to be authorities, levy fraudulent taxes. One example of this is the numerous "syndicates" which charge illegal duties on the baskets of foodstuffs which women bring to sell in the market. Under the threat of violence and prohibition of sales these women pay every day, unaware that the "syndicates" have no legal basis.

In some respects activity in the informal sector is not considered as "work" or "employment". Nevertheless, the resulting earnings have become more and more necessary during the present economic crisis. For instance, many market women selling foodstuffs declare that they alone supply their families' needs (food, clothing, rent, school fees, medical care, etc.), thus earning the respect of their husbands, who are often out of work, and of the entire extended family. Indeed, husbands increasingly encourage their wives to start up a "little business".

The informal sector is rarely considered in official policy, whether national or local. For example, women who have sold their goods at the same place in the market for many years can be suddenly pushed out from one day to the next in spite of having regularly paid their daily fees for years. As a result of this precarious condition, market women consider that they pay their fees but neither benefit from any of

* General Secretary, DIGNITE.

the promised amenities such as paved market-places, storage depots and public lavatories for which those fees are supposed to pay, nor even have the slightest sense of security in return for their regular payments.

Trade union background

At present Côte d'Ivoire has two national trade union confederations. These are the General Union of Workers of Côte d'Ivoire (UGTCI) and the Confederation of Free Trade Unions of Côte d'Ivoire (DIGNITE). In addition, there are autonomous unions grouped in the Federation of Independent Trade Unions of Côte d'Ivoire (FESACI).

DIGNITE has existed in practice since 1988, but only received official recognition in July 1992. It unites four federations, 16 cooperatives and 75 trade unions (including SYNAFSI, the subject of this case study), representing more than 100,000 members from among every sector of economic activity.

The emergence of SYNAFSI

The National Union of Informal Sector Women (SYNAFSI), which is affiliated to DIGNITE, was formed in 1990 at the initiative of DIGNITE's Executive Bureau. It was the leadership of the Confederation which acted upon the Executive Board's decision and set out first to organize the women in the markets. In September 1991 SYNAFSI submitted the papers necessary for the union's official registration but as of September 1992 it had not been recognized by the Government.

Registering women's cooperatives

The goal of SYNAFSI is to group women working in the informal sector according to their particular sphere of activity (fish sellers, vegetable sellers and fruit sellers, for example) and to give some structure to these groups. In Abidjan, only 5 per cent of the women belong to officially recognized cooperatives. It is often the case that they believe themselves to be organized because they have formed a group with elected officials, but these groups are in fact completely informal. They are neither official nor formally recognized and they engage in neither collective bargaining nor defence of their members' rights. Some 65 per cent of women in the informal sector in Abidjan and over 20 per cent of those in provincial cities find themselves in this situation. As a first step, SYNAFSI tries to form such groups into officially registered buyers' and sellers' cooperatives.

Each such cooperative has a bureau whose staff is elected by the women members (most frequently those elected for the former group). Since the groups are often ethnically based, SYNAFSI tries to ensure that each bureau contains at least one woman who can speak French in addition to her mother tongue.

SYNAFSI has over 2,000 members who work as farmers or selling food (such as fish, fruit, vegetables, meat, and soft drinks), as well as gourds, shoes, jewellery, cloth, beauty products and many other goods. They have no experience with real trade union organizations other than the above-mentioned informal groups.

Prior misfortunes leave women suspicious

However, women in the informal sector have had experience with other types of organization which have promised a good deal and ended by inevitably disappointing them. In one organization their money was taken but they never received the services for which they paid. Although this organization is still in existence, it has reportedly lost all credence among women of the informal sector. Another experience was the closing of a local bank in which many women's cooperatives had deposited their savings. The women have not been able to recover their savings.

These incidents have naturally left the women discouraged and highly suspicious of any talk of new schemes or organizations forming. They feel that they have been deceived too often by those who, in proposing one form of organization or another, were really serving their own interests. Some, for example, offered to draw up all the accounts for a cooperative, demanding an excessive advance payment for administrative costs, and then disappeared with the money. Others registered women as members of non-existent trade unions.

Thus the task of DIGNITE recruiters has been and still is a very difficult one. Informal sector women want tangible proof before committing themselves to anything at all. Little by little SYNAFSI is gaining their confidence and their membership by negotiating the registration of cooperatives while charging no more than the genuinely incurred administrative costs.

Dues structure

The message is gradually getting through and the members of SYNAFSI are highly motivated and ready to pay their dues. These amount to 2,000 CFA-francs per year, and are collected in one payment when the membership card is issued. It is very difficult to ascertain the average income of women in the informal sector. Some of them do not know how much profit they make; some may earn up to 200,000 CFA-francs per month, whereas the majority get along on 50,000-60,000 or even less. Nevertheless, they consider the fee of 2,000 CFA-francs entirely reasonable.

Leadership

It should be noted that SYNAFSI is a young trade union. It has not yet held a congress and is still at the recruitment stage. Up to now working sessions have not followed any formal agenda but have proceeded as a function of the programme of activities drawn up by SYNAFSI's Executive Bureau. These activities have mainly been carried out by the Bureau members themselves and permanent staff, of whom there are 12. These women — who are still unpaid volunteers owing to the union's lack of funds — carry out recruitment, follow up the administrative process of getting cooperatives registered, and hold information and awareness-raising meetings in conjunction with the cooperatives. They meet with local authorities to explain their members' immediate problems.

Most of the executive and permanent staff of SYNAFSI have completed the first cycle of secondary education, and all of them have completed the primary cycle. They had no trade union training prior to joining DIGNITE. The General Secretary was given a two-month training course in Belgium in 1991. Like the other executive and permanent staff, she has learnt on the job and follows weekend training courses at DIGNITE headquarters. Respected by the Executive Bureau and the members as a whole the General Secretary is considered important for the stability of the trade union. Nevertheless, the members insist that the post depends on competence and the work accomplished, and if the incumbent failed in either of these respects she would very soon be replaced.[1]

Socio-economic activities

For the time being, SYNAFSI does not undertake income-generating activities on behalf of its members. However, when circumstances permit it intends to provide certain cooperatives with income-generating equipment, notably:

— a fish-drying machine (for the fishmongers' cooperative);

— a rice-husking machine (for rice sellers);

— a manioc flour grinder for the women who sell fermented cassava or manioc flour.

DIGNITE planned to begin a savings bank and a mutual fund during 1992. SYNAFSI members, in their capacity as DIGNITE affiliates, would be invited to take advantage of these services.

Training activities

SYNAFSI proposes in the very near future to begin training counsellors who in turn will train the members in:

— household management and family budgeting;

— the rights and obligations of citizens, wives and mothers;

— basic administrative procedures;

— commerce (capital, investment, profit, etc.).

In addition, it is intended to set up study groups to discuss the different experiences of the women concerning their lives in general, their children's education or

[1] Ed. note: It has been observed that some trade unions organized for women in the informal sector, although highly successful, tend to revolve around the charismatic personality of the founder/leader. Case study authors were asked to address this question because it can have an impact on the future of the organization.

any other aspect, in the company of a counsellor who will be able to suggest possible solutions to their problems.

Potential drawbacks to joining

So far, the members have not suffered any prejudice as a result of having joined the union. They pay no more taxes than before and do not expect to have any further demands made of them on account of having joined DIGNITE. They are gradually learning that a trade union looks after their interests better than an association because, thanks to its official status and its affiliation to a national confederation, it has more power of negotiation and organization than other types of group.

The national confederation, DIGNITE

DIGNITE headquarters consists of 35 permanent staff, nine of whom are women. Two of the six Assistant General Secretaries are women, one of whom is responsible for matters relating to women in the formal sector while the other, who for the time being is also General Secretary of SYNAFSI, is responsible for the informal sector. However, there is no formal separation into men's and women's sections at headquarters. DIGNITE's permanent staff have played a very active part in the founding of SYNAFSI and continue to support its development. Indeed, as mentioned above, the very idea of creating SYNAFSI originated in DIGNITE's Executive Bureau, embodying its desire to promote organization in the informal sector.

DIGNITE's constitution expressly provides for the struggle for women's emancipation, so that supporting the informal sector is a self-imposed moral obligation. Moreover, the Confederation is very much aware of the role which women's small businesses play in the informal sector and in the country's economy. A certain linkage effect is also observable, in that women encourage their husbands to join the DIGNITE branch at their place of work. The presence of women from the informal sector has contributed to the Confederation's acceptance by the public; and all the more so because, despite its obvious lack of funds, SYNAFSI has already won a number of victories.

It is still too early to judge whether SYNAFSI will be a success or not. Once again, it is necessary to emphasize the difficulty of mobilizing women in the informal sector because they have so often been cheated by more literate but unscrupulous people who tricked them with visions of cooperatives, unions and other sorts of organization. Thus they are extremely wary of any further proposal of association. Many of them say: "Do something for us first, and then we'll see."

DIGNITE supports the development of SYNAFSI in various ways: it lends its premises for meetings; it types documents; it supplies funds for the security deposit required in setting up cooperatives; and it helps to recruit women in the interior of the country by asking its members to promote contacts in their own districts.

Finally, DIGNITE has introduced SYNAFSI to those overseas organizations likely to be supportive of its activities, for example the Belgian trade union Women of the CSC, which invited the General Secretary to a seminar on women and development. The Dutch NGO Actie Kom-over also invited the General Secretary to take part in a workshop/seminar for Third World women trade unionists in October 1992. Finally, the Belgian NGO Solidarité Mondiale (World Solidarity) has made a gift of 2.4 million CFA-francs to finance a project on behalf of women fishmongers' cooperatives in Abidjan and the interior.

Relations with the authorities

As in the case of the Self-Employed Women's Association (SEWA), in India, the Government did not react well at first to the creation of a trade union for those without employers. It takes time to convince others that the self-employed, homeworkers and rural workers are all just as much in need of labour rights, and often more so, as those in the more formal sector.

Conditions have already begun to improve for the women in the market-place and soon SYNAFSI intends to take action to compel local authorities to improve the working conditions of these women by demanding:

— the provision of drinking fountains, lavatories and washing facilities in market-places;
— the asphalt paving of market-places (veritable bogs on rainy days);
— the provision of first aid posts, etc.

It should be noted that nowadays certain local authorities are beginning to view SYNAFSI as a potential partner in the organization, management and regulation of working conditions in the informal sector.

16

The informal sector in an industrialized country: Textile and garment workers in northern Italy

Vicky Franzinetti *

Background

Biella is a mountainous area in the north of Italy, not far from Turin, a highly industrialized area. The textile and garment industry in the region dates back over 100 years. In earlier years there was a good deal of sheep farming, hence the district had a virtually complete cycle, from the raising of sheep to producing the finished garment.

In 1982 the area experienced a strong economic downturn which was overcome by specialization, introducing new technologies and focusing on exports. In fact, since 1986 exports to the EC countries, and especially to Germany, have exceeded domestic demand.[1]

Compared to the rest of the country, the area has a very low unemployment rate and a growing number of small cottage industries. However, unlike regions which traditionally had a large informal network, such as Emilia Romagna in Central Italy, this activity is relatively new to this area. Neither does it compare to areas such as Tuscany which have a tradition of women embroidering at home, with a network managing the collection and marketing of garments. Lastly, the switch to informal and cottage industries does not in any way appear to correspond to a lower level of technology. The sector works in heckling, spinning, spinning and heckling, garment making (subcontracted by large enterprises such as the Carpi knitwear industry) and decorative stitching of top-quality materials for the expensive range of the garment industry.

Two other significant points should be made. First, Italy now has one of the lowest birth rates of Western Europe, and Biella has an especially low birth rate,[2] which has meant a dwindling local labour force. The area experienced a strong wave of migration from the south of Italy in the late 1960s and early 1970s. Second, the State and local government, as well as industry, have invested heavily in training for this sector. Tecnotex — a multidisciplinary training centre for the textile industry — was established and this, combined with a long-standing apprenticeship system, guarantees a highly trained female and male labour force supply in the area.

* Founding member of Sindacato Donna and part-time researcher for the Union Research Unit (Ires), Turin.

[1] Roberto Garavini et al.: *La quarta Italia* (Rome, EDIESSE, 1987).

[2] Data on Biella, Oct. 1991, from ISTAT (Italian Institute of Statistics) and Eurostat-ISTAT data ("Cifre per conoscersi" [Data to know yourself], suppl. to *Mondo Economico* (Milan, 1992).

The informal sector in the Biella area

The Biella area has a number of large and medium-sized enterprises, although only one, the Ermenegildo Zegna, is quoted on the stock exchange. Unlike other areas of the country there is not much homeworking or outwork, but a growing number of small and cottage industries (under 15 employees), where the labour force is virtually exclusively female. The textile sector is by far the largest employer in the area, and in 1991 accounted for 68.6 per cent of all employment.[3] Data show[4] a growing number of productive units — from 907 in 1971 to 1,563 in 1981, accompanied by a decreasing overall number of employees (from 18,681 to 16,941); according to both trade unionists and employers, this was also accompanied by the introduction of new technologies into cottage industries. In the late 1980s, the average cottage industry (out of a total of about 800 for the district and 310 in and around Biella itself[5]) had 4.4 employees.

The percentage of women of the area in the labour force is much higher than the national level (37 per cent).[6] This is also true of the percentage of women registered as unemployed, which is higher than that of men (20 per cent compared with 15 per cent), with a prevalence of younger people under 25 (39.4 per cent). The impact of gender segregation is seen throughout the sector, although it is reportedly lower than in other areas. According to the local FILTEA Secretary, Marisa Lucano, the average wage in the mechanical sector (the other large industry of the area) is about 10-15 per cent higher than in textiles. Preliminary data from Law 125/91 on Equal Opportunities (which refers exclusively to large enterprises) show that women earn 87.5 per cent of men's wages. Considering that women workers in the informal sector earn less than those in large enterprises, one may estimate that there is a difference of about 25 per cent between an average male metalworker in the area and a woman in the informal sector for comparable work. The data should be considered as representing a situation of high employment in a long-industrialized area which has succeeded in reviving its industrial base, making this a rather privileged district.

Informal sector workers tend to be native to the area or fairly long-standing migrants. They are generally recruited through informal channels (acquaintances or relatives). The period of apprenticeship is quite long (one to three years), and women either start at age 14 or 15 (the end of compulsory education) or come from the larger textile enterprises.

One important difference between the formal and more informal sectors of the textile industry is that in the latter the distinction between women's personal and working lives tends to become blurred. The women in this group appear to be more established in the community, with a strong network of personal relationships. This also means there is a higher degree of social control on the part of employers who are

[3] Data from the *Quarterly Report* (1/91) published by the Industrialists' Association, according to the Agreement signed on 17 October 1980 for the Biella district.

[4] Istituto Nazionale della Previdenza Sociale (INPS), national pension and social security data for 1981-91; FILTEA; Biella chapter data.

[5] Garavini et al., op. cit., table 7, p. 196.

[6] European Community data on employment in Europe, 1992, from *Crew Reports* (Brussels), Aug.-Sept. 1992, p. 16.

also part of the community. This factor leads to many cases of sexual harassment (which exists in the larger enterprises as well), and to instances of employers demanding that workers perform their domestic chores, and even insisting that not more than one worker per year is allowed to become pregnant. Carmela Brancato, who migrated to the area from Sicily in the 1970s when the sector was expanding, remembers that employers would go directly to the young women's houses trying to attract the most skilled to their establishments.

Most of the women interviewed for this study would have preferred to work in larger enterprises for these reasons and for the higher pay, although others felt that the informal sector afforded a higher degree of flexibility. In other words, the more "informal" environment appears to be conducive to balancing women's domestic and job-related roles, but also tends to infringe too much on their private lives.

Although some trade unionists said that husbands shared child rearing and domestic tasks, this was not confirmed by the women interviewed. Instead, in addition to a full day's work, women still have responsibility for the multitude of chores involved in raising a family. It is particularly in this respect that flexibility is important. Mothers, sisters, daughters and female in-laws all appear to share their family burdens, and to arrange work on different shifts according to the demands of their productive and reproductive roles.[7] This is possible in the community work environment but would be more difficult to arrange in the larger enterprises.

Union access to the informal sector

In 1985 a national agreement was signed pertaining to wages in both formal and informal sectors — the *Contratto Territoriale*. Although the agreement itself has since been superseded by the new *Contratto Nationale*[8] described below, it marked a turning-point in that unions were authorized information rights for the informal sector, which until then had not been possible.

In 1987 a new national agreement[9] was signed for the entire sector, setting many more constraints on the cottage industries. All the women interviewed (workers and trade union officials) stressed the importance of this agreement as it allowed external trade union representatives (Carmela Brancato for FILTEA) to have the right of access to even the smallest productive units. They were then able to negotiate on behalf of the workers.

[7] Caroline O. Moser: "Gender planning in the Third World: Meeting practical and strategic gender needs" in *World Development*, Vol. 17, No. 11, 1989, pp. 1799-1825.

[8] *Contratto Collettivo Nazionale di Lavoro, per i lavoratori dipendenti delle imprese artigiane dei settori tessili, abbigliamento e calzaturiero* [National Collective Labour Agreement for workers in the small-scale textile, clothing and footwear industry] (Rome, July 1988).

[9] ibid.

The union: FILTEA

FILTEA is a textile and garment union affiliated to the Italian General Federation of Labour (CGIL), the largest of the three trade union confederations in Italy.[10] About one-and-a-half years ago the CGIL introduced a quota system whereby at least 25 per cent of all trade union officials must be women. FILTEA's statistics for 1991 in Biella show that in the cottage industries 80 per cent of all members are women, and that membership is 314 out of a workforce of 3,500 (as opposed to 4,771 out of approximately 25,000 in the medium and large enterprises in 1990).[11] The area has had trade unions for about 100 years.

The Union offers two types of membership: full membership *(tessera diretta)*, with dues amounting to 1 per cent of wages, where the employer is informed of the membership; or indirect membership, where the person pays an annual L60,000 (about US$50 in October 1992) directly to the trade union, and the employer is not informed of the membership. There is also a "service fee" (0.5 per cent of wages) established by an agreement between the unions and the Employers' Association, paid by the employers to the unions regardless of the number of members.

Among the main reasons given by women in the informal sector for joining the union were: legal services (in the case of unfair dismissal, severance pay, or other such cases); assistance with filling out tax forms, pension claims and other types of documents required by the State (services provided by the union to members which would be very expensive if purchased on the open market); and organized travel and group outings.

As well as being responsible for collective bargaining for the sector, FILTEA was also party to the struggle for the implementation of Act No. 125 of 10 April 1991 on Equal Opportunities and Act No. 223 of 23 July 1991 on Extension of Redundancy Rights to the informal sector, as well as the right to maternity leave. To date the union does not have a policy on equal pay for comparative worth, nor has it carried out any studies on the impact of job segregation. Ms. Lucano, the General Secretary for Textiles for the area, is the first woman ever to hold the post. Women account for 50 per cent of the *direttivo*, the elected union body, whereas one might expect the figure to be between 75 per cent and 90 per cent if the sex distribution of the workforce and the importance of women's contribution throughout the sector were taken into account.

The process of unionization

Compared to the larger enterprises, the process of unionization in the informal sector appears to follow a different pattern: in the former most recruitment occurs

[10] Each of the three confederal unions — CGIL, Italian Confederation of Workers' Unions (CISL) and Italian Labour Union (UIL) — groups a number of trade or sectoral unions (also known as vertical unions, as opposed to the horizontal or confederal ones). Some sectors also have other "independent" unions, not affiliated to any of the confederal unions. This is not the case in the textile and garment sector.

[11] Membership survey by the Biella FILTEA, 31 Dec. 1990.

at the time of strikes or plant disputes, whereas in cottage industries strikes appear to be themselves a result of unionization. The presence of an external trade union official appears to be a key factor. For instance, the presence of Ms. Brancato, a full-time official who had formally worked in one of the large textile firms, had a visible impact on membership. Following her appointment membership rose, and the union's decision to move her out of the area following cutbacks within the union has led to a slow but consistent decline in membership. No comparable figure was available in larger industries, and the impact of external stimuli was not as visible.

Both Carmela Brancato and the women interviewed spoke of the importance of having a trade union representative present on a regular basis. Such officials play a very important role, particularly in some of the following key areas: the dissemination of information on rights and national legislation; as a deterrent against sexual harassment (a problem which appears harder to deal with in the cottage industries); help with the night work issue and checking pay packets. In general, a charismatic and forceful personality engendered respect for the union and its representatives. As union officials they also had much more freedom in entering into negotiations.

The fact that there is no longer a full-time official in the area for the informal sector (they now have become part of subdistricts) appears to have had a very negative effect on the members' situation. Some have put forward the argument that such a decision is an indication of the union's image of the informal sector as weak and politically not as important as the larger industries. In other words, resources have been taken away from a virtually all-female sector which greatly benefited from them. Most of the women interviewed did not believe it was necessary to have a woman official, although some said that it was easier to talk to a woman representative. This would be quite understandable when discussing personal issues such as sexual harassment, particularly when workers and employers usually live in the same neighbourhood. FILTEA reiterated its commitment to the informal sector in the course of its 1991 National Conference.

There is not only a women's caucus in FILTEA but also a separate women's union, Sindacato Donna.[12] A small number of women hold membership both in FILTEA and in the Women's Union. Sindacato Donna has organized several courses for women. In September 1992 it organized discussions on government measures and gender discrimination which were also attended by FILTEA members.

Group discussions with FILTEA members working in cottage industries

A meeting was organized with 23 women from six different cottage industries. This made it possible to speak to the women directly about their working condi-

[12] Sindacato Donna, the Women's Union, is mainly present in Piedmont, with a membership of about 2,000 and double membership for those who already belong to another union. About one-third of its membership are not union members. The basic philosophy of Sindacato Donna is the importance of negotiating the cost of both productive and reproductive labour, maintaining that, if unions only negotiate the cost and value of productive labour exchangeable on the market, a substantial part of women's work will remain unpaid. It also aims at fighting discrimination at work and calculating comparable worth among sectors and gender differences in disposable income.

tions and the differences they perceive between themselves and FILTEA members in larger firms. The main points of discussion are outlined below. Two individual profiles are included (see box) to provide a better picture of the women and their concerns. Although 80 per cent of the female textile labour force are employed in spinning and related activities (*"fusi"* as they are known), in the Biella area as a whole union membership is relatively higher in the garment-making and weaving sections.

Working conditions

Working conditions in the cottage industry were estimated to be worse than those in larger enterprises, productivity was higher, and any mistakes (yarn, spinning or decorative stitching) were considered the worker's responsibility and therefore to be remedied in her own time. Bargaining power was estimated to be much lower in spite of the fact that "we pay the same tax, work harder and are more skilled".

Women who had also worked in large enterprises felt that they were more personally involved in the actual production process. This gave them more of a sense of accomplishment, which they appeared to enjoy. Furthermore, the women appear to put in longer hours (often without extra payment) but, as mentioned above, they enjoy a higher degree of flexibility which enables them to cope with family commitments.

Indignities suffered

What may be a common occurrence in the informal sector, such as employers checking the toilets or not allowing women to take breaks together, is unheard of in larger enterprises. Furthermore, employers do not give advances on sick pay or the redundancy fund, as is possible in larger firms.

Unionization

Joining the union (this pertains to any of the three main confederations) often means ending up blacklisted. One woman, who had been a court witness in a case against an employer in an industrial tribunal, was "blacked" for over a year — meaning that her name was placed on a list which is reported to exist at the headquarters of the Association of Employers of Small and Cottage Industries.

The right to information appears to be one of the main reasons for joining the union, as well as the services it offers. Members preferred a woman representative because they feel more at ease in confiding in a woman. However, they thought that a man might be perceived to have more authority.

Maternity leave

In most cases women on maternity leave are not replaced. They receive five months' leave (two months before delivery and three months afterwards), and some employers tell their workers to "take it in turns".

Interviews with members

Susanna M. is 32 years old, married with no children. She started work at 15 as an apprentice. When the large company where she had been employed (and where she had been a shop steward for two years) closed seven years ago, she was unable to find work in any medium-sized or large company. She has been in the informal sector ever since. "We are constantly told that we are not worth anything . . . we are useless . . . and we get shouted at if we go to the toilet more than twice a day." She works from 8 a.m. to 4.40 p.m. with a 40-minute lunch break.

Susanna found it especially difficult to get work when she was first married, as prospective employers were concerned that she might have children in the coming years.

Her unit is quite large (14 employees) and does contract work for a larger textile company. Her employer is involved in the marketing side of the business, and is therefore away for periods, leaving one worker as the de facto manager although she is not compensated for this extra work. Susanna feels that the informal sector lacks any sort of career structure (unlike the larger enterprises) and that the workers' flexibility (knowing how to do a bit of everything) is not recognized.

Although she has been a union member for nearly 20 years and feels that "a lot was done in the 1970s and 1980s", she stressed the importance of laws for the cottage industry because "recourse to the courts is often all you have", unlike the larger industries where in-plant bargaining power is stronger. However, she worked in larger enterprises at a time when both the economy and the trade unions were stronger.

Elisabetta is 20 and has been working in knitwear (weaving) since she was 15. She joined the company as an apprentice for the first three years. She says that she likes her work but not the job. Even so, Elisabetta expects that she will probably continue with the job even after marriage and possibly children. She had first learned about the firm when a friend of hers who worked there said that there was an opening.

She says that working conditions are very stressful, all the more so because the employer, "who also works and is very skilled" has a board where she writes the names of those who have made mistakes or broken needles and she then circles them in red, which, according to Elisabetta, "is not good for your pride or your pocket". Virtually all the workers and the employers (husband and wife) live in the same neighbourhood, and she considers her employers to be "nice people outside work . . . very pleasant when you meet them". However, during working hours they are not allowed to chat ("it affects our concentration, they say"), nor listen to the radio, which apparently was allowed about 30 years ago. She sees the union as a bargaining force concerned with the more basic issues (pensions, basic wage rates, unfair dismissals) but not with local conditions.

She would be happy to have either a part-time job for the same amount of money, or more money for the job. She also feels that in her job she will be at her best at about 30, in terms of experience and speed. After that she thinks you get slower, and therefore compensate with extra skill or lose out to the younger women.

She joined the union following Ms Brancato's "information assemblies" on the national contract, and felt she got more information as a member, which increased her confidence in negotiating on a day-to-day basis. Both she and Susanna also felt that being a member offered some sort of protection against sexual harassment.

Changes in the informal sector

The older women said that 20 years ago these were "family-run businesses". Today they usually consist of a husband and wife with four to five employees, and a high capital investment. Most employers work on either the production or marketing side. The male employer is often the only man in the enterprise.

Summary

A. *The relationship between the union and the informal sector*

1. The presence of a full-time union official has a major impact in the case of cottage industry and the entire informal sector, compared to the role the official can play in larger factories.

2. The informal sector appears to play a less important role in terms of union politics. This means that in times of union cutbacks (as was the case), officials are likely to be moved from sectors where they are very effective, to sectors which are more important from a policy point of view.

3. Gender awareness in the unions has led to greater attention to women in the larger sectors, but has not yet led to a shift in overall union priorities, i.e. investing in sectors which are entirely or the majority female. Some objectives, however, such as legislation on sexual harassment and equal opportunities, seem to be widely accepted. Comparable worth among sectors appears to be less of an objective for the union, compared to career opportunities within the same sector. In other words the type of negotiation that the unions have developed in Italy is more plant and sector based (i.e. negotiating within the sector or enterprise) as opposed to across the board (i.e. comparable worth negotiations or court cases).

B. *Areas where the unions have had a positive effect*

1. In-plant negotiation plays a marginal role in the informal sector, with some notable exceptions. However, the impact of the union as a negotiating party at the national level, and the resulting legislation, is very important for the informal sector.

2. The dissemination of information on existing agreements and legislation appeared essential, and was perceived as an element of strength. Negotiation at district level also appeared to have a positive effect on the weaker sections of the industry.

3. The presence of a female rather than a male official was not considered to be essential, although results indicate that women are more effective. For instance, the female representatives were able to cover a wider range of issues and "explain" more.

C. *Important differences between women in the cottage industries and women in the main industrial plants*

1. The women in cottage industries appeared to be more rooted in the area, which makes possible the informal methods of recruitment and the close intermingling of women's working and home lives. Unlike the formal sector, no new migrants

work here. Although they experience a substantial amount of social control (made even stronger by employers and employees often living in the same area), the women enjoyed a slightly higher degree of autonomy at work. Nevertheless, this autonomy did not correspond to a monetary recognition of their greater skills and longer working hours.

2. The women were more skilled and less well paid than their counterparts in the large plants. Union membership appeared to be the result of union organizing, rather than the opposite, as one might expect in a large concern.

3. The greater the overlap between productive and reproductive spheres, and especially the greater the presence of children, the more difficult was the situation for the women, although in this case child-rearing was shared, mostly among the women of the same family. Women in large plants can negotiate shifts and avail themselves of extended maternity leave and paid "permits", which entitle either parent to take leave to care for a sick child under 3 years old. While "non-working" mothers are ignored by the Italian welfare system, "working" women have or have had some of the most favourable maternity and family leave provisions. In other words, rights dependent on employment are much stronger than general welfare rights.

Part VI

Organizing women workers in export processing zones

Introduction to Part VI

Margaret Hosmer Martens

Most of the case studies gathered for this report have focused on organizing women in the informal and rural sectors. Although export processing zones (EPZs) cannot be considered as belonging to either of these sectors, they are included here because of their large number of women workers and their general lack of access to collective bargaining.

EPZs have long presented a special challenge to trade unions. Although they can be found all over the world, they are predominantly located in developing countries. During the 1970s the World Bank and other international development agencies promoted export-led industrialization in order to bring in foreign exchange, encourage the transfer of technology and build up industrialization in the host countries. Developing countries were also anxious for EPZs to alleviate local unemployment. In order to attract industrial investment, countries have competed in offering incentives to foreign enterprises. Governments make every effort to present the available workforce as young, educated, inexpensive and free of labour problems.[1] Although few governments actually prohibit trade unions in the zones, they are actively discouraged and it is often impossible for unions to gain access.

Young women make up the vast majority of the labour force in these zones, and for many of them it is their first job. They have little, if any, knowledge of their rights as workers and often their working conditions are deplorable, with much mandatory overtime. Health and safety precautions are frequently overlooked. Although most have been educated, the work is invariably unskilled and semi-skilled, involving very basic tasks which correspond to specific phases of the production process. The women work very hard for long hours trying to meet their quotas, and after four or five years they are often exhausted and in poor health. Clearly any study of organizing women workers could not afford to ignore EPZ workers.

A detailed study on the Mauritius experience of EPZs was prepared for this volume. Although, as will be seen, this case is atypical for several reasons, it was chosen for analysis because it had been recommended for the unions' reportedly successful organizing techniques. Instead the report itself is quite pessimistic about

[1] A recent advertisement found in an employers' publication for the garment industry shows a picture of a young woman at a sewing-machine. The message reads: "Rosa Martinez produces apparel for US markets on her sewing-machine in El Salvador. *You* can hire her for 57 cents an hour. Rosa is more than just colorful. She and her co-workers are known for their industriousness, reliability and quick learning. They make El Salvador one of the best buys . . ." In subsequent versions of this advertisement Rosa's wage had dropped to 33 cents an hour.

recruitment in the zone and closes by stating that it would appear highly unlikely that the union could recruit the remaining number of unorganized workers, as the majority of these are women.

Taken at face value such a statement would be quite discouraging, but when other parts of the chapter are studied and contrasted with experiences in EPZs in other countries, some important lessons can be learned about the process of organizing women workers, as well as the impact of these zones on the culture of the host countries. Therefore, by way of comparison, the Mauritius study is followed by a report on experiences in organizing women in EPZs in several other countries.

17

Women in trade unions in the Mauritius export processing zones

Dev Luchmun *

Background

Mauritius, an island republic off the coast of East Africa, has one of the highest population densities in the world, approximately 555 per km^2. Agriculture is vulnerable to severe tropical storms and, other than tourism, the country's chief resource is its well-educated population. The years following independence in 1960 were characterized by low economic growth combined with rising levels of unemployment. Estimates indicated that no less than one-fifth of the labour force was either jobless or underemployed. It was in this light that the first export processing zone was created in Mauritius in 1970 in the hope of creating employment.

Since that time the zones have been so successful for the economy, growing at a rate of 25 per cent per annum since 1984, that they have been allowed to expand over the entire island. In fact, EPZs in Mauritius are not geographical concepts limited to particular regions, but legal ones. Today the Mauritian economy is based principally on industry, although tourism and sugar cane production are still important.

The Mauritius experience with EPZs must be considered as atypical for several reasons:

1. As explained above, it has never been restricted to one geographical location, as is often the case. Rather than having to bring employees from increasingly greater distances as the zone grew and employment opportunities increased, employers could locate in areas where the labour supply was more readily available.[1]

2. The employment effects of the EPZs are considerable. Whereas in many Asian EPZs those employed in this sector may represent from 2 to 10 per cent of the workforce, in 1992 Mauritius had approximately 90,000 employed in the sector out of a potentially active workforce estimated at 440,000 in 1990.[2] In June 1992, the EPZ sector comprised 568 enterprises employing 90,000 workers, of whom 63,400 were female and 26,600 male.

3. The most striking feature of EPZ workers in Mauritius is the predomi-

* Education Director, Mauritius Labour Congress. As Mr. Luchmun's case study was too lengthy to reprint in entirety, only the sections most pertinent to women workers were included. Material from several additional sources has also been included.

[1] Catherine Hein: *Multinational enterprises and employment in the Mauritian export processing zones*, Working Paper No. 52 (Geneva, ILO, Multinational Enterprises Programme, 1988).

[2] ILO: *Economically active population projections, 1950-2025*, Vol. II, *Africa* (Geneva, 1986), p. 46.

nance of women, who accounted for about 80 per cent of the workers until 1985. This proportion started to decline, reaching 66 per cent in 1987, and since then it has remained more or less static. Women in the EPZs entered the labour force as a new and distinct group of workers. A survey conducted by the University of Mauritius in 1987 showed that 70 per cent of the female workers were under 25; three-quarters had never been married; almost all had attended primary school; one-quarter had some secondary schooling and 90 per cent were initial entrants to the labour force.

4. There is a higher proportion of Mauritian-owned enterprises or joint ventures than in most countries and more Mauritians are found in management and supervisory positions than has been the case for nationals in other countries.

5. The available workforce in Mauritius is unable to keep pace with the expansion of industry and there is competition for skilled workers not seen in countries such as the Dominican Republic, the Philippines, Sri Lanka and elsewhere. Surprisingly, this may have negative ramifications for trade union organizing. As an example, Sheira Toofany, organizer and head of the Mauritius Free Zones and Secondary Industry Employees' Union, has reported a problem increasingly encountered in organizing women in EPZs. The union has succeeded in organizing women in an EPZ factory only to learn later that they have left for a firm elsewhere in the EPZs which is not yet organized.[3] This is a phenomenon that has not been encountered elsewhere in the research, and that can cause major problems because if the union does not represent 25 per cent of the firm's workforce it may have trouble in gaining recognition and negotiating on behalf of its members.

6. The labour shortage has also convinced the Government to allow "compulsory" overtime in the EPZs. Employees are required to work for 45 hours a week plus 10 hours compulsory overtime, whenever necessary. Over 55 hours, employers can ask but not force employees to work overtime to meet quotas and delivery deadlines, although there is reportedly considerable pressure for voluntary overtime. These long hours are very hard on the women, and it is estimated that this is the cause of the comparatively high rate of absenteeism (as compared with Sri Lanka, for example, where the women fear being dismissed if they are absent because of illness).

7. The Government has made a specific effort to create jobs for men in the EPZs. As can be imagined when an employment sector is the mainstay of a country's economy as in Mauritius, and 80 per cent of its employees are women as was the case in early 1985, this is certain to have a strong impact on society. As will be seen, in late 1984 the Government abolished a minimum wage for men and two years later women were down to 66 per cent of the EPZ workforce.

The social impact and the effects of industrialization on women workers

The availability of a low-wage, well-educated labour force, particularly female, played an important role in the development of the EPZs in Mauritius. The female labour force participation rate increased from 18 per cent in 1962 to 42 per

[3] Personal communication from the International Textile, Garment and Leather Workers' Federation (ITGLWF), Brussels.

cent in 1988. In the 1970s female labour in the EPZs was in the 18-25 age group. These women did not possess any basic skills for entry into the employment market. Although some had attended secondary school, the majority were primary school leavers.

This scene was to change dramatically with the institution of free education in 1976, with the result that today many of the women workers in the EPZs have completed their school certificate. It should be pointed out, however, that these women turned to the EPZs for employment as a last resort because they were not absorbed within the preferred public sector.

The early years of the EPZs were characterized by a social stigma attached to female workers in the factories because the jobs were considered to be low in social status and offered poor wages. Negative public opinion against the so-called "kitchen to factory" women workers was rampant. To work in an EPZ company was considered to be low status, even for a professional. No upper- or middle-class family would consider sending their children to work in an EPZ factory. If they did enter the EPZs it was only temporary, while awaiting a more appropriate and higher-status job in the civil service or the service sector.

Cultural norms and traditions regarding woman's appropriate role in the family and community limited her working opportunities; but when it came to supplementing the family income, especially at a time of high unemployment among men, the woman's desire to work was legitimated. Gradually parents accepted that their daughters could work in factories, but for most young couples, husbands or fiancés would not tolerate it. Upon becoming engaged or married, it was noticed that many women resigned from their jobs, if there was no pressing economic need for them to work.

The rate of male unemployment increased between 1979 and 1984, and this situation gave rise to a number of serious problems. The women were, in the majority of families, the sole income earners and this caused definite resentment from the men because of the availability of work for women. It was hard for the men to acknowledge women's contribution within the family. Women had to cope with factory work as well as their household responsibilities and the alienation of the men. The frustrations of men resulted in increasing social problems associated with male unemployment such as drug abuse, alcoholism and petty crime.

As a result of measures initiated by the Government, important changes occurred in 1984 which had economic and social repercussions. The Government decided to deregulate wages in the EPZs. Until that time, minimum wages for men had been higher than those for women, and in that sector this was removed from labour legislation. From 1970 until 1984 women had been discriminated against.[4]

[4] Ed. note: According to Hein (op. cit., pp. 44-45), minimum wages and working conditions in the EPZs are regulated by Export Enterprises Remuneration Orders. Until December 1984 minimum wages were set according to four categories of employees: men under 18 years; men over 18 years; women in their first year of employment; women after their first year. The minimum wage set for men was always substantially higher than that for women, the minimum for women with at least one year's experience being only 63 per cent of the male wage. Even in comparison with a man under 18 years, the same woman's salary would only be 76 per cent. Following the "liberation of wages" for the EPZs, the practice of setting lower minimum wages for women was not modified for workers in the sugar industry and other agricultural sectors. This was on the grounds that women in these sectors are legally exempted from heavy work, and thus they should earn less than men.

The consequences were important:

— more men could be employed at the same wage level as women;

— women were no longer discriminated against in terms of wages;

— men and women could be employed in the same job with equal pay.

The late 1980s witnessed an increase in male employment in the EPZ sector as Mauritius started experiencing an economic boom. Industrialization gradually brought in its wake a more permissive society. Parents tended to become more liberal and open-minded. The stigma which was formerly attached to work in the EPZs has now disappeared. More and more women from the urban as well as from the rural areas are taking up jobs, whatever their family and educational background. The EPZs have also been able to absorb women professionals at middle and top management level as general managers, personnel managers, production managers, computer programmers, accountants, supervisors and designers.

It is undeniable that the EPZs have largely contributed to providing women with a new social status through their newly found economic independence. It is equally true that the additional income brought home has greatly contributed to improving the standard of living of the family. However, there also exists the other side of the coin regarding the negative effects of industrialization, particularly on women.

A.G. Mitchel, in a report prepared in 1989 at the request of the Ministry of Labour, Industrial Relations, Women's Rights and Family Welfare, rightly analyses the socio-economic problems and the effects of industrialization on women in Mauritius. His observations are summarized as follows:

1. The availability of a low-wage, well-educated female labour force played an important role in this process of industrialization. Women workers have thus become both a major force in industrialization and the primary subject of its impact.

2. Industrialization radically transformed the way in which men and women need to organize their work and their lives. Traditional Mauritian society has not yet adapted to the changes brought about by rapid industrialization, since the process of social change takes much longer than economic change.

3. The adverse effects of industrialization brought into focus the social dimensions of development. The society has witnessed the breakdown of the extended family system, higher divorce rates, and increased child abuse, juvenile delinquency and nutritional deficiencies. It is reported that children are left at home unattended, or girls of 11-12 years are taken from school to care for their siblings. Women and family members are reluctant to change the traditional ways, for instance by using institutional child care or laundry services. Household tasks still remain the responsibility of women. Domestic help is unavailable, particularly for poorly paid factory workers.

4. An unusual feature of the Mauritian economy which contributes to social problems is its labour shortage. Workers in the EPZs are required to work regularly beyond normal hours (45 hours a week plus ten hours compulsory overtime), possibly to rectify the labour shortage and meet delivery deadlines. (In other sectors overtime is defined by daily rather than weekly working hours and is not compulsory.) There seems to be considerable pressure for voluntary overtime beyond 55 hours per

week. Absenteeism is a major employer concern. Because overtime is defined on a weekly basis, employers are able to require employees who have been absent, upon their return, to work in excess of normal working hours at the end of the week without paying overtime rates. Unions indicate excessive hours of work as the main cause of absenteeism.

5. Taking into account the low and stable population growth and the labour shortage, the future growth of the economy will rest largely on female labour.

6. Women workers, who increasingly choose to remain in the workforce after marriage and childbirth, prefer to work in the manufacturing sector rather than in agriculture. This is because, in spite of the relatively better working conditions, the agricultural sector is considered to be lower in status.

7. The question of total hours worked at home and outside is a major problem which particularly affects women workers, creating continued stress and adversely affecting workers' health, nutrition, family welfare and productivity.

8. It is urgent that an environment and conditions be created to enable female workers to assume their roles as productive workers and family members.

The above observations quite rightly situate the social impact and the effects of industrialization on women in Mauritius. It should also be added that EPZ women workers spend between ten and 12 hours daily away from home and that by 6 a.m. they must be on their way to work. In the evening, after a hard day's work, they must again spend between one and two hours travelling home. Much of the time is spent queueing for the bus, after prolonged standing in the factories all day.

This situation, therefore, puts the women in the EPZs in a very different category from their counterparts in other sectors of the economy. It provides the necessary arguments to demonstrate the very low level of women's participation in unions, both as members and leaders, and tends to demonstrate also why even outside the union structure and in informal discussion groups, women are passive and silent. Women's involvement in trade unions, particularly in the EPZ sector, should therefore take into consideration their backgrounds (sociocultural and economic) and the conditions of such a demanding sector as the EPZs.

Trade unions in the EPZs

Although the laws regulating trade union activity in the EPZs are the same as those applicable in other sectors, the Mauritius EPZs are considered as the least organized sector in the country in terms of unionization. Trade unions have been active in the EPZs since the very beginnings of this sector, but the proportion of workers unionized has been very low since the conditions for the development of unions have been less favourable than in other sectors. Most of the enterprises controlled by multinationals operating from areas with little union activity have been particularly reticent to deal with trade unions. Also, for various reasons which will be seen later in the chapter, women workers in the EPZ have proved most difficult to organize.

Although the EPZs today employ over 90,000 workers, the latest figures (December 1990) clearly show the existence of some nine unions active in that sector, catering for a total membership of only 10,943 workers. In proportional terms, therefore, only 12 per cent of the EPZ workers are unionized; through their nine unions they represent 18 per cent of organized labour in the private sector (60,771 in 1989) and only 9.7 per cent of the total organized workforce in the country (112,526 in 1989).

Although the EPZ labour force is made up largely of women, the situation is quite different as regards the trade union movement in the sector. The EPZ trade union movement is characterized by a very low level of participation of women workers at all levels, from rank and file to top leadership.

The absence of the designation by sex of key office bearers of trade unions (i.e. president, secretary and treasurer in the Official Return of Trade Unions as published by the Registrar of Associations) makes it difficult to determine the exact percentage of female office-bearers and executive members of trade unions. It is, however, known that there are very few women holding trade union office and that they have practically no influence in the running of the unions, even though the majority of rank-and-file members are women. The women, officers or not, tend to remain in the background while giving a free hand to their male colleagues to act as official spokespersons, delegates or negotiators of the union, even when the majority of the executive members are women. It is also true that, in the case of at least three important unions active in the EPZs,[5] non-elected officials run the show, because of the absence or unwillingness of women members to take up the challenging position of union leader.

Recruitment methods

The trade unions in the EPZs, as in the other sectors of the Mauritian economy, use traditional methods of recruitment:

1. The women workers are encouraged by their colleagues or friends to join the union voluntarily. They join only after having been advised to do so by those who are already members.

2. Recruitment is carried out by the union representatives at the worksites, and is normally successful provided the union is already recognized by the employer.

3. Recruitment is also carried out during or after meetings organized by the union. Most of these meetings take place outside the workplace at the regional level — in towns or villages and outside working hours. They have to be organized during the weekend, either on Saturday or Sunday morning.

4. Seminars and other workers' education activities are organized by some unions such as the Mauritius Textile and Garment Workers Union with the primary aim of recruiting new members through the help of participants. These participants are trained and informed on a host of subjects such as the significance of trade unionism, collective bargaining, organizing techniques, and so on.

[5] Textiles and Clothes Manufacturing Workers' Union, Mauritius Free Zone and Secondary Industries Employees' Union and Mauritius Textile and Garment Workers' Union (5,989, 2,971 and 1,338 members respectively in 1990).

5. Attempts at unionization are also made through forging links with other unions, especially between unions belonging to the same federation. The officials or representatives of unions in the sugar industry are used in the membership drive in the rural areas for the benefit of unions in the EPZs. These possibilities, however, are not fully utilized even though the unions may be aware of all the advantages of making use of experienced and trained representatives from other unions.[6]

6. Incentives in the form of cash allowances, travelling allowances or commissions are given by unions to some members or union representatives for their services in the recruitment drive. During the years of high unemployment, young people were recruited on a temporary basis against payment of commission based on the number of workers recruited as members. Although this practice of using unemployed persons has ended, these incentives have been extended to some active union representatives.

7. Some unions in other sectors (i.e. the Plantation Workers' Union, the Artisans and General Workers' Union) have diversified their services by setting up cooperatives, credit unions and provident funds for the benefit of their members. Non-members are thus encouraged to join these unions in order to benefit from these services. However, no union in the EPZ sector has taken such initiatives.

Constraints

It would be too exhaustive to enumerate all the constraints facing the Mauritian trade unions in their endeavour to organize the unorganized, particularly women workers in the EPZs. However, analysing a few of these constraints will help to clarify two fundamental points, namely: (a) why the EPZ has the lowest level of unionization in the country; and (b) why women's involvement in trade unions is almost nonexistent.

1. There is a general misconception of the role and importance of women in unions and other social activities, and generally women tend to think that trade union matters concern men only.

2. Most of the EPZ enterprises, whether multinationals or foreign-owned, are particularly reticent to deal with trade unions. This situation may, to a large extent, be attributed to the management culture of the countries of ownership. The fundamental approach of the enterprise towards workers' organizations depends upon their country of origin. The anti-union mentality is more pronouced among the Asian investors than their European counterparts.

3. Various cultural influences bar women from participating actively in social or trade union activities. They cannot stay away from home after working hours or at weekends when most trade union activities are held. Besides working in an EPZ factory, the women are expected to fulfil their roles as housewives and mothers with family commitments. The household tasks still remain the responsibility of women.

[6] Ed. note: According to Dan Coonea, former General Secretary of the Mauritius Labour Congress (MLC), there have often been cases of the women workers' parents, themselves members of the union in the sugar sector, convincing their daughters to join the union.

This family commitment leaves hardly any time to spare for social or trade union activities even though the women might personally be willing to participate. Traditional attitudes, therefore, tend to hinder women from obtaining the support of their families and parents to participate in trade union activities, which are considered to be a man's world.

4. Lack of time is another major constraint on the part of the women workers. Women workers in the EPZs spend between ten and 12 hours daily away from home. Tired as they are, they have hardly any time to spare to attend trade union meetings.

5. Most anti-union employers in the EPZs often resort to victimization and retaliatory measures against any worker who attempts to organize his or her fellow workers within trade unions. Some are transferred, others lose their chances for promotion, while others are suspended if not simply dismissed under some pretext. Potential trade union leaders are readily identified and eventually promoted against the guarantee of not becoming involved in trade union affairs. Certain supervisors, especially men, in the textile factories try everything to dissuade women from participating in trade union activities. Since most of the women workers are more concerned with their job security, they prefer not to invite trouble from the employers by becoming involved.

6. There is a lack of effective communication between union leaders and workers due to inaccessibility of the worksites. Most factories have high fencing and enclosures fixed around their premises, with security officers posted at the entrance. Access for union leaders or representatives is therefore difficult unless they are invited by management for negotiating purposes. Union leaders are not allowed inside the factory premises to recruit members or hold union meetings, unlike in other sectors such as the sugar industry. Recognition and negotiating rights are not easily granted to a union by EPZ employers unless it represents about 25 per cent of the workforce in the enterprise.

7. In the EPZs many enterprises have encouraged the establishment of works councils composed of employers and workers' representatives, although the latter does not imply union representatives. It has been observed that some of these works councils are used as an instrument to diminish the importance of the unions by dealing with issues that should normally fall under the purview of trade unions. This is in spite of the fact that the Industrial Relations Act 1973 states that the councils should maintain a consultative arrangement with the union and that this "arrangement should not be used to bypass or discourage trade unions".

8. A top priority for the Government is to launch the country into its second phase of industrialization. This means persuading potential investors that Mauritius is a country of political and social stability. The Government is also stressing to trade unions and workers that in any labour conflict all existing labour relations machinery should be used before any strike action is taken, and that unwarranted strikes would not be tolerated. The Government has made it clear that it will not allow the reoccurrence of the traumatic experience of the 1970s, when prolonged strikes led to serious economic disaster and to the closure of several factories.

This argument, repeatedly emphasized, has created a climate of apprehension among workers and has tended to make them more cautious in taking trade union action. This is more apparent among women workers in the EPZs where discipline is the keyword for economic success, according to the Government.

9. A lack of trade union education has been identified as a major constraint to women's participation in the trade union movement. Workers' education is practically non-existent in the EPZs, and it is considered that an intensive education campaign to mobilize the women could make a distinct difference in their participation.

However, the ability of the EPZ unions to organize workers' education activities is quite limited. They have neither the necessary means, know-how, nor infrastructure. A particular problem is the reluctance of employers to grant time off for trade union education.

Workers' education in Mauritius does not operate within a legal framework. The Government, although committed to the cause, organizes very few seminars for women workers in the EPZs. Through an ILO project funded by the United Nations Development Programme (UNDP), it has set up a Workers' Education Unit within the Ministry of Labour and Industrial Relations. National workers' education activities have been conducted under the programme. The Workers' Education Advisory Committee has also set up a subcommittee to advise on the general orientation of the activities of the Workers' Education Unit so as to arouse women's consciousness in trade union matters and their role in the socio-economic development of the country. However, the Ministry is criticized by trade unions for not giving enough importance to the EPZs, particularly when this sector has the highest percentage of unorganized labour in the country.

The lack of trainers, and of physical and financial resources, has also impeded trade union educational programmes. However, in recent years a few union federations have organized short training programmes for their leaders and rank-and-file members, some of them on a regular basis and others on an ad hoc basis, or when funds are available. The Mauritius Labour Congress (MLC), the country's largest trade union federation, is the only exception since it has its own Workers' Education Centre and carries out its programme on a more systematic, permanent and continuous basis. The MLC Workers' Education Centre is fully equipped with all the logistic support required for conducting its educational activities. The Mauritius Textile and Garment Workers' Union, an MLC affiliate, has benefited from their training programme. However, for the past few years the MLC has not been able to organize one seminar for trade union members from the EPZs. This is in comparison to 45 three-day seminars organized by the MLC each year for other sectors.

Two EPZ unions, the Mauritius Textile and Garment Workers' Union (MT&GWU) and the Mauritius Free Zone and Secondary Industries Employees' Union, are both affiliated to the ITGLWF, which assists them in running one or two seminars each year. The ITGLWF is presently aiding the MT&GWU with a short-term education project in the context of a recruitment campaign among women workers in the EPZs.

In spite of assistance from their federations, whether at the national or international level, the EPZ unions are unable to carry out successfully any workers' education programme. A lack of time-off facilities in the EPZs has been identified as a major factor affecting workers' education activities and the trade union movement in general.

10. A lack of time off for union activities, as a major constraint, is more pronounced in the EPZs. Employers in this sector have such an uncompromising attitude to the subject that it is practically impossible to organize seminars or any workers' education activity.

The Industrial Relations Act protects the individual employee's right to choose whether or not to be a trade union member and to take part in trade union activities, including the right to seek appointment or election as a trade union officer and to hold office. Appropriate time for training and activities is defined as a period which is (a) outside the employee's working hours, or (b) within working hours in accordance with arrangements agreed to by the employer. This implies that the employer has absolute discretion on whether to approve or refuse such facilities to union officials and members.

Management in the private sector is generally quite rigid over the issue. Granting time off for union or workers' education activities is considered as an additional cost. Further, management is reluctant to have trained union officials in the organization, and the very presence of a trade union is viewed as a threat. This applies more to the employers in the EPZs than to sectors such as the sugar industry where time off is included in collective agreements. The practice is to offset leave entitlements against time off for union or workers' eduction activities. As the approval of such facilities is at the discretion of the employer, workers in fact face much hardship to enjoy this privilege. It should be noted that the Paid Educational Leave Convention, 1974 (No. 140), has never been ratified by the Mauritian Government despite persistent requests of the unions.

Conclusion

Complicated legislation, a proliferation of unions, internal union rivalry, limited union finances and infrastructure, a heavy concentration on wages, conditions of work and job security in union bargaining, and the institutional constraints of the Industrial Relations Act — all these seem to have characterized the trade union movement in Mauritius. Taking these constraints into consideration, the trade unions in the EPZs find themselves in a far worse sitution than their counterparts in other sectors of the economy. The task seems almost impossible for the trade unions in their endeavour to organize the remaining 88 per cent of the unorganized labour force in the EPZ sector, the more so when 66 per cent of workers in the EPZs consists of women..

18

Organizing experiences in export processing zones in other countries

Margaret Hosmer Martens

Introduction

Although formal organizing is firmly discouraged in most export processing zones, there are a few exceptions. Workers have been successfully organized in EPZs in *Tunisia* and in the Bataan EPZ in the *Philippines*.[1] In *Malaysia* workers in light industries such as garment manufacturing have been organized, although the electronics industry has long been adverse to any outside trade unions. In certain countries where organizing is legal, EPZ industries are sometimes declared as essential to the economy and the President or Labour Minister can refer the strike for arbitration and an immediate back-to-work order. In others the government grants "pioneer status" to certain companies (including those in the EPZs), which means that collective bargaining is severely restricted.

This chapter consists mainly of three case studies on organizing women in EPZs in the Dominican Republic, Jamaica and Sri Lanka. First, however, two short examples are given. The chapter ends with some general remarks on building links with other groups.

The Bataan EPZ in the Philippines

The Bataan EPZ in the Philippines was established in 1972 shortly after the declaration of martial law. Since then three others have been added in Baguio, Caite and Mactan. Bataan is the largest, with on-site housing and medical services available for workers. Three-quarters of EPZ employees are women, most of whom are under 29 years of age. Contrary to experience in the other three zones, Bataan is heavily organized but most trade union activity has taken place since 1980 and some surmise that it takes a while for the unions to become installed. It has also been reported that employers in Baguio are careful to offer better treatment than elsewhere in order to avoid an influx of trade unions. Labour legislation is applied throughout the Philippines and freedom of association is guaranteed in the Constitution and applied.[2]

[1] "Worker rights in export processing zones", in *Foreign Labor Trends* (Washington, DC, US Department of Labor, Bureau of International Labor Affairs), 1989-90, FLT 90-32.

[2] ibid.

The Penang EPZ in Malaysia

It is frequently observed that women workers are rarely assertive in the workplace and will avoid confrontation at all costs in favour of mediation. Therefore it was a surprise to many, including some of the women themselves, when this proved erroneous in Penang in 1985. There were massive lay-offs in the unorganized electronics sector, and when women realized their jobs were threatened they rose up in protest.[3] The Mostek electronics firm gradually laid off all but 200 workers from its original workforce of 2,590.

The women were particularly incensed because Mostek's management style had previously been faithful to the Malay tradition of pledging loyalty to a protector who in return offers moral and political support and protection. When this relationship broke down the women were infuriated, all the more so because Mostek apparently showed disregard for seniority and the effect on families (both husbands and wives were dismissed). Although the electronics sector still resists attempts at organization, the struggle, which led to the emergence of a strong, committed women's leadership, challenged many of the assumptions made about women workers' capacity to take action on their own behalf.

The Dominican Republic[4]

Allegations that employers refuse to allow unions to organize EPZ workers in the Dominican Republic have made that country a focus for concern of national and international trade union organizations for some time. On 26 September 1992:

> the six Dominican labor confederations and the Free Trade Zone Industry Association (ADOZONA) signed a tentative pact in which the unions renounced the right to seek economic adjustments for six months and the right to strike for 30 months, in return for a commitment by EPZ employers to respect the Labor Code and the right of freedom of association. ADOZONA members rejected ratification of the pact, and the Association subsequently submitted a counter proposal, which the labour confederations rejected; negotiations remained stalled at year's end.[5]

A consortium of major trade union federations from other countries is preparing to pressure the Government again.[6]

[3] James Lochead: "Retrenchment in a Malaysian free trade zone", in Noleen Heyzer (ed.): *Daughters in industry: Work, skills and consciousness of women workers in Asia* (Kuala Lumpur, Asia and Pacific Development Centre, 1988).

[4] For more information on organizing women in EPZs in the Dominican Republic and Jamaica, see Leith L. Dunn: *Women organising for change in Caribbean free zones: Strategies and methods*, Paper presented to the International Workshop on Women Organizing in the Process of Industrialization, The Hague, April 1991. Ms. Dunn is currently conducting research in these countries for a doctoral dissertation.

[5] US Department of State: *Country reports on human rights practices for 1992*, Report submitted to the Committee on Foreign Relations, US Senate, and the Committee on Foreign Relations, US House of Representatives, by the Department of State (Washington, DC, US Government Printing Office, Feb. 1992), pp. 387-388.

[6] Personal interview with Luis Andersen, Secretary-General of ORIT, the regional office for North and South America of the ICFTU, 26 March 1993.

There are over 15 EPZs spread throughout the Dominican Republic and, as usual, most of the workers are women. Until the developments of 1992 described above, one union in particular, the San Pedro de Macoris Free Zone Trade Union (SPMFZU), had been fighting for recognition. The union was established in 1987 following massive demonstrations over a woman employee who had suffered a miscarriage after being kicked by her supervisor.

Building mutual support

One woman, a founding member of the union, had worked as a supervisor in a garment factory and was dismissed and blacklisted for being an activist — which meant that she could not obtain employment anywhere in the Zone. She described how mutual support can be built up among the factory women at the workplace.

The work in each factory is divided into sections and each section has a supervisor who is responsible for quotas or production targets being attained. In her job as a supervisor she motivated the other women by providing small incentives and building friendships with them. The women in her section became mutually supportive and continue to celebrate birthdays or special events together. Over time these exchanges helped to build up solidarity among the women and evolve a cohesive group.

Building links with women in the community

Two dedicated women trade unionists, who are by now too well known by management to go near the EPZs, visit the women's homes at night after work. The two women attend meetings in several communities, often in the same evening, discussing situations at work and giving advice. They talk about problems in the various factories and try to help the women to develop strategies to address them. A tremendous investment in time and energy has been made to build up links and a communication network across a broad spectrum of women working in the EPZs.

Building links with other unions

FENAZUCAR, the union which represents many workers in the sugar industry, has been particularly helpful to the SPMFZU. There have been massive layoffs in this sector and some of FENAZUCAR's members have found employment in the EPZs. This has helped to establish a link between the SPMFZU and FENAZUCAR, and the latter's long history of trade union activity has been instructive. Although the majority of the leadership is male, they are reportedly sensitive to women's needs and make an effort to include them.

A women's section was formed at the FENAZUCAR's Sixth Congress in 1991, and women trade unionists have been able to build up links in Central America and the Caribbean through the ILO's DANIDA-sponsored project, Workers' Education Assistance for Rural Women Workers in Central American Countries and the Dominican Republic.[7]

Although FENAZUCAR has been very supportive of the SPMFZU both nationally and internationally, its confrontational manner is viewed as somewhat radical for operating in the free zone environment. This has sometimes alienated women workers who would prefer more subtle attempts to improve working conditions and wages without risking dismissal. Women officers in the SPMFZU believe "that women have a different style of trade unionism from men and there is a need to affirm this when organizing within the free zone".[8]

Jamaica

Jamaica has large export processing or free trade zones distributed throughout the country, particularly along the coasts. Most of these are garment factories. The Constitution specifies that workers have the right to organize and approximately 25 per cent of the labour force is unionized. However, although trade unions play an important role in the economy and there have been serious attempts to organize in the EPZs, managers of most enterprises have persistently refused to allow organizing. Some have set up workers' councils to discuss problems and one company has long been unionized, but these are the exception.

Community-based organizing

Women workers have found support in several organizations. One of these is the Women's Action Committee, a group of individuals and organizations concerned about the free zone.

Another source of support has been the St. Peter Claver Roman Catholic Church, which is located in Western Kingston, an area where many of the free zone workers live. The St. Peter Claver Free Zone Women's Group was formed in 1988 and from the beginning has provided a forum for women to share their problems, both at home and at work. Classes were started in sewing and literacy, mathematics and English, and workshops held on problem areas such as parenting, sexual violence, grievance procedure and budgeting. The group gradually became more cohesive, organizing family outings and parties, and becoming more active in the women's movement.

In 1989 the group decided to form a housing cooperative to take on one of the most pressing problems in the area, the lack of housing. A number of international organizations assisted, in particular the Canadian International Development Agency (CIDA), which made it possible for the group to obtain the necessary funds. With this money they were able to buy and renovate eight houses, which were to pro-

[7] See Chapter 11 of this volume for a case study of this project.
[8] Dunn, op. cit.

vide housing for 16 cooperative members[9] and their families. There are plans to expand the programme.

The experience which the women have gained through working together in the St. Peter Claver Women's Housing Cooperative has proved invaluable in building their sense of themselves as individuals and as an organization working for change. They are often asked to speak to other groups and they have produced a video tape of their experience to share with others. The cooperative has become a model for others on how an organization of working women can come together to discuss their common problems and develop strategies to work collectively to improve their lives and those of their families. This is an excellent example of women's empowerment under adverse conditions.

Sri Lanka[10]

EPZs have had a profound impact on women's lives in Sri Lanka, although the shift from the agricultural or plantation sector to the industrial sector was seen even earlier than in Mauritius. Between 1953 and 1971 alone, women in the industrial sector rose from 18.5 per cent to 81.6 per cent of the total workforce while the category of self-employed and unpaid family workers declined from 15 per cent to 2.1 per cent.[11] In 1985 women accounted for 28,414 out of a total workforce of 35,786 employed in industry.[12]

The Katunayake Investment Promotion Zone (KIPZ) was established in 1978 and, although legally employees have the right to form and join a trade union, recognition of such unions by employers is not regulated by law. The Greater Colombo Economic Commission (GCEC), the legal arm of the Government which is responsible for the zone, requires industries to have Joint Consultative Councils to promote labour-management cooperation and resolve disputes. These Councils have equal representation of workers and management, but have no links with trade unions. Special entry passes are checked by police, and trade union representatives report that they cannot gain access to the zone to organize the workers.[13] Therefore, although trade unions are not openly forbidden in the zone, to date there are no recognized trade unions. This is in strong contrast to conditions for trade unions in Mauritius.

The Sri Lanka experience offers a useful comparison with the Mauritius case because both groups of workers are young women from traditionally conservative Asian cultural backgrounds. Although EPZs developed somewhat later in Sri Lanka

[9] It is the women who hold the leases to these homes, so that if the man were to leave home the woman and her children would still be guaranteed a place to live.

[10] For an excellent article on the Sri Lankan experience, see Kumudhini Rosa: "Strategies of organisation and resistance: Women workers in Sri Lankan free trade zones", in *Capital and Class* (London), No. 45, Autumn 1991, pp. 27-34.

[11] Hema Goonatilae and Savitri Goonesekere: "Industrialization and women workers in Sri Lanka: Working conditions inside and outside the investment promotion zone", in Heyzer, op. cit., p. 185.

[12] ibid.

[13] "Worker rights in export processing zones", op. cit.

and the climate is far more hostile to trade unions, Sri Lankan women display a sense of cohesiveness which did not emerge from the Mauritius case study.

One important difference between the two cases is that because of the geographical spread of the EPZ sector in Mauritius, the women workers live at home with their families. In Sri Lanka and in other countries in Asia, the women are far from home and lodge together in boarding-houses. Although this has obviously helped to build alliances, it is not essential for the women's empowerment. Instead it is the experience gained in working together for change in their communities which has been so important in Sri Lanka and in other countries where unions are not allowed to organize.

Community-based support

Since the EPZ was first established in the area, a variety of organizations have set up centres for women workers. Although they may have different approaches and ideologies, their support is important to the women and they have devised ways to work together on specific issues.

Religious organizations have worked with the women since the beginning of the EPZ in 1979. They have established centres and organized activities in an attempt to integrate the women into the village communities where they board. Seven Catholic centres adjoin the EPZ; some provide boarding-house facilities and opportunities for the women to go to the nuns with their problems. The centres serve as meeting-places where they can socialize and discuss issues. Some have library facilities and run seminars or social activities.

These centres have been able to fill a real need in the women's lives. Particularly helpful has been a food cooperative which was started by one of the centres to combat the rising prices of food in the area (the increase had caused tension as the villagers evidently blamed it on the women's presence). Women workers bought shares to build up capital to establish the cooperative. As a result, prices of basic food items went down and local shopkeepers were forced to lower their own prices. This experience demonstrated to the women how by working together they were able to develop strategies. This was a boost to both them and the villagers, and also helped to win the confidence of the community.

Other groups helped the women workers to organize campaigns to stop sexual harassment of women walking to and from work after dark. This had been a serious problem, in particular because in 1982 Sri Lanka denounced the Night Work (Women) Convention (Revised), 1948 (No. 89), prohibiting night work for women. Industries had insisted that in order to be competitive, night shifts were absolutely necessary.

As it was well known that the women were forced to frequent unlit areas at night, thieves and rapists had been drawn to the region and it was dangerous for women to be alone after dark. At first their only recourse was to form groups to walk together, but soon they developed posters and pamphlets and campaigned from door to door. Their message was preached in every church and Buddhist temple. Petitions were sent to the GCEC requesting security and transportation for the women. By bringing such sensitive subjects out into the open, these experiences helped to unite the women and the organizations assisting them.

Although the women workers do not control the operation of the religious centres, they do participate in the committees where decisions are taken. Key persons who are not themselves women workers sit in to guide the discussions. In spite of the ideological nature of these centres, they do provide the women with a place that they can rely upon and relate to.

There is also a Women's Centre which was organized by a group of women who had themselves previously been factory workers. They offer EPZ workers a multifaceted programme including legal and medical assistance, library facilities and training in alternative skills. Also provided are seminars and discussions on women's rights.

Although most of these centres provide some legal advice, the Legal Advice Centre (LAC) specializes in giving free professional advice to the EPZ workers as well as intervening on their behalf, either free of charge or at a minimum basic charge. The centre prepares and distributes pamphlets on legal issues of interest to the workers, as well as organizing seminars and discussions in which they are invited to participate. Such an organization is clearly beneficial to the women, who are traditionally lacking in awareness of their rights.

Another organizing method that has been successfully adopted in Sri Lanka is the publication and distribution of an EPZ newspaper. The paper has been published since 1984 by an independent women's collective. The EPZ women are free to use it to express their opinions and share their ideas with other women. About 8,000 copies are sold to the women at a minimal charge. Although the newspaper is not allowed inside the zone, it has been known to be passed along an assembly line or found on a bulletin board. The paper provokes mixed reactions from the managers — some try to find out who has written about them but others find it useful to know their workers' views. It has been an important instrument for campaigns on issues such as night work, sexual harassment, problems relating to organizing, and the difficulties of women travelling to and from work.

Resistance on the job

As the women gradually gain confidence in their ability to organize in the community, spontaneous and subtle types of resistance are being heard of on the factory floor. For instance, the women have taken to manifesting their independence by signalling to each other through eye contact or, where talking is allowed, using a local language in the presence of foreign management. Other forms of resistance have developed such as lowering production targets when pressure is placed on workers to increase their productivity or helping others who are slow to reach their targets. Although these acts may not appear to be very significant in themselves to outsiders, they demonstrate the sense of mutual support and cohesion which has developed among the women. Management tries to counter this by forbidding talking among co-workers or only allowing one woman at a time in the lavatory. This naturally serves to anger the women even more.

The Sri Lankan experience shows how various methods and approaches have gradually evolved to help these women cope in situations where they originally felt powerless to improve their lives. These young workers live in a culture where women are traditionally submissive and obedient to authority, and they have not had access to trade union representation and collective bargaining. In spite of these handicaps, the combination of forces both on the factory floor and in their community is building in these women a new sense of themselves and their capacity to change their surroundings.

Building alliances with other groups

As seen throughout this volume, there are a multitude of groups throughout the world attempting to improve conditions for working women. Two of these are found in Part II of this book, on domestic workers: SOS CORPO in Brazil and the ATABAL Collective in Mexico. Some groups working with women in EPZs are church based and some are women's organizations. An article in *News from IRENE* (International Restructuring Education Network Europe) talked about the visit to the Netherlands of two representatives of women's organizations in Latin America, CIPAF (Centro de Investigación Para la Acción Feminina) in the Dominican Republic and CIDHAL (Communication, Interchange and Human Development Latin America) in Mexico.[14]

CIPAF is a women's organization which specializes in research on the living and working conditions of lower-class working women in the Dominican Republic. Typical research projects have been on violence against women and prostitution. The results of these investigations are aimed at bringing about action to improve the lives of the women they study. Since the women themselves are the target group, the data is prepared in easily understood forms, often illustrated with cartoons. CIPAF is active among women workers in the Dominican Republic EPZ.

CIDHAL was founded as one of the first women's organizations in Mexico in the 1960s. Its original work revolved around research, documentation and the organization of conferences. From the mid-1970s its action was redirected to working closely with women, particularly among the poor. CIDHA sees itself as an instrument helping the women to empower themselves. It worked with the "19 September garment union", which was formed as an autonomous trade union following the Mexican earthquake, and has also collaborated with rural women and women in the urban popular movement. It operates a documentation centre and a health clinic, and conducts educational and awareness-raising activities.

CIDHAL reported that with the restructuring of the industrial sector in Mexico and the decentralization of the labour force, it is necessary to re-examine the work process again and find new ways of organizing the workers.

[14] "Supporting women workers in free trade zones in Latin America", in *News from IRENE* (Tilburg), May 1992.

Conclusions to Part VI

Margaret Hosmer Martens

The incentive and support for organizing

We have seen in Sri Lanka, the Dominican Republic and Jamaica that, in spite of the lack of organized trade unions, women will organize around a common objective. The incentive or problem could be the fear of rape in Sri Lanka or the severe lack of housing in Jamaica. These were problems which concerned the women as a group and, with support from others in the community, they learned that they could do something about it. As they developed a sense of their own empowerment, they were ready to take on other efforts as a group.

Whereas this process is traditionally considered to occur within the trade union movement, it is not always possible. In some cases the union cannot reach the women to organize them and in others, as in Mauritius, few women have seen the need to join trade unions. Although conditions in Sri Lanka, the Dominican Republic and Jamaica make it very difficult for trade unions to enter the zones, many of the women workers have been mobilized through this process and are bringing pressure from within.

The EPZ women workers in Mauritius do not appear to have had a catalysing force which sensitized them to the many possibilities of working together. These women certainly have reason to join together for change — their compulsory overtime calculated on a weekly basis should be reason enough — but it is unclear what opportunities exist for them to meet together in the community, if this is not possible in the EPZ. It is this important first step, which did exist in the other cases, that appears to be lacking. The women need support from the outside and experience in working together, not perhaps on a major issue at first but on something which is vital to them and offers a good prospect for success.

The impact on society of EPZs

The potential for increasing employment opportunities in countries where unemployment is a major social problem has often been cited as one of the main reasons for establishing EPZs. However, foreign investors have almost uniformly shown a preference to hire young women in the EPZs. In countries such as Mauritius and Sri Lanka this has meant providing work for a population which had never been active in the formal labour force. The phenomenon of young women from a very conservative society emerging to work in large numbers in factories is, in itself, a strain on society. When this is combined with high male unemployment — and it is suddenly the young women who are supporting their families — it is sure to cause far-reaching social problems, as seen in the Mauritius case.

These women's lives have changed dramatically in a comparatively short time. They are caught in a period of profound change for their culture and are pulled between two opposite poles, both demanding more of their time. In exchange for a small income, they are harangued at work to put in more hours to meet the company's quota and at home for not taking proper care of their families. Nevertheless, they appear to feel powerless to influence some of the issues around them which make their working and living conditions almost intolerable.

It is at this point that community-based support groups could have an important impact on their problems, while being (as a first step in the process) more acceptable to the culture than trade union activity for women. For in Mauritius, although there are several reasons for the poor rate of organizing in the EPZ, the strongest would appear to be the cultural factor exacerbated by the fact that the women are living at home, as compared to Sri Lanka where they live in lodgings.

The fact that Mauritius women "... cannot stay away from home after working hours or at the weekends when most trade union activities are held" shows clearly the direct impact of the family. According to the 1987 survey cited in Chapter 17, three-quarters of these women have not yet married, thus it is not a question of leaving children unattended at home. It would appear that just as it originally took time before parents could accept the idea of their daughters working in the EPZs, it will be necessary for society as a whole to understand the benefit of women participating in the trade union movement to defend their interests. The multitude of trade unions in Mauritius may also tend to confuse prospective members.

Two steps are vital to improve this situation, the first is applicable to other similar situations and the second is particular to Mauritius.

— The need for creating a sense of solidarity can be deduced from experiences in other countries: the women must be given support from groups within the communities and learn how they can join together to solve a problem which affects them as a whole. Once a sense of empowerment and cohesion has evolved, then they should be ready to continue working together in the union.
— Many families in Mauritius have long been involved with the sugar industry and have their own ties with the trade union movement. The unions should try harder to build support for women workers in the EPZs by forging solidarity linkages with the families.

In addition, more workers' education programmes for women, particularly those who are already members, are clearly essential and some help is forthcoming from the International Textile, Garment and Leather Workers' Federation.

Other issues for organizing

An important issue in the Mauritius case study is the fact that there are cases of elected women officers allowing male colleagues to represent the union. Furthermore, in at least three important unions active in the EPZ non-elected male officials are effectively in charge, reportedly because the women are unprepared to demonstrate their leadership abilities.

This is an important question for women's participation in trade unions and we can cite the experience of Malaysian women in Penang:

During the Mostek (EPZ) picket four representatives were selected to meet with state government officials. Despite the fact that the picket was overwhelmingly supported by women, two of the representatives chosen were men. The women later explained that they were still unsure of themselves and thought that the Government might not have listened to them if men had not been in the delegation.

This is often the case; women are afraid that they will not be taken as seriously as men would be and they do not want to jeopardize their action. This insecurity is entirely understandable for women raised to be unassuming. However, it does not have to remain the norm. This realization is one step along the path of women's becoming more actively involved and gaining experience in making themselves heard.

Part VII

Conclusion

19

Lessons for organizing the unorganized

Margaret Hosmer Martens

The case studies in this volume have offered a wide range of experiences in organizing women workers. A variety of significant issues, including some of the common features and differences, have already been discussed in Chapter 1 and in conclusions to individual parts of the book. The present chapter will merely serve to highlight a few lessons for organizing.

It is clearly possible to organize women in the informal and rural sectors, as in those other sectors where women's employment has become casualized, but organization can begin only with a clear understanding of the women and their particular situation. As women workers' needs are different the world over, each milieu calls for its own organizing methods. As Kathini Maloba-Caines put it so well when referring to the rural sector on the African continent, it must be assumed that women are not homogeneous and therefore "the approach to their learning differs from country to country, region to region and even crop to crop".

Several approaches to organizing women in unorganized sectors emerge in this report, and they are outlined below.

Empowerment and organizing

A pattern or process has emerged from several of these studies, in particular those which received even a minimum of outside support. This approach is very relevant to organizing:

(a) the women workers perceive a need which is shared by their peers;

(b) they are helped, usually by outsiders friendly to the group, to see that together they might be able to improve their situation;

(c) they work together to resolve a problem touching on one of the three key areas in their lives — home, community and work;

(d) once they have gone through these steps and resolved a basic problem, they understand the possibilities which are within their reach and wish to take on more issues;

(e) at this point:

(i) if they are members of a trade union, as in the case of the RWOs, they become active members and some move on to leadership positions;

(ii) if they do not belong to a trade union, they are more easily convinced of their need for a union in order to be able to negotiate on their own behalf and receive a variety of other benefits not otherwise obtainable.

This process is conducive both to organizing women workers and to helping them become more independent and active in their unions. Once women gain the confidence which comes from working together on issues important to them as a group, they will be ready to become full partners in the labour movement.

If any of these steps is missing, successful organizing is unlikely. There has to be a perceived need that is sufficiently a problem to move the women to act. Other people must be supportive enough to allow them to be effective, but it must be the women themselves who plan and carry out their strategy. Particularly important, this must be an issue which is attainable through group action. Otherwise the women will grow discouraged and abandon their campaign.

Outside support, as seen from the case studies, is often necessary from the very beginning to help the women meet together, discuss their concerns and review possible plans of action. From this initial point onward, linkages with other groups have proved rewarding for both sides. Domestic workers in Brazil and Mexico readily acknowledge the importance of those in SOS CORPO and the ATABAL Collective who are working closely with them. They consider that the feminist movement can bring about changes in the way society views domestic service and women's work in the home in general. In the UWDE's opinion, any hope of improving the status accorded to domestic service lies with the feminists.

At some point the link with the trade union is formed. This can be at the beginning, as in Côte d'Ivoire and Namibia, or later, as in Brazil. Unions can offer benefits which associations cannot provide, but at first associations may appear less threatening and more "women-friendly". Whether the union is prepared to receive these workers is an important question and will be discussed below.

Organizing the inaccessible

Jane Tate's case studies show that despite the obvious differences involved, there are important similarities in some of the methods adopted in Australia, Canada and the Netherlands to organize homeworkers. Interestingly, these methods are just as valid for organizing domestic workers, who also risk invisibility in their work. Both of these sectors have long been ignored by trade unionists and deemed to have no future. Unfortunately, this has not proved true. Both sectors, for a variety of reasons, are expanding and these women workers need to be acknowledged and provided with the protection which only trade unions can offer.

Following is a summary of the methods used for homeworkers:

1. **Establish contact** through community organizations, groups and individuals who can work in these communities. Establish a hotline (a free information service) which provides both a place to go for advice and a contact point.

2. **Collect information** from the women themselves after contact is established. Once gathered, the information can be used to generate support for activities to improve their situation. This, for instance, is the work currently being carried out

by the domestic workers' unions in Brazil in order to determine a profile of potential members.

3. **Advocate legislative reform** depending on the particular situation. In some countries, portions of homeworking may be illegal; migrant women working illegally as domestics need to have their situation addressed — this latter has just become obvious in the United States. Domestic workers and homeworkers need to be legally considered as workers and given the advantages of other workers.

Trade unions as the instigator of organizing

Another approach was seen in Côte d'Ivoire, Italy and Namibia, and in the homeworking studies, in which it was the trade union which set about organizing women in the informal sector.

Under the right circumstances, where for instance there are no cultural hindrances to organizing women, this is an excellent approach. However, it is very important for the unions to pay heed to some of the women's concerns in these case studies, in particular regarding their fear of being marginalized. The women in Italy believed that those in the informal sector, even though union members, were less important politically than workers in large factories. Therefore, they considered that they were the first to suffer when cutbacks had to be made. Most revealing are the concerns of the UWDE in Brazil on affiliating with the CUT.

A holistic approach

An important lesson for organizing is that just as women's work in the informal sector, and in casualized employment in general, differs from that of the formal sector, their situation calls for a more holistic type of organizing. These women view their lives in their homes, at the workplace and in their communities as an integral whole. In order for organizing to succeed and for trade unions to become more relevant for women in general, this fundamental requirement must be acknowledged. Such an understanding could also help to assure that women member's needs are properly represented.

This need for a holistic strategy was also seen in EPZs, where it was possible to begin to organize the women around problems in their communities. This is a good approach in circumstances where it is difficult for trade unions to step in directly, either because they are not welcome in the area or because cultural attitudes inhibit women from joining.

Women's holistic view of life also makes them initially more conservative regarding strikes and the more confrontational methods of dispute resolution. Such approaches risk alienating women who would alternatively support more subtle attempts to improve working conditions and wages without risking dismissal. Yet again, this clearly depends on the sector, as in the case of FENAZUCAR in the Dominican Republic where union behaviour which might have been appropriate for the sugar industry was viewed as too confrontational for EPZs. For women who are heads of households, as are many in Central America, the Caribbean and elsewhere, assuring food for their children is too important to risk endangering their families. Thus they would usually prefer mediation to confrontation. However, as the women's action in the Penang EPZ shows, when women are convinced that their jobs are at risk, they will rise to the occasion and fight to protest against injustice and protect their dependents.

Are trade unions ready for women from unorganized sectors?

We have seen several instances of newly empowered women ready to move into decision-making positions in their unions only to find resistance among the leadership. This was particularly obvious in the rural sector studies, but it is encountered elsewhere.

What happens when women are convinced of the value of trade unions and recognize that they as members should be active participants, only to find that they are blocked?

A good example is the concerns of UWDE in Brazil about affiliating with the CUT. These are very valid issues which the union raises and it will be interesting to observe how the relationship evolves. Other confederations in Mexico were less enthusiastic than the CUT about representing these women workers. Other affiliations which should be observed in the future are those of the informal sector women's unions and the confederations which have organized them, as in Burkina Faso, Côte d'Ivoire and Namibia.

This point will not be laboured here, but these case studies have shown us that women are organizing and, for the sake of solidarity alone, trade unions should be cognizant of their needs and be ready to receive them.

Actions for the future

There are many associations already working with women in the unorganized sectors and which have linkages with the academic community and international trade union organizations. These links should be reinforced wherever possible to continue this exchange of experience and awareness-building which is so crucial for these unprotected women workers. It would be particularly helpful if the type of information found in these case studies could be collected more systematically and distributed widely to encourage others.

20

Final remarks

Swasti Mitter

In the 1990s and beyond, the question of organizing unorganized workers will assume special significance for trade unionists, employers' organizations and governmental bodies.

In the 1980s and early 1990s, spectacular shifts in the international economic and political situation have created uncertainties which make it difficult for decision-makers, at all levels, to define policy frameworks that would allow the dignity and security of the working population to be compatible with market efficiency. Decentralization of work to smaller units of production was among the measures adopted in order to circumvent labour market rigidities, so that the poor countries could meet the requirements of structural adjustment programmes as imposed by the World Bank and the International Monetary Fund (IMF). In addition, a disillusionment with centrally planned economies and inefficient state-owned industries contributed to the breaking up of large public sector companies into smaller, privatized production units. The aim was to achieve greater efficiency in production; the objective was also to lower wage costs through flexible employment contracts. Deregulation and liberalization of the labour market were viewed as essential conditions for achieving competitiveness and market efficiency. However, this also led to erosion of workers' rights and security.

An expansion of the unorganized sector arose also from the survival strategies of the workers themselves. The world recession, the negative consequences of debt crises and the formation of strong trading blocs among rich countries led to a deeply disturbing rise in the level of unemployment in weaker developing countries. In this scenario, increased reliance on self-employment was an indication of the desperation of workers, as the opportunities in the organized sector declined over time.

For present policy-makers and researchers, it is thus important to be aware of the diverse factors that led to a rise of employment in the unorganized sector, in both rich and poor countries. It would be counterproductive, from the point of view of policy-making, to analyse all types of unorganized casualized employment as if these belonged to a single undifferentiated category. The mobilizing strategies geared towards domestic servants or street vendors, for example, are not likely to be appropriate for wage employees of the local subcontractors of multinational enterprises. Likewise modes of collective action that are suitable for the employees of export processing zones are likely to be distinct from those that are targeted at home-based workers in manufacturing or service industries.

If the differences among diverse groups of unorganized workers are significant, the case studies in this volume highlight that it is important also to be clear about the common features in the situations of poor self-employed and casualized workers. A large proportion of them are women who, besides their responsibilities at the workplace, bear a major share of unpaid work at home and in the community. These multiple roles generally leave women with inadequate energy and time to devote to organizing activities. The current type of trade union work for collective action is thus scarcely compatible with women's patterns of work, life-cycle and rhythm of living. As in the organized sector, women workers in the unorganized sector often feel incapable of responding to the traditional trade union modes of operating. However, as the volume of employment increasingly shifts to the unorganized sector, the trade unions, in order to retain their institutional strength, need to examine the innovative activities followed by women workers' organizations in order to promote the value of collective actions among poor self-employed and casualized workers. Until recently, there has been only a limited amount of documentation of such efforts.[1] The case studies here add some new material in this rather unexplored and under- researched field.

A more detailed understanding of the possibility of organizing workers in casualized employment is likely to benefit the employers as well. The involvement and commitment of employees in the production process enhances the quality of products and services. In many markets, the quality of goods or services ranks with, or even above, the price in considerations of market efficiency. A reliance on scattered or insecure employees in some cases seriously jeopardizes companies' share of markets and profitability.

One of the consequences of a rise in non-bargainable, casualized jobs is a perceptible decline in the quality of working lives. Inadequate workplace safety, health hazards, poverty wages, sexual harassment — all contribute to a depletion of human resources, a vital condition for a nation's competitiveness in the world economy. The growth of a flexible and scattered workforce may in the short run lower the wage cost, but in the long run it may also entail inefficiency in terms of lowering employee involvement and the quality of labour input.

Therefore, in the interests of employees, employers and governments, further policy-oriented research should be geared towards assessing the benefits and costs of different ways of organizing flexible workers and the poor self-employed, by:

— evaluating the effectiveness of existing legislative frameworks that aim to give workers in the unorganized sector security of contracts and employment benefits;
— highlighting the importance of women-specific demands in making collective action relevant to a large section of unorganized employees;
— documenting innovative mobilizing experiences, undertaken generally by women activists, in the sectors dominated by poor self-employed and casualized workers;
— investigating the points of collaboration between employer and employees in initiating collective action to improve the quality of employees' working lives.

[1] For the most recent documentation see Sheila Rowbotham: *Homeworking worldwide* (London, Merlin Press, 1993); and Swasti Mitter: "On organising women in casualised trades: A global overview", in Sheila Rowbotham and Swasti Mitter (eds.): *Dignity and daily bread: New forms of economic organising among poor women in the Third World and the First* (London and New York, Routledge, 1993).

Research in this direction will indeed be in the new spirit of trade unionism that relies more on cooperation than on confrontation among governments, employees and workers.